D0162726

# The Police Manager
## Professional Leadership Skills

## Ronald G. Lynch
University of North Carolina at Chapel Hill

## THIRD EDITION

**McGraw-Hill, Inc.**
New York St. Louis San Francisco Auckland Bogotá
Caracas Lisbon London Madrid Mexico City Milan
Montreal New Delhi San Juan Singapore
Sydney Tokyo Toronto

**Charles R. Swanson, Jr.**
*University of Georgia*
ADVISORY EDITOR

 This book is printed on recycled, acid-free paper containing a minimum of 50% recycled de-inked fiber.

**THE POLICE MANAGER**
Third Edition

7 8 9 10 11 12 13 14 BKMBKM 9 9 8 7 6 5 4

Library of Congress Cataloging in Publication Data

Lynch, Ronald G.
   The police manager.

   Bibliography: p.
   Includes index.
   1. Police administration.   2. Organizational
behavior.   3. Leadership.   I. Title.
HV7935.L9   1986      350.74      85-14205
ISBN 0-07-554818-6

# PREFACE

The goal of the third edition of *The Police Manager: Professional Leadership Skills* continues to be to provide selected step-by-step procedures to help police administrators execute their duties and fulfill responsibilities more efficiently, effectively, and productively.

This book does not pretend to be a complete source for all the management information necessary to operate a modern police department. It should be read along with a number of other excellent books in the fast-growing field of criminal justice management.

This revision includes the following new chapters, "Understanding Personnel Through MBTI" (Chapter 6), "Use of Power" (Chapter 12), "Civil Liability" (Chapter 13), "Assessment Center Process" (Chapter 15), and "The Future" (Chapter 18). In addition, other chapters have been upgraded to reflect both theory and experience.

The sequence of chapters has been changed in response to users' suggestions, and a number of other chapters have been substantially rewritten. In addition, an instructor's manual outlines the major points of each chapter and provides examples of projects that may be undertaken by individual students or groups of students within the program.

This book can be supplemented by the use of programmed instruments that are mentioned in the instructor's manual. Sufficient flexibility is left to the individual instructor, who may wish to round out the information in this book with personal experiences.

I hope that readers will use techniques and theories discussed in this book to assist them on an individual basis. By joining theoretical understanding to practical application of the techniques, they should be better prepared to serve their communities and upgrade law enforcement as a profession.

I am in great debt to a number of experts in the law-enforcement field for their kind assistance, dedication, and patience in helping to develop the techniques presented in this text. Every effort has been made to acknowledge the sources and to give credit when due.

I want to thank specifically the following individuals, not just for their contribution to the subject matter but also for the influence they have had in helping me mature and develop during my law-enforcement career:

S. B. BILLBROUGH
*Regional Director, DEA*
*Miami, Florida*

GEORGE MURPHY
*Mobil Corp.*
*New York*

JOHN VERMILYE, Former Director
*Department of Public Safety*
*Lakewood, Colorado*

ROBERT DVORIN
*Consultant, ESD*
*Hartford, Connecticut*

MIKE SWANSON
*Institute of Government*
*University of Georgia*

Special thanks go to my friend and colleague Dick McMahon of the Institute of Government, University of North Carolina. The chapter on transactional analysis is the product of his thought and hard work.

Further special thanks go to G. Patrick Gallagher, Director of the Institute for Liability Management, Vienna, Virginia, for developing and writing the chapter on civil liability.

One person in particular—my wife, Anne—has helped me to adopt the life goal of understanding and helping people. Others have helped me grow and mature as a man and find ways of making my life worthwhile, but none was more demanding and supportive than my three children, Scott, Chris, and Stacy. The many "warm fuzzies" my family gave me during the time it took to carry the idea for this book to the point of publication have sustained me and helped me to overcome any doubts I may have had.

Finally, a grateful thanks to God; without His blessings, none of this could have been achieved.

Ronald Lynch

# CONTENTS

## 17 Organizational Development 209

## 18 The Future 228

# CHAPTER 1

# A History and Philosophy of Police Management

Are the problems that confront police managers on a day-to-day basis very different from problems confronting managers in industry and government? Are these problems different from the ones occurring in schools, hospitals, or churches? If we carefully examine the material geared specifically for industry or government, the answer is an obvious and resounding *no*. The problems facing police managers are similar to those that concern business executives, social leaders, and university personnel; though the purpose of the organization may differ greatly from agency to agency, the management process remains quite similar.

What, then, distinguishes the successful and effective police organization from one that is poorly run and under constant pressure because of its ineffectiveness? What is it that causes one police department to be exciting, interesting, and challenging while another is boring, suffers from high turnover rates, and is basically losing its battle against crime?

The major difference between the effective and ineffective can usually be traced to the management of the organization and, more specifically, to a difference in the philosophies of management that are employed. The differences can be seen in the organizational structure and in the amount of decision-making power granted to captains, lieutenants, and sergeants. The difference is clearly reflected in the attitude and managerial philosophy of top management personnel.

## THE POLICE MANAGER'S ROLE

What do police managers do? They listen, talk, read, write, confer, think, decide—about men, money, materials, methods, facilities—in order to plan, organize, direct, coordinate, and control their research service, production, public relations, employee relations, and all other activities so that they may more effectively serve the citizens to whom they are responsible. Police managers, therefore, must be skilled in listening, talking, reading, conferring, and deciding. They must know how to use their personnel, money, materials, and facilities so as to reach whatever stated objectives are important to their organizations.

1

A study conducted by the Harvard Business School identifies the three elements common to all successful managers in government and industry. These elements are:

1. The will to power
2. The will to manage
3. Empathy

This study defined the will to power as the manager's ability to deal in a competitive environment in an honest and ethical manner and, once this power is obtained, to use it to accomplish the goals of the organization. The will to manage was described as the pleasure the manager receives in seeing these objectives accomplished by the people within the organization. It is important to note that the third quality does not stress the manager's technical ability but rather the ability to sense and feel where other people are and how they can best be helped to develop their potential to the fullest.

The police manager's responsibility is to unify his or her organization. There are commonly four levels of organization: (a) *the system*—the total organization and its environment, (b) *the subsystem*—the major divisions or bureaus, (c) *the event*—a series of individual activities of similar type (normally a patrol watch or detective unit), and (d) *the element*—the incidents from which service to the community is measured. This relationship is shown in Figure 1.1.

The police manager's role is to combine these four levels of the police department so they may reach their stated objectives and justify the trust and respect placed in their hands by the citizens of their community.

Many police departments today have more than these four typical levels of organization. As a result, there is overlapping between the different levels and lines of authority and responsibility become unclear. A common problem might exist where the division is commanded by a captain who is assisted by a lieutenant. The assistant chief in the organization might not be clear on his specific role within the division and might make decisions that rightfully belong to the captain and the lieutenant. As a result of this interference, the lieutenant might begin to find himself making decisions that really belong to the sergeant. The sergeant, in turn, might make line operation decisions that should be made by the police officer. The result is that there is very little area for decision making by the individual police officer at the element, or bottom, level of the department.

| Level | Organizational Unit | Primary Responsibility |
|---|---|---|
| System | Department | Chief, assistant chiefs |
| Subsystem | Bureau or division | Majors, captains |
| Event | Division, section, watch | Captain, lieutenant |
| Element | Squad | Lieutenant, sergeant, police officer |

**Figure 1.1**  Organizational Levels

Team policing helps to maintain a balance among the four major levels within the police department. In agencies where team policing has been successful, usually the only ranks required at the working level are the police officer, the investigator, or the special police officer, all of whom are members of the element level of the department. At the first-line supervisory level, the sergeant is designated as the individual responsible for the coordination of the team's activities. She is a first-line supervisor and deals in the element and the event level. She makes decisions at the event level but assists at the element level. At the subsystem or team level, the commander is designated as the lieutenant. He is responsible for the individual team achievements but leaves the choice of method to the sergeants and officers involved. At the system level is the chief of police and some form of key assistant, who is called the captain or assistant chief.

Police departments are beginning to reorganize with a stronger emphasis on the reduction of levels between the top of the department (the chief of police) and the bottom of the organization (the police officer). The typical pyramid hierarchy that we have been accustomed to in the past is slowly beginning to flatten out, and this trend seems likely to continue, at least in the immediate future.

## THE MANAGEMENT PROCESS

Effectiveness in reaching the objectives of the organization depends on the management process. That process is composed of three major areas:

1. Technical factors
2. Behavioral (psychological) factors
3. Functional factors

The technical factors comprise those skills that are common to all police agencies. They include the ability to investigate crimes and accidents as well as to perform preventive patrol and execute other routine procedures. These skills are not a subject of this text.

In any organization, especially a law enforcement organization, the behavioral factors involve the circular flow of verbal and nonverbal communication that is a part of everyday operations; these factors deal with human interaction.

The functional factors are those involved in producing desired results. They are designed to assist the police manager in controlling his organization. These factors include planning, organizing, control, problem solving, decision making, and management by objectives.

The *management process* is the integration of all of these factors, with the purpose of achieving stated objectives (Figure 1.2). Police managers must utilize both theory and tools so that they may more effectively use the functional factors and behavioral factors in unison with the technical factors, thereby raising the overall level of service provided to the community.

| Technical Factors | Behavioral Factors | Functional Factors |
|---|---|---|
| Investigation | Leading | Planning |
| Preventive patrol | Values | Organizing |
| Fingerprinting | Conflict resolution | Decision making |
| Calls for service | Change process | Problem solving |
| Property management | Communications | Management by |
| Record keeping | | objectives |
| Manpower allocation | | Planned program |
| Traffic control | | budget |

Results

**Figure 1.2**   Integration Through Management

# HISTORY OF MANAGEMENT

The history of management can be divided into three broad philosophical approaches and time periods.

1. Scientific management (1900–1940)
2. Human relations management (1930–1970)
3. Systems management (1965–present)

The *scientific management theory* dominated the period from the beginning of the twentieth century to about 1940. Frederick Taylor (1910),[1] "the father of scientific management," emphasized time and motion studies.

His study of determining how pig iron should be lifted and carried is one of the classics of the scientific management approach. His recommendations for faster and better methods of production, in this case in the shoveling of pig iron, stress the importance of efficiency of operation through a high degree of specialization. The "best method" for each job was determined, and the employees were expected to conform to the recommended procedures. Employees were seen as economic tools. They were expected to behave rationally and held to be motivated by the wish to satisfy basic needs.

Frederick Taylor theorized that any organization could best accomplish its assigned tasks through definite work assignments, standardized rules and regulations, clear-cut authority relationships, close supervision, and strict controls. Emphasis was placed entirely on the formal administrative structure, and such terms as "authority," "chain of command," "span of control," and "division of labor" were generated during this time.

In 1935, Luther Gulick formulated the now famous PODSCORB. This acronym—representing planning, organizing, directing, controlling, reporting, and budgeting—has been emphasized in police management for many years.

Gulick emphasized the technical and engineering side of management, virtually disregarding the human side. Any changes in management during this period were designed to improve efficiency; little or no thought was given to the effect that the change process would have on the officer.

The major criticisms of the scientific management theory as it relates to law enforcement are that:

1. Officers were considered to be passive instruments; their personal feelings were completely disregarded. Any differences, especially with regard to motivation, were ignored. All employees were basically treated alike.
2. The employee was considered to be "an economic man" who could be motivated through wage-incentive plans or through the fear of job loss.
3. The focus was on technical efficiency and not on the effectiveness of the organization.
4. The efficiency of operation was to be obtained only through:
   a. the division of labor—the breaking down of the police task into its smallest components.
   b. the specialization of police activities, resulting in vertical and horizontal groupings that were each headed by a single supervisor.
   c. the orderly arrangement of administrative units into a simple but rigid structure of line and staff departments.
   d. the use of a small span of control whereby the managers supervised only a few subordinates.

Beginning in 1930, the negative features of the scientific approach began to outweigh many of the established principles and practices. Strong criticism was brought against the failure of police management personnel to recognize the necessity for instilling dignity and pride in their employees. The impetus for the *human relations management* approach came from studies conducted in the Hawthorne plant of the Western Electric Company by Harvard scholar Elton Mayo.[2] The studies were initially designed to improve the existing physical facilities that affected work output. These studies focused on finding ways to bring about changes in production by changing working conditions, such as the number of hours, the number of work breaks per day, and the physical environment.

One of the first studies involved the effect of lighting on the output of each worker. A research group and a control group were established, with the research group being introduced to varying levels of light. It was first believed that the stronger the light, the greater would be the output of the employee. As the researchers increased the light intensity, output did go up. However, as they lowered the intensity of light below the original base level, output continued to rise. It was this startling fact that led the researchers to examine more carefully the causes for the increased output.

The researchers then began initiating smaller research groups, and they worked very closely with the employees in revamping working hours, rest periods, and complaint procedures. They constantly invited creative comments on the part of employees. The researchers soon realized that the organization comprised more than just the formal organizational structure. The informal organizational structure—comprising the rumor process, cliques, and informal status systems—was soon recognized as being an important factor in the increase or decrease of productivity. The individual employees involved in the study began to feel a sense of belongingness and felt they were being treated as more than just tools to be used in the completion of a task.

In the 1940s and '50s, police departments also began to recognize the strong effect of the informal structure on the organization. Police agencies began to use such techniques as job enlargement and job enrichment at all levels in order to generate a greater interest in law enforcement as a profession.

Police departments began to realize that the classical concepts of the formal structure, with strong separation of staff and line operations, were not adequately meeting the goals of law enforcement. The trend began to change, allowing staff personnel to have direct authority over some line functions, and community relations units were created within the administrative function of the department.

The communication process within police agencies became one of the major problems for the police manager. The span of control originally established as an aid to effective police operations soon became a massive problem. Levels developed within the organization that did more to thwart effective communication between the police manager at the top of the organization and the police officer at the bottom.

During this same time period, industry recognized the difficulties created by the scientific management approach and began to deemphasize the tall organizational structure. Sears Roebuck, for example, developed the flat type of organizational structure, which provided for fewer levels of supervision. This type of structure required the delegation of responsibilities and emphasized careful selection, training, and placement of new employees.

During the 1950s, the management structure began to shift toward the more democratic or participatory management that is familiar in law enforcement today. Studies indicated that the supervisor who was "employee centered" was usually more effective than the one who was "production centered." The behavioral sciences became a source of information for police managers.

The human relations management approach also had its limitations. With the emphasis being placed upon the employee, the role of the organizational structure and its importance became secondary. The primary goal seemed to be social rewards, and little attention was given to the necessity for completion of tasks. Many police managers saw this structure as being unrealistic. Douglas McGregor pointed out in his studies that the "soft" approach to management in many instances led to an abdication of management authority. Employees began to expect more and give less in return.

Management professionals in all fields of government and industry soon recognized the need for developing a third management approach that would encompass the positive features of both the scientific management and human relations structures.

In the mid-1960s, the features of the human relations and scientific management approaches were brought together in the *systems management* approach. This approach fused the individual and the organization; it was designed to help managers use their employees in the most effective way while reaching the desired production goals.

The systems management approach emphasized the organization as a unit, rather than concentrating on one element such as the employees or organizational structure. The importance of the elements within any organization cannot be minimized, but the total system came to be seen in terms of definitive levels such as system, subsystem, event, and element.

The systems management approach recognized (1) that it was still necessary to have some hierarchical arrangement to bring about cooperation and coordination; (2) that authority and responsibility were essential; and (3) that overall organization was required. This approach went still further by recognizing that the organization can reach its stated objectives and goals only through the interrelationship of its parts. In 1950, Abraham Maslow[3] developed his "hierarchy of needs," in which he classified the needs of people at different levels. Studies by Frederick Herzberg reinforced Maslow's theories concerning the motivation practices that produce the most effective results in any organization.

Further studies by Douglas McGregor[4] in the 1950s, as discussed in his book *The Human Side of Enterprise*, stressed the general theory of human motivation as developed by Maslow. McGregor developed a set of assumptions about human behavior in which he showed how the scientific management approach was based on a specific set of assumptions; these McGregor labeled Theory X. McGregor's Theory Y, on the other hand, comprised the assumptions of the systems management approach.

In 1964, R. R. Blake and J. S. Mouton,[5] in their book *The Managerial Grid*®, emphasized two universal ingredients or concerns that each manager must have. They defined these as the concern for production and the concern for people, using these as the basis for their "managerial grid." They identified, for example, the manager who was heavily production-oriented and minimally people-oriented as a "9, 1 manager." The reverse, the manager who had low concern for production but a very high concern for people, was a "1, 9 manager." As the theories developed by McGregor, Blake and Mouton, and others are carefully examined, it becomes obvious that under the systems management approach the concern for reaching objectives and performing assigned tasks requires more than an emphasis on control or autocratic behavior patterns. The police manager, in order to be effective, must have a sense of interdependence with others and the ability to recognize and deal with conflict and change.

The police manager must develop meaningful tools and methods to implement the latest theoretical approaches to the field of management. Tools are designed to assist the police manager to be effective and efficient in performing daily tasks. This means that the manager must possess more than simple knowledge of rational and technical management skills. The ability to handle people is also a necessary part of the manager's day-to-day operation. Stated simply, it is the police manager's role to achieve the goals of the organizational unit through the most effective and efficient use of the available resources—people, money, time, and equipment. The goals of the organization can only be reached through team cooperation, not by an individual. Police managers can best obtain these organizational goals through the police officers who work with them on a day-to-day basis.

How far procedures will go in the future is hard to predict with any degree of certainty. One direction, however, seems fairly obvious. Law enforcement personnel of both lower and upper levels will be more qualified to do their respective jobs in the future, and they will be increasingly rewarded for their abilities and production. These rewards will come not only in the form of pay increases and the upgrading of fringe benefits but also by virtue of the manner in which the agency itself is run. The people within the agency will have an opportunity to develop pride, to increase their skills, and to feel worthwhile and that they are achieving some form of success while working for a specific police department within the police profession as a whole.

## NOTES

1. Frederick W. Taylor, *The Principles of Scientific Management* (New York: Harper and Brothers, 1911)
2. Elton Mayo, *The Human Problems of an Industrial Civilization* (New York: The Macmillan Company, 1933)
3. Abraham H. Maslow, *Motivation and Personality* (New York: Harper & Row, Publishers, 1954)
4. Douglas McGregor, *The Human Side of Enterprise* (New York: McGraw-Hill Book Company, 1960)
5. Robert R. Blake and Jane S. Mouton, *The Managerial Grid* (Houston, Texas: Gulf Publishing Company, 1964)

## PART ONE

# Behavioral Aspects of Police Management

The police manager's role demands a knowledge and understanding of the psychological aspects of management. The police manager must be aware of the effect that operations has upon the people within the police department.

Part I deals with the organizational environment facing the police manager. Included is a discussion of the various theories about people in organizations, including police departments.

Chapter 2 discusses leadership behavior styles and shows the varied behaviors available to a police manager. This chapter also considers the qualities necessary to be a successful police manager and places strong emphasis upon use of the managerial grid. This section provides criteria that may be used in helping police managers decide which style of leadership is best for them within their own given environments.

Chapter 3 deals with management communications. It attempts to clarify and explain the styles of communication available to the police manager and to demonstrate the consequences of each approach. Special attention is given to the processing model called the "Johari window."

Chapter 4 talks about Maslow's hierarchy of needs, Herzberg's motivation-hygiene theory, and the relationship between these two theories and Douglas McGregor's Theory X–Theory Y.

Chapter 5 deals with the latest techniques available to management concerning the issue of human behavior. This chapter on transactional analysis will not only help police managers analyze their personal behavior but also give them tools with which to gain insight into the behavior of others. Through the implementation of some of the techniques mentioned in this chapter, police managers will eventually gain a greater insight into themselves and will thus be in a better position to help bring about changes in their departments.

Chapter 6 deals with another human behavior model that can help the police chief to understand department personnel. Such understanding can, of course, allow for smoother operations and easier implementation of policies and goals.

In short, the psychological aspects of management discussed in this section provide a base on which police managers can build specific procedures and techniques to be implemented within their own agencies.

# CHAPTER 2

# *Leadership Behavior Styles*

The qualities of leaders and the processes of leadership have long been considered an important field of inquiry. Early speculation about the personality traits and qualities of a successful leader has given way to the study of actual leadership behavior and analysis of situational factors such as the type of group and the nature of the group's task.

Several people have studied leadership behavior and have sought to classify the different approaches to leadership and the different ways of exercising the leadership role. The style of leadership chosen by a manager largely depends on what he or she intends to accomplish.

Police managers must understand that their subordinates will follow their leadership for one or a combination of four reasons:

1. Fear of their authority and the manner in which they control, direct, and plan
2. Personal liking
3. Personal respect, based on the manager's actions, values, and consistent manner of dealing with subordinates
4. Trust, based on the manager's professional competence and proven ability to make decisions and manage conflict and change

Trust is a result of numerous personal contacts between the manager and the people he or she directly supervises. This kind of leadership is the most lasting and surely the most effective.

## QUALITIES OF A SUCCESSFUL POLICE MANAGER

Managers need to exhibit certain outstanding qualities in order to be successful, regardless of the style of management behavior they use. The following qualities, when exhibited by managers, have helped the individual to reach success in his day-to-day operations.

1. *Patience*—managers must be calm and steadfast, despite opposition to their beliefs, opinions, and attitudes.
2. *Wisdom*—managers must have the ability to judge fairly and equitably the behaviors and actions of subordinates.
3. *Virtue*—managers must show moral excellence, not only by word of mouth but also by everyday actions in dealing with departmental problems and personal issues.

11

4. *Empathy*—managers must learn to accept and understand the feelings of their subordinates, always being prepared to see others in a positive light.
5. *Kindness*—managers must try to be kind and gentle in all their dealings with others.
6. *Trust*—managers must develop confidence in subordinates, not just respecting their position or knowledge but also allowing them to achieve their personal goals as well as those of the organization.
7. *Knowledge*—managers must constantly attempt to upgrade their knowledge of technical matters, the management theories being developed and implemented in government and industry, facts as they occur within their own departments.
8. *Self-control*—managers must be able to restrain their emotions.

Police managers can develop these qualities by:

1. Showing a high frustration tolerance
2. Encouraging full participation of subordinates
3. Emphasizing the subordinate's right to express another point of view
4. Understanding the rules and acts of ethical competitive warfare
5. Expressing hostility tactfully
6. Accepting victory with controlled emotions
7. Never permitting setbacks to defeat them
8. Knowing how to "be your own boss"
9. Continually seeking success
10. Being experts in their fields

## STYLES OF LEADERSHIP

Leadership can be defined as the role of the manager in influencing subordinates to work willingly to achieve the stated objectives of the organization. In essence, leadership involves accomplishing stated departmental objectives through other people in the department. Therefore, leaders have two major concerns: they must be concerned with purpose and they must show concern for people.

Many writers have attempted to define styles of leadership. Writers emphasizing the scientific management[1] approach of the 1920s argued that the primary function of the leader was to set up and enforce performance criteria in order to meet the goals and objectives of the agencies. The manager's main concern was for purpose or production, with very little concern for the needs of the employees within the agency.

With the dawning of the human relations movement, initiated by Elton Mayo,[2] the function of the leader was to focus on the individual needs of employees and not on those of the organization itself.

In essence, the scientific management movement emphasized concern for purpose or task and the human relations movement stressed concern for people. Leaders who were concerned primarily with tasks were said to be "task-oriented" or "authoritarian" leaders, while those who emphasized the concern for interpersonal relationships were said to be "democratic" leaders. The style chosen by the leader depended on the assumptions he made concerning the members of the department. If the police manager felt and believed in Theory X assumptions, he was predominantly an authoritarian leader. If he believed in Theory Y assumptions, he was more democratic. In 1958, Robert Tannenbaum and Warren H. Schmidt[3] suggested that leadership varies along a continuum from boss-centered at one extreme to subordinate-centered at the other. Based on this analysis, they defined four styles of leadership, tell, sell, consult, and join. (See Figure 2.1.)

Under the "tell" style of leadership, the manager would make his own decisions and announce them to subordinates, expecting them to be carried out without question. An example of this type of leadership would be that of a police chief who makes all the decisions in the daily operation of his agency. He establishes schedules, assigns personnel, gives specific orders on how each crime must be investigated, chooses who should attend what training program. After reaching all these decisions, he proceeds to advise his immediate subordinates—the middle managers—who, in turn, advise supervisors, who advise the officers. In essence, there has been no input by any member of the department below the chief's level and the chief has made his decisions based upon his own personal experiences.

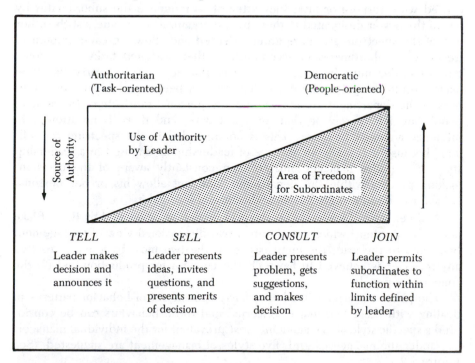

**Figure 2.1**  Continuum of Styles of Leadership
SOURCE: From Paul Hersey and Kenneth H. Blanchard, *Management of Organizational Behavior*, 2nd ed., © 1972. By permission of Prentice-Hall, Inc.

The manager who chooses the "sell" style of leadership makes all the decisions but, rather than simply announcing them to subordinates, attempts to persuade them to accept the decisions. Recognizing the potential for resistance on the part of subordinates, the manager concentrates on selling them ideas.

Under the "consult" style of leadership, the manager does not make any decision until the problem has been presented to members of her group and until she has listened to their advice and suggestions. The decision is still hers, but it is not made until after consultation with members of the staff.

The manager who uses the "join" style delegates the authority for making decisions to subordinates. She may reserve the right to be part of the decision-making process, but she views her primary function as one of helping to define the problem and to indicate the limits within which the decisions must be made. After the problem has been freely discussed by the subordinates, either a consensus or majority opinion will bring forth the final decision. There are three major disadvantages to the "join" type of leadership. First, it is time-consuming; second, it is frustrating; and third, it calls for mature subordinates who have the ability and willingness to arbitrate and arrive at some form of agreement.

Leaders who are at the "tell" end of the continuum are primarily concerned with purpose or task; they attempt to influence the subordinates by use of the power designated to them by the organization. Leaders at the other end of the spectrum are more group-oriented and allow a greater amount of freedom to subordinates in accomplishing their assigned tasks. The "join" type of leader must be aware of the fact that it is easy to carry this type leadership to the point where decisions are not being reached and the members of the department are not gaining any personal satisfaction. In essence, people are left to rely on their own initiative, and there is no attempt to influence anyone's behavior. This is not included in the spectrum of "tell-join" because it is really an absence of leadership as opposed to a leadership style. The police manager must remain constantly aware of the decision-making process within the department, and not allow his or her personal behavior to be interpreted as an abdication of leadership.

Another style of leadership is the grid model, as developed by R. R. Blake and J. S. Mouton,[4] which represents a two-dimensional view of management behavior. In the grid, the emphasis is on the two most basic concerns that any manager is believed to have: (1) the concern for production and (2) the concern for people.

The police manager will adopt a fairly specific set of behavior patterns in dealing with these two major concerns, and these behaviors can be considered a specific style of management most prevalent for the individual manager.

Under the managerial grid, five styles of management are suggested. (See Figure 2.2.)

According to the grid concept, the concern for production and concern for people have been rated on a scale of 0 to 9. The five predominant styles have

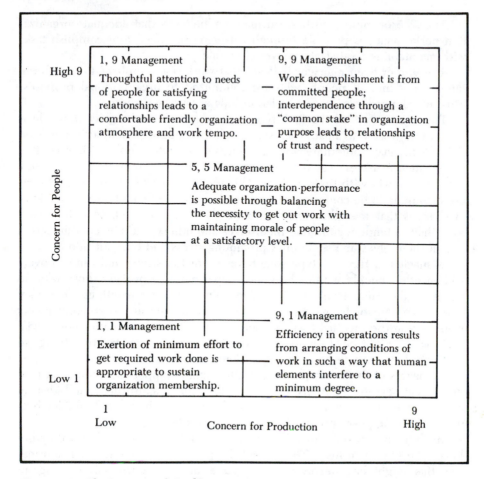

**Figure 2.2** The Managerial Grid®
SOURCE: Robert R. Blake and Jane Srygley Mouton, *The Managerial Grid* (Houston: Gulf Publishing Company, 1964). Reproduced by permission.

then been identified as 9, 1, task-oriented; 1, 9, country club; 1, 1, avoidance; 5, 5, middle of the road; and 9, 9, team.

The 9, 1 or task-oriented manager believes that efficiency in operations comes from arranging work conditions in such a way that interference by human elements is minimal.

The 1, 9 or country club manager pays thoughtful attention to the needs of people on the theory that satisfying relationships lead to a comfortable, friendly organizational atmosphere and work tempo.

The 1, 1 or avoidance-type manager exerts the minimum effort to get the required work done, and is concerned with people only to the degree that sustains organizational membership.

The 5, 5 or middle-of-the-road manager believes that adequate organization performance is possible through balancing the need to accomplish tasks with maintaining a satisfactory level of morale.

The 9, 9 or team manager believes that work is accomplished through the interdependence of people who are committed to organizational purposes. This interdependence leads to relationships of trust and respect.

Police managers of the 9, 1 type make decisions and expect these decisions to be treated as final. They stand for ideas, opinions, and attitudes even though this may sometimes appear offensive to other people. When conflict arises, such managers cut it off or allow it to continue only if they feel they are going to win with their position. When operations within the department are beginning to be confusing, they defend, resist, and counterargue any kind of changes that may threaten their individual positions. These police managers have a tendency to drive themselves and others, thereby creating stress within themselves and sometimes promoting stress and burnout in others.

Managers of the 9, 1 type sometimes seem too strong and tend to overwhelm other people within the police department, especially those who do not have the same level of knowledge. When holding meetings, they may attempt to control by monopolizing the conversation and correcting points made within the meeting that they feel are not correct, no matter how trivial such points might be. In most meetings, 9, 1's attempt to structure things so that only *how* as opposed to *why* questions are discussed.

Managers of the 1, 9 type, on the other hand, support decisions that promote good personal relations, embracing the opinions, attitudes, and ideas of others rather than attempting to push their own. They avoid conflict but, when it does appear, attempt to soothe people's feelings.

Such managers seem to value acceptance and tend to say things they believe others want to hear. They dread the possibility of mentioning information that might be interpreted as negative and are continually striving, in meetings and elsewhere, to please people. The result is that productivity tends to be low or may even grind to a halt.

The 1, 1 manager is indifferent to others and normally accepts the decisions of both superiors and subordinates. Such managers avoid taking positions and are not likely to reveal their opinions, attitudes, or ideas. They strive for a neutrality. Because they remain uninvolved on issues, they rarely show feelings of approval or disapproval and may seem indifferent to the processes within the police department.

In a management sense, such people appear passive. In meetings, they have a tendency to let others lead the conversation. They volunteer little or no information; when asked direct questions, they tend to give short answers and to avoid elaborating on any additional information. In some meetings, in fact, they may appear to be bored.

Managers of the 5, 5 type search for workable, if not perfect, decisions; they are willing to meet halfway people who hold opinions, ideas, and attitudes different from their own. When conflict arises, they try to negotiate them away through compromise.

In meetings, they try to impress others regardless of their status, reputation, or prestige. When they are asked questions, they tend to be tentative; they prefer to avoid giving direct answers until they understand everyone else's position fully. This caution may sometimes look like fear of being wrong, but it is actually a way of testing and probing the positions of others in order eventually to support the majority viewpoint.

A 9, 9 manager places a high value on creative decisions that result in understanding and agreement. Such managers listen for and seek out ideas, opinions, and attitudes different from their own. They have strong convictions but are willing to respond to sounder ideas and are more than willing to change when such ideas tend to achieve the purposes of the police department and are acceptable to the personnel within the agency. When conflict does arise, the 9, 9 manager attempts to identify the reasons for the conflict and seeks to resolve underlying causes, thereby reducing the number of conflicts that may eventually arise within the agency.

In meetings, 9, 9's command the respect of others by their behavior. They seem to enjoy the give-and-take processes within meetings but are usually geared toward keeping the meeting focused on its original stated purposes. They listen keenly and are able to tell the difference between fact and opinion.

In attempting to determine whether his or her management style is affected more by the scores on a managerial grid instrument or those on the Johari window, individual managers place more weight on the grid scores. In reality, subordinates have a tendency to describe the police manager's communication style more accurately; therefore police managers who are aware of both their managerial grid and Johari scores are more likely to be among those whose style is accurately described by subordinates. This is especially true when the subordinate is at least two levels away from the manager's present position. For example, sergeants identify the styles of captains more quickly and more accurately than they do the styles of higher-level managers.

When the managerial and communicative style are identical, little confusion will arise. However, when managerial style, which might be 9, 9, is confused with communication style, which might appear to be closer to 9, 1, the manager must be aware of these differences as perceived by subordinates. Only through a more open communication process will subordinates be able to identify both the management and communicative styles accurately.

Effective police managers strive for consistency in these respects.

## IS THERE A BEST STYLE?

Emphasizing that the police manager has two primary concerns—for people and for production—is there really a best style for effective direction, planning, and control of a police agency?

Research conducted in industry indicates that the manager who is able to balance both concerns is more effective than the manager who deals with only one. Likewise, successful police managers must contribute to the specific objectives of the police department while also helping individuals within the agency to achieve their personal goals.

Rensis Likert[5] did extensive research in analyzing high- as opposed to low-production managers. His studies indicated that the managers who focused primary attention on the human aspects while building effective teams were more successful than managers who were job-centered. The manager who achieved high production used general rather than close supervision of subordinates.

Even though Likert's studies suggest that the employee-centered, democratic leader is most successful, his findings leave some doubt as to whether or not a single style of leadership behavior can or should apply to all situations. The recommendation for using a single style of leadership leaves to chance the cultural or traditional differences that may exist and does not provide clear explanations of the effect of education and standard of living on the employees. Therefore, most studies indicate that the effective leader does not use a single style of leadership behavior but instead takes into consideration the numerous existing variables.

## Adaptive Leadership

It has become apparent that police managers are often trained to seek an ideal leadership behavior pattern that they can employ to maximize the effective operation of their individual agencies. In reality, however, the effective police manager is one who is able to integrate all the available styles and adapt to meet each given situation. In essence, police managers who are able to change their style of leadership according to the situation and the needs of their employees are those who will be most effective in attaining both personal and organizational objectives.

In choosing a leadership style, there are three major variables to be considered by the police manager:

1. Personal relationships with members of the department
2. The degree of structure in the task that the agency has been assigned to perform
3. The authority, power, and responsibility provided by the manager's position
   within the organization

The effectiveness of the leadership style chosen by the police manager will depend on the closeness of the relationship between the manager and subordinates, the degree of structure in the task, and the authority of the manager. In essence, the more flexibility given to the manager, the higher the possibility for effective decisions.

For example, the police manager who is assigned the task of eliminating corruption and unethical conduct within an agency will find that a democratic leadership style or an attempt to develop team decision making will be the most ineffective method of controlling the situation. Under such conditions, the manager who is more autocratic and has a high regard for production will be more successful on a short-term basis. Another example is the police manager who is faced with a riot or emergency condition. His success will depend on his immediate response to the issues. He may not have time to explain the situation to his subordinates and engage in team decision making. Once the crisis is over, however, the manager may find a different leadership style much more effective.

## Reality Leadership

Reality leadership focuses on the realities in a given situation. The police manager must develop the best kind of executive behavior for each administrative situation to be faced. The most effective manager will advise subordinates ahead of time regarding which conditions will produce which style of leadership. For example, a police chief may employ group decision making in general while reserving the authority to make all decisions concerning promotions of key personnel.

Police managers must realize that their leadership style must be judged in light of the departmental goals and purposes of the organization. Furthermore, depending on its nature and its location within the agency, a group may need a particular kind of leadership. For example, the police manager may find an open, team-style of management most effective in dealing with units composed of intelligent, mature employees. However, in other units where the tasks are mundane in nature, such as simple record filing, the police manager may find that the more effective style would be one that is more autocratic. Police managers must always realize that they, as leaders, are only as effective as their subordinates will allow them to be, and in most group situations the entire group is really responsible for the success or failure of the stated objectives.

## Deciding How to Lead

In reaching decisions, police managers are affected by (a) forces within themselves and (b) forces in the situation.

Police managers, in deciding which style of leadership or management is most applicable, are affected by their value systems, by the amount of confidence they have in their subordinates, and by their leadership inclinations. These inclinations have been brought about by the success they have achieved within their organizations to date. For example, if they have been successful by being heavily autocratic in leadership style, chances are that they will continue this style, regardless of the levels they reach in the bureaucratic structure. In situations where there is an element of uncertainty, managers will not jeopardize their own security by delegating too much responsibility and authority to subordinates.

Subordinates usually will receive greater freedom if they have clearly demonstrated the need for independence and have exhibited a readiness to assume responsibility. In choosing a leadership style, the manager will consider the amount of interest shown in the problem by subordinates. For example, when the first-line supervisor has received the necessary knowledge and experience to deal with the situation, understands the goals of the organization, and has learned to share in the decision-making process, the chances become greater that the style of leadership chosen by the manager will be more democratic.

There are forces in the total situation that greatly affect the leadership style employed by the manager. The effectiveness of the group itself in its past decision-making processes will tend to give some indication of how much freedom it should be given in each individual situation. If the organizational structure is highly bureaucratic in both principle and policy, with numerous levels between top and bottom, the chances of effective group decision making are greatly reduced. The problem itself and the pressure of time also affects the style of leadership that can be employed.

The effective police manager should choose a style of management that attempts to bridge the gap between the management process and actual line operations. The manager must learn to be a "multicrat"—being flexible enough to deal with each situation.

Consider the effective police chief who deals with the department's command and internal operations by employing techniques that bring about high-quality team decisions. But in dealing with the political structure of the community, this chief becomes a more compromising manager. Depending upon the demands of particular pressure groups, the chief may employ a different style of leadership and be most effective in bringing about peace and tranquillity to the community.

---

## NOTES

1. Frederick W. Taylor, *The Principles of Scientific Management* (New York: Harper and Brothers, 1911)
2. Elton Mayo, *The Social Problems of an Industrial Civilization* (Boston: Harvard Business School, 1945)
3. Paul Hersey and Kenneth H. Blanchard, *Management of Organizational Behavior*, 2d ed. (Englewood Cliffs, N.J.: Prentice-Hall, Inc., 1972)
4. Robert R. Blake and Jane Srygley Mouton, *The Managerial Grid* (Houston: Gulf Publishing Company, 1964), p. 10
5. Rensis Likert, *New Patterns of Management* (New York: McGraw-Hill Book Company, 1961)

# CHAPTER 3

# *Management Communication Behavior*

Communication has been defined in numerous ways, but the most appropriate definition is "behavior that results in an exchange of meaning." There are many examples of communication in an organization such as a police department. This process includes the facial expressions of police managers, spoken or written messages, the notices placed on bulletin boards, interactions in staff meetings, and the issuance of general orders. This varied output from the manager transmits the feelings, attitudes, and ideas of management to the other personnel in the department. The exchange between the sender, usually the management, and the receiver, usually the employees, carries meaning and intent.

When a misunderstanding or "communication misfire" occurs, it can generally be traced to either (1) the sender, having conveyed unclear expressions, words, or ideas or (2) the receiver, having misinterpreted the transmission or having been distracted while receiving it.

The critical question that the police manager should answer is, "What is effective communication for my department?"

## LEVELS OF COMMUNICATION

The communication process in a police department involves two levels. The primary level may be observed or heard. It is a single transaction in the form of either a written or oral statement from one person to another. There is, in addition to this first level, a second level of communication. This second level is built by the prior history of interactions between the manager and personnel.

Consider the statement "I want you to make as many decisions as possible." If managers in two different police agencies were to make this statement, the agencies would have identical first-level communication. However, in one agency the true meaning, or second level of communication, may be that before implementing decisions, the subordinate must receive approval from the manager. In the other agency, the same words may mean that the individual has complete authority to act on the manager's decision.

The police manager should constantly be aware of both levels of communication and should realize that actions taken on a day-to-day basis will have a greater effect on communication than will a statement made only once.

## HIERARCHY OF EFFECTIVE COMMUNICATIONS

Through effective communication, a manager in any police organization attempts to establish a specific behavior pattern in subordinates. Effective communication may be described as a four-step process.

In the first step, information is exchanged between manager and subordinates. Step two involves the development of understanding. The manager may have to clarify a message to the subordinates so that they clearly understand the boundaries of their authority in making decisions on a daily basis. Again, such development of understanding requires openness, trust, and the willingness on the part of both to talk and listen. The third step is the resolution of the issues communicated in steps one and two. If, for example, orders are clearly explained by the management and the subordinates understand but do not accept them, then the goals of the communication process have not been achieved. For example, a manager may order subordinates to arrive on time for roll call, but the officers do not agree with the order, refuse to accept it, and continue to arrive approximately five minutes before roll call. Here the communication process, for all intents and purposes, has failed.

The function of the fourth step is to produce appropriate behavior in both the sender and the receiver. In the example given above, the manager should stop, reevaluate the process, and either issue stronger orders with more control or reopen the communications, thus attempting to develop understanding and acceptance.

## FACT VERSUS INFERENCE

In organizational communications, confusion occurs when people are not able to differentiate between fact and inference. If the police manager makes an inference and fails to be aware of having done so, the manager will not be able to calculate the chances for failure involved in the process. If the subordinate acts upon the inference made by the manager, she may be taking an unrecognized and unnecessary risk.

Certain characteristics distinguish statements of fact from statements of inference. Statements of fact should be based on the individual's firsthand observation, not on assumptions. Statements of inference, however, can go well beyond what the individual has actually observed; they are limited only by his or her imagination. Statements of inference involve probability as opposed to certainty.

The effective communicator sets specific behavioral goals that may be stated as follows:

1. To make all the inferences I want but know when I am doing so and to understand the difference between fact and inference.
2. To check my inferences, perceptions, and reflections, since appearances can be deceiving, and not to give them the same weight I give to my personal observations.
3. To try not to pass on inferences as if they were statements of fact and not to accept the inferences of others as facts.
4. To avoid acting on inferences as if they were facts.
5. To base my life on the assumption of probability, not on the assumption of certainty; to continually check my assumptions and be willing to say, "I don't know."

## THE JOHARI WINDOW

The Johari Window[1] (Figure 3.1) is an information processing model by which the manager can judge his effectiveness in dealing with the concerns of feedback and exposure. The model is graphically expressed by a square. This four-celled figure shows the interaction of manager and subordinates, and it lists the behavioral processes required in utilizing feedback and exposure.

The Johari Window may be viewed as comprising numerous pieces of information that the manager can use in establishing interpersonal and team relationships. The window represents all the available communicative processes. As shown in Figure 3.1, it is divided into four regions, each repre-

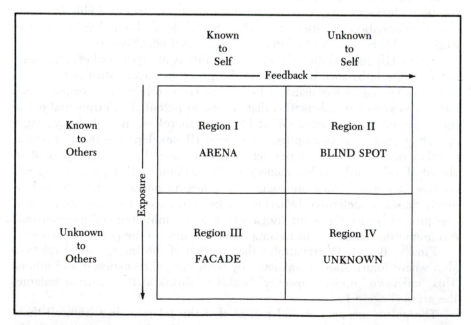

**Figure 3.1** The Johari Window
SOURCE: Adapted from *Styles of Management Inventory*, Jay Hall and Martha Williams, Teleometrics Intl., Conroe, Texas.

senting relevant information about the quality of the relationships. In order
to fully appreciate the effect of each region and the manner in which they
intertwine to create interpersonal and team effectiveness, the police manager
should not only consider the size and shape of each region but also the reason
for their presence within the total structure of the Johari Window.

As stated, the window deals with two kinds of communication—feedback
and exposure—each of which is subdivided into categories that are known by
the manager, unknown by the manager, known by others, and unknown by
others.

Region I, for example, represents open communications, where information is equally shared and understood. This information, known by the manager and known by others, is the facet of the interpersonal communication
relationship that controls interpersonal productivity. This region helps to develop an effective hierarchy of communication. The assumption behind this
principle is that interpersonal effectiveness and productivity are directly related to the amount of information that is mutually held within the relationship. Therefore, as the police manager increases the size of Region I, his
interpersonal and team relationships will become more rewarding, effective,
and productive. Region I is called the "Arena."

In Region II, information is known by others but unknown by the manager. This situation handicaps the manager, since it becomes difficult for her
to understand the behavior, decisions, or potential of others if she does not
have the necessary data upon which to base conclusions about their motives.
In addition, the other person has the advantage in knowing his or her own
reactions, feelings, and perceptions. Region II, an area of hidden, unper-
ceived information, is titled the "Blind Spot." More limited in scope than
Region I, this is an area of inhibited interpersonal effectiveness.

Region III, termed the "Facade," also inhibits interpersonal effectiveness,
but here the imbalance is in favor of the police manager. Most of the information is known by the manager but unknown by others. The manager may
attempt to keep any information that is seen as potentially detrimental out of
the communicative process. What happens, therefore, is that the manager
operating under the assumptions of Region III develops a series of communication facades. These facades act as his defense. Facades are present in
almost all relationships, but damage to the communication process depends
on how extensively they are used. The police manager should decide how
much conscious defensive behavior can be introduced into the communication process before the arena (Region I) becomes inhibited and interpersonal
communications suffer, thus causing ineffectiveness in the police department.

Finally, Region IV constitutes that portion of the interpersonal relationship where information is unknown by both the police manager and others.
This "unknown" region, however, begins to shrink as the manager enlarges
the arena (Region I).

The police manager should realize that the information within all these
regions constitutes both primary- and secondary-level communication. At the
secondary level, the manager should constantly be aware of how assumptions,
prejudices, and attitudes relate to factual information. Furthermore, the Jo-

hari Window concept deals with data that is relevant to the decision-making process and it is not designed to examine irrelevant information.

## Basic Interpersonal Processes

The police manager should be aware that the development of effective communication in any police department requires a combination of exposure and feedback. It is up to the manager to encourage downward communication and at the same time to enlarge the feedback process in a horizontal direction. The police manager should understand that in order to develop a climate of mutual exposure, the necessity for honest and realistic feedback must be emphasized. The manager must also be willing to solicit such feedback by encouraging subordinates to expose their information.

In order to reduce his blind spot, the police manager must receive the cooperation of his subordinates. His willingness to deal openly with issues will dictate the level of cooperation and trust that his subordinates give to him.

Police managers should realize that, theoretically, we all strive for a high degree of exposure and feedback, but we fail to achieve an optimum within organizational communication. The police manager usually has a preference for either exposure or feedback and has a tendency to overuse one and neglect the other. Imbalance results, causing tension, frustration, and confusion that decrease the effectiveness of the communication process. Figure 3.2[2] presents some commonly used approaches to the exposure and feedback processes. Each process may be described as an interpersonal style, and each is associated with fairly predictable behavior patterns exhibited by the police manager.

Four possible behavior types are demonstrated in Figure 3.2.

*Type A.*    Under this type, there is little use of either exposure or feedback. Here, the police manager is not very concerned about communication with subordinates. The "unknown" region dominates this type, and an analysis usually indicates that the type A individual withdraws from decision making and does not emphasize creativity or risk taking. Type A police managers are usually only personally motivated to create safety and security for their present positions. These managers are usually rigid, aloof, and uncommunicative with their subordinates. The police manager who believes in the 1, 1 style as defined in the management grid would have a window similar to that of the type A.

*Type B.*    This type of police manager has an aversion to exposure but also exhibits some desire for interaction with subordinates. The emphasis, however, is on feedback, to the extent that it is overused. Personnel and police managers with this type of communication window usually mistrust those with whom they come in contact; they believe in developing a facade behind which they can hide their intentions. The feedback, in many instances, may simply denote a probing on the part of the manager because of lack of trust

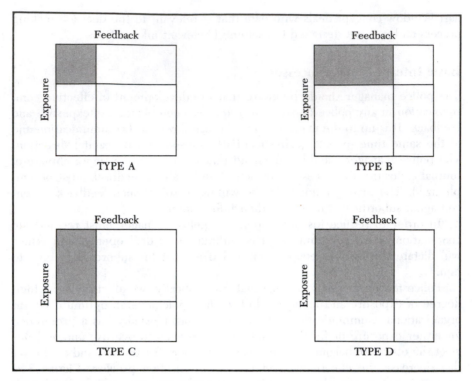

**Figure 3.2**  Exposure–Feedback Styles

in subordinates. Once this factor is realized by the subordinates, the manager's facade is easily recognizable and effective communication ceases to exist.

*Type C.*    In type C, exposure is overemphasized and feedback is neglected. The police manager within this kind of window is usually ego-striving and does not trust the people with whom he or she communicates. Such managers usually feel confident about their own values, opinions, and decisions and like to emphasize their authority. They are usually unaware of the impact of others in assisting in the decision-making process. A large blind spot usually results from this type of behavior. Persons with whom the manager communicates usually feel that their thoughts, ideas, and feelings are not being valued. This attitude often results in the subordinates' feeling insecure, hostile, and rebellious. Many times the personnel in the department will deliberately withhold important information from the manager or attempt to offer only that feedback that they feel the manager wants to hear. This results in decision making that is not based on all the facts.

*Type D.*    In the type D manager, exposure and feedback are balanced. The result is openness, trust, candor, and sensitivity to the needs of others. The arena becomes the dominant feature of the communication relationship; therefore, the productivity of the entire department increases. The police manager should be aware that attempts to increase the arena may lead some subordinates to react defensively. This is especially true if they are not accustomed to honest and trusting relationships with their superiors. Although those managers who want to increase the size of the arena should be aware of such possible defensive behavior, they should continue to promote and create the trust and respect that is so important to effective communication.

Generally speaking, the larger the manager's arena, the more effective his or her relationships with subordinates, peers, and superiors will be. The manager should be aware that not only the size of the arena but also its shape tends to be related to effectiveness. The size of the arena is usually related to the quantity of production stimulated by the communication process. The shape of the arena is directly associated with the quality of the work produced as a result of interpersonal communications. A balanced arena is preferred, for this means that both the exposure and the feedback processes are equal or as close as possible to being equal. Such equality allows the manager to establish a foundation from which further enlargement of the arena may be accomplished.

## Giving Useful Feedback

In order to have an effective police organization, the police manager should be concerned with growth and development and able to devote time and effort to problem solving and decision making within the department. Effective decision making requires open relationships among those involved in the process. This type of open relationship—based on candor, honesty, and trust—allows individuals within the department to express their feelings freely; it also helps reduce existing barriers that hamper effective decision making.

One way in which the police manager can develop open communication is through the effective use of feedback. The question the manager should ask before becoming involved in the process of feedback is, "Do I really feel that the information I am about to give to my subordinates can be used to help them improve and grow?" It is important that police managers first examine their own motives. If they find that they are only trying to unload a burden of hostility, then the feedback will bring about more harm than good. The three important criteria are that:

1. The other person needs to understand the feedback information.
2. The other person must be willing to accept the feedback.
3. The other person must be able to change his or her behavior or otherwise act on the feedback.

The manager should realize that there will be times when it will be extremely difficult to demand that the subordinate accept critical and negative feedback. In attempting to gain acceptance of feedback, the manager should follow certain general principles.

First, managers should develop a foundation of trust with their subordinates before beginning to use feedback.

Second, managers should be aware of the manner in which they discuss feedback with subordinates. They must constantly be aware of tone of voice, facial expressions, choice of words, and all behavior indicating second-level communications to the recipient of the feedback.

Third, managers should realize that their subordinates will be more likely to listen to negative feedback if they simply describe to a subordinate what they, as managers, have seen and what effect it has had on them. For example, a statement to the subordinate such as, "I think that's a nasty way to act towards people, and I think you ought to grow up," does not really help the subordinate to change and may bring out feelings of hostility. However, if the manager points to a specific situation and carefully describes his or her feelings about the incident that occurred, then the feedback, although negative in nature, is more likely to be accepted by the subordinate.

Finally, the manager should be careful to time the feedback correctly and be able to judge whether or not the subordinate is in a proper state of mind to receive negative feedback. For example, if the subordinate appears to be confused, angry, upset, or defensive, the feedback should be postponed. However, if the subordinate seems to be in an open state of mind, then the time would be right and the feedback would have a greater chance of being accepted.

There are some general rules for establishing and understanding feedback. First, the feedback should be specific rather than general. For example, if the police manager merely says she feels that her subordinate does not produce quality work but does not state facts to support this criticism, then the feedback is not very useful to the subordinate. The manager should cite specific instances and examples to show clearly to the subordinate why she feels that he is not acting in a proper manner.

The second rule for establishing understanding is to use recent examples of the employee's behavior rather than old ones. It is not advisable to give feedback to the subordinate concerning alleged behavior of three or four months earlier. In many instances, police departments force themselves into this situation by completing performance evaluation reports only once or twice a year. Because these performance evaluations are the only feedback from manager to subordinates, the manager should begin the feedback process as soon as possible after a given incident so that the event is still vivid in the minds of both the manager and the subordinate.

The third rule states that the feedback must be conducive to being acted upon by the subordinate. Frustration is only increased when the subordinate is reminded of a shortcoming over which he has no control. If the police manager feels that the subordinate is not acting with the degree of commitment necessary to perform his patrol duties effectively, then the manager should be able to give him specific instances that will help him to understand the feelings and opinions of the police manager. Merely stating that the officer does not adequately perform his assignments and functions usually does not help him to change his behavior.

Whether or not the police manager elects to give negative feedback to a subordinate depends upon the manager's estimate of the subordinate's ability to change the behavior.

The fourth rule states that feedback must be influenced by the needs of both the subordinate and the manager. Feedback can be destructive when it serves only the manager's need and fails to encompass the needs of the subordinate.

Fifth, the feedback should be solicited rather than imposed. Feedback is most useful when it is the subordinate who formulates the kinds of questions that the police manager, through observation, can best answer.

Last, the feedback should be checked to ensure effective communication. One way of doing this is for the subordinate to rephrase the feedback received from the manager to see if it corresponds with what the manager originally intended.

## Receiving Feedback

In order to keep the Johari window as open as possible, the police manager must also receive feedback. There are some overall criteria that should govern the manager's conduct in receiving feedback.

The police manager should make a sincere attempt to avoid being defensive. One of the quickest ways to stifle feedback is for the police manager to insist that the subordinate does not understand him or her and that therefore the premises of the feedback are erroneous. Such a manager would end up receiving nothing more than reinforcement of his or her own thoughts and opinions. Within a short time, this manager would become isolated from the facts about the department.

If police managers do not clearly understand the information their subordinates are trying to offer, they are unable to help their personnel. On the other hand, an open response from the manager can help to clarify his or her behavior. Examples will sometimes zero in on the true issues brought about within the feedback process—for example, such statements by the manager as, "Remember when we met last Thursday and I did not allow all members of the staff to express their ideas? Is this the kind of behavior you are talking about?"

Once the feedback session has been completed, it is a good idea for the police manager to briefly summarize what has been said. This gives a final check and an opportunity to clarify any misunderstandings that may have occurred during the meeting.

## Rules on Exposure

The police manager should also be aware that there are rules governing exposure as well as feedback.

First, the exposure should come about as part of the ongoing relationship between police managers and subordinates. The exposure should be properly timed so that it fits into the existing realities of the department. Police managers should also be aware of the effects that such exposure will have upon them as well as their subordinates. As they drop their facade, these managers will also reduce their blind spots in relation to their subordinates. Of course, once the subordinates also decrease their facade, the two-way communication process begins to be effective.

Exposure should also carry with it a reasonable but not overly high risk. Police managers should not be so open that they create a win-or-lose situation with subordinates. Constantly criticizing or downgrading subordinates may be a form of exposure, but the manager who does this runs the risk of never receiving any feedback from the subordinates.

## Principles of Change in the Johari Window

Actions and interactions between individuals have definite effects on the size and shape of the Johari window. Some of the basic principles of change operating within the Johari window are as follows:

1. A change in one quadrant will affect all other quadrants. As the size of the arena increases, the facade, blind spot, and unknown begin to decrease.
2. It takes energy to hide, deny, or be blind to behavior involved in interaction. In other words, it becomes a sheer impossibility on the part of a police manager not to witness and give some interpretation of the actions of other members within the department, whether they are peers, superiors, or subordinates.
3. Threats tend to decrease awareness, whereas mutual trust tends to increase awareness. This principle emphasizes the necessity for the high degree of trust that must exist within any police agency in order for the police manager to partake in effective and open communications.
4. Forced awareness is undesirable. In the communication process as in other processes, to force someone to give exposure or feedback usually carries little long-range effect; in many instances it does more harm than good in the short term.
5. Interpersonal learning comes about through an increase in the arena. Only by having a moderate to large arena can a police manager expect to grow in technical, rational, and psychological skills. The police manager who emphasizes the autocratic 9, 1 approach to management will, in the long run, develop a fixed arena that, depending on the manager's position of power and authority, will very quickly cease to grow.
6. Working with others is facilitated by a large area of mutually shared information. The larger the arena, the easier it is for the police manager to work with superiors, peers, and subordinates. On the other hand, the smaller the arena, the poorer will be the communicative process between the manager and other members of the department.

## What Affects the Size of the Arena in an Agency?

The trust between management and subordinates strongly affects the size of the arena in any police agency. Consider what happens when police officers do not believe their superiors. In that case, the only information flowing upward is that which the lower levels of the organization believe the upper levels want to hear. Very quickly, the police manager ends up in the proverbial ivory tower, not really aware of day-to-day activities within the department.

The rank and structure of the police agency also affect the size of the arena. If the structure contains five steps between the police officer and the chief, each level begins to filter out, accept, and reject information in different ways. The arena begins to shrink in such agencies, especially where superiors have only one or two people under their direct control.

Probably one of the most important factors existing in any police agency is the unwise use of power by the police manager. If the police manager feels obliged to make as many of the decisions as possible, continually attempts to justify his or her positions, avoids any kind of conflict, and tries to guarantee that no mistakes will occur, an extremely small amount of effective communications will exist within that agency. Usually the communications will deal with nebulous problems or with social activities within the agency; never would they address the more important issues that require team decision making.

Police managers should be aware of the different types of information that they and others possess. First of all, they have different feelings about each other. They know different facts concerning a given issue and have separate sets of assumptions, prejudices, and opinions. Each person possesses skills that enable him or her to deal with issues and each has an individual way of confronting or avoiding conflict. All of these factors directly affect the size of the arena.

## PATTERNS OF COMMUNICATION[3]

There are four basic patterns of communicative behavior that the police manager can implement in influencing subordinates. "Influence" has been defined as the major process, function, or activity involved in the leadership role. The four basic patterns of influence available to the police manager are:

1. Controlling pattern
2. Relinquishing pattern
3. Defensive pattern
4. Developmental pattern

In Figure 3.3, the circle is divided into four quadrants indicating the four approaches to another person:

| Style | Approach |
|---|---|
| Controlling | "I want to have most of the influence." |
| Relinquishing | "I want to give you influence." |
| Defensive | "I want to stay uninvolved and neither exert nor respond to influence." |
| Developmental | "I want to use my influence and yours to solve a problem." |

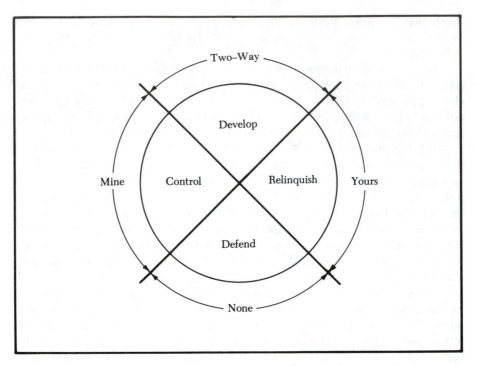

**Figure 3.3**   Patterns of Communication as They Relate to Influence
SOURCE: From *Management Models—The Communication Process*, copyright © 1967 by
Educational Systems & Designs, Inc., Westport, Connecticut. Reprinted with ESD's specific
permission.

## Controlling Pattern

Under the controlling pattern, the police manager uses his influence to force
his subordinates to do exactly as he, the leader, desires. Police managers who
constantly try to lead by using sell techniques are exhibiting a control type of
leadership behavior.

Police managers who rely on their power or threats to control their subordinates are indicating constraining behavior, and they attempt to maintain
full and total influence over the decision-making process. The influence belongs solely to the leader, and he shares none with his subordinates. On some
occasions, the police manager may not have stated authority, but he will attempt to use superior knowledge or threats of some negative consequence in
order to influence the behavior of subordinates. For example, "If you don't
follow this rule then I'll have you suspended," or "The chief says that you'd
better get this done as quickly as possible," or "I'm sure the chief would want
it done my way." These statements are typical of a police manager who is
attempting to control the influence and not share with the subordinates in
the decision-making process.

## Relinquishing Pattern

Under this pattern the police manager is giving up part or all of her influence in making the decision. She wants her subordinates to accept her as a leader or is attempting to be "one of the boys."

The police manager may attempt to relinquish her influence by complying with her subordinates' point of view. She does not totally withdraw from the situation but is still involved through compliance. She offers little or no resistance to suggestions made by other people in the group, even though she may strongly disagree with their opinions or conclusions.

Managers who, in the decision-making process, make such statements as "Well, you're the boss, I gotta follow what you say, so I'll go ahead and do it," or "I'm sure we won't have any trouble if we do it exactly the way the men want it" are really examples of the manager abdicating the leadership role.

## Defensive Pattern

In this pattern the police manager or leader totally withdraws from the problem-solving process. He doesn't contribute or solicit ideas and usually avoids any involvement with the problem. Statements such as "Well I've done all I can, there's nothing else for me," or "That's not my job, let somebody else figure it out," are examples of defensive behavior.

Sometimes, this withdrawal will be exhibited by emotional outbursts on the part of the police manager. He begins to move away from the problem and begins to attack other people involved in the decision-making process. Such statements as "That was a dumb thing to do," or "I'm tired of the way you've been behaving, and I sure wish you'd get yourself straightened out," are examples of withdrawal communicative behavior. The responses are really directed at other individuals within the group, not at the issue or problem at hand. Many times, these statements build hostility and cause other people to be defensive, and very little is accomplished in the problem-solving, decision-making process.

## Developmental Pattern

Under the developmental pattern, the influence flows between the police manager and her subordinates. Each participant in the decision-making group is allowed to contribute opinions and ideas, and the group in turn attempts to draw out the ideas of all members involved in the decision-making process. The desire on the part of the leader is to find the best possible alternatives for the resolution of the problem. In order to accomplish this, the police manager must be willing to listen, explore, and test out new ideas. The developmental pattern consists of two types of action-reaction. First, the police manager can attempt to develop some course of action by developing commitment and understanding and by dispensing information to the other people involved in the decision-making process. Her role as a leader is one of stimulating discussion and interaction with other members of the decision-making group. Before entering the decision-making discussions, the manager must plan how she can stimulate thinking, challenge the other people in her group, and decide what she can contribute to the growth of the group.

Police managers may begin the discussion of issues with such statements as "I saw a report the other day that indicated that 20 percent of our population causes about 80 percent of our crime problem. I think this has real significance for us on how we are going to allocate our resources." By beginning the discussion with such a statement, the manager is attempting to develop alternatives, to bring in new facts for the knowledge and awareness of other people in the group, and to provide information from which the problem can be solved. Second, the police manager who wants to implement such patterns of behavior can attempt to seek out the ideas and opinions of others in the agency. She should take the role of asking questions, of reflecting opinions of others, giving support, and showing an interest in the other members' points of view. Such responses as "How do you feel about this" or "What is your opinion" are ways in which the police manager can develop a developmental pattern of communicative behavior.

In essence then, the influence in the decision-making process and the role of leadership is really a two-way process, being shared by the police managers with their subordinates.

## APPLYING PATTERNS OF COMMUNICATION[4]

The four patterns of communicative behavior and their relationship to the influence process have been described. It is important that police managers understand the four basic patterns of communication and, more importantly, that they be aware of when a given pattern of communication is most appropriate.

### Controlling Pattern

The leader who chooses a controlling pattern of behavior uses his authority to apply pressure, and he attempts to persuade people to do what he wants accomplished. The issue for the police manager is whether this approach would ever be appropriate. The answer is *yes*.

First, if the manager wants to control his personnel so as to achieve his objectives, he must first have the facts, information, and experience to justify his adoption of the controlling pattern of behavior. For example, when the police manager is first assigned to a unit, he should not attempt to use the controlling pattern because he is not familiar with the qualifications of his subordinates.

Therefore, when the police manager is first given a new supervisory position within the police department and is unfamiliar with the job, the developmental pattern or even the relinquishing approach may prove more effective in problem solving. If, however, the police manager has all of the facts, understands the situation clearly, and has the necessary experience and knowledge to make the high-quality decisions, then the controlling approach is more appropriate.

In emergency or crisis situations where action and direction are needed immediately, the controlling approach is the most appropriate pattern of communication for the police manager. For example, if a disturbance broke out during a specific tour of duty, it would be inappropriate for the manager to sit down with his superiors and subordinates and attempt to develop some course of action. Directive, specific controlling behavior is much more appropriate in that situation. Usually, the police manager who shows some presence of mind and knowledge in giving directions and organizing his people to fight the disturbance and control it is behaving in the most effective way. Therefore, in crisis and emergency situations, the controlling pattern of behavior is often appropriate.

Another situation where the manager may choose this behavior pattern is where the joint commitment and motivation of the subordinates are unimportant and unnecessary. Any situation that is positive or useful from the subordinates' point of view can be handled effectively by the controlling pattern. For example, if the city manager's office allowed office personnel to leave early with pay, the joint decision-making process would be unnecessary.

Recognizing that there are occasions when the controlling pattern is appropriate, the manager must realize that certain circumstances have to exist in order for this approach to be effective.

There are two basic ingredients. First, the manager must have some authority or control over the alternatives available for solving the problem. For example, when managers of equal rank attempt to use a controlling approach on each other, this approach rarely works. The one police sergeant would not give a direct order to a fellow sergeant, especially when he has no authority or responsibility over the other's affairs. By the same token, when the police manager has no authority or responsibility over activities of subordinates, he would not use the controlling approach. Consider what would happen if the police manager attempted to define in detail what church his police officers should attend or how they should deal with their private lives. In essence, the authoritarian or controlling approach would have no effect. Also, with the trend today of increasing the authority, responsibility, and freedom of subordinates, the controlling pattern is becoming less and less effective.

Police managers in some instances are being legally restricted in the degree to which they can use controlling methods. As a result of such issues as mandatory collective bargaining, civil service rules and regulations, and threats of lawsuits, the police manager has lost much of the control that he had over his subordinates' activities in the past. Even in those instances when the police manager has legal or stated authority over the alternatives, he must always remember that he does not have complete control of the individual's motives, feelings, or attitudes. If the subordinate decides that the controlling pattern as exhibited by his manager is overcontrolling and overdirecting him, he will usually find some quiet and subtle way of resisting the orders. This passive resistance shows up in many police agencies. Police officers begin to perform only the amount of work necessary to keep from being dismissed or having charges brought against them. Therefore, the police manager, even though he has legal and stated authority over the alternatives, must always balance that against how much control he really has over the alternatives.

In summary, then, the following ingredients must be present if the controlling pattern is to be effective:

1. The police manager must have all or most of the facts, experience, or knowledge related to the issue.
2. The manager must have full control of the alternative solutions.
3. The manager must feel that joint commitment with subordinates is not necessary or important.
4. Speed is an important consideration.
5. Resistance to change is low.

The last item on the list, low resistance to change, is probably the most important, because when resistance is high, controlling techniques have rarely been found to be effective. If they are, the effectiveness lasts for a short time period only. When the police manager attempts to force a specific change upon police officers who are vehemently opposed to the new course of action, rarely will commitment and self-motivation be developed by the controlling pattern. Usually the manager would have to take the time and effort to discuss the issue with the staff in order to develop understanding and get them personally involved.

This does not mean, however, that the police manager must never implement change against these forces. The real professional recognizes the management situations where such difficult decisions must be made and where the changes must be imposed, regardless of the resistance from internal or external sources. In many instances, when resistance is great, the manager would be required to use more controlling techniques than usual. Nevertheless, the police manager must always realize that the controlling pattern of leadership is not the best way of introducing new ideas into an organization.

## Relinquishing Pattern

The process of relinquishing means that the police manager gives up her influence and reduces her contribution or role in the problem-solving process. It occurs most often when the manager is concerned about losing acceptance. Unfortunately, in many situations, this pattern of communication is used to avoid unpleasant situations or keep subordinates happy. Rarely is this sufficient reason for a manager to relinquish influence and authority.

The police manager must always be concerned with the goals and objectives of the police department and with the various precedents she is in the process of establishing. In dealing with subordinates, the police manager cannot always act merely to keep her people happy but must be concerned with the total situation.

There certainly are some circumstances when the relinquishing pattern is appropriate. For example, when the police manager finds that her subordinates are in a highly emotional state, then this relinquishing of her influence may be the most suitable way to handle the issue. Even though the manager may feel that the subordinates are misinformed, she may be willing to go along with them until they calm down and can be approached logically. Remember, however, that it is dangerous to assume that emotional people can be handled effectively by relinquishing influence. However, if the subordinates are irrational, the police manager may find it more advantageous in the long run to allow them to express their personal feelings. After the emotional outburst, the manager may find it more appropriate to restrict the conversation to the issue at hand.

There is a second set of circumstances under which the relinquishing approach may be the most effective for the police manager. In situations where the subordinates have all the information, experience, and facts necessary for the decision-making process, the manager may very well want to give up her influence in the decisions. In essence, the manager is exhibiting trust in her subordinates and in their ability to make the right and proper decisions. For example, if the police manager was required to approve the decision concerning which computer system to employ or which police radio to purchase, she may find it more effective to follow the advice of technically qualified subordinates.

In emergency situations, when the police manager first arrives at the scene, she may be willing to give up her influence in the decision-making process until she becomes more familiar with the facts. Under such circumstances, the relinquishing of influence would be only temporary. Once the facts are known to the police manager, she must decide whether to take the controlling pattern or the developmental pattern in reaching the remaining decisions.

Finally, when the police manager wants her subordinates to learn by experience, she may very well decide to give up her influence. This is especially true when the employee is highly motivated. For example, when the police officer approaches the police manager with a new program to reduce the number of armed robberies in a specific area of the community, then the police manager may, assuming the project is reasonable in nature, allow the officer to plan, implement, and evaluate the entire operation. In essence, she has relinquished her influence in the decision-making process concerning the development of the project itself. Obviously, if the subordinate's program is too costly, too dangerous, or not consistent with department objectives, the police manager must take a direct role, denying permission to implement the project. Usually after a careful explanation, the subordinates would either accept the manager's decision or attempt to redesign their project to meet the specific guidelines outlined by the manager.

In review, then, when the following key factors exist, the police manager may find the relinquishing pattern to be appropriate:

1. When the other person has most of the facts and experience related to the issue
2. When the issue is highly personal and is not directly related to the police activities

3. When the subordinate is highly motivated and wants to implement a specific project
4. When the other individual is highly emotional or disturbed by the issue at hand

## Defensive Pattern

This pattern of communicative behavior is usually inappropriate. However, there are a few situations where this approach might prove effective. In considering issues that are legal, moral, or ethical, the police manager may find it appropriate to withdraw from the issue. For example, when dealing with union agitators, the police manager may refuse to comment on a practice or procedure. In essence, he would withdraw from the situation and avoid involvement.

If a police manager is approached by either a superior or a subordinate and asked to engage in some practice that might be illegal, the manager may express a strong withdrawal action. He may become angry at the person rather than at the problem. Thus, there are circumstances where this approach would be both understandable and even appropriate. These situations rarely emerge in most law-enforcement agencies, but the police manager must also realize that managers, supervisors, and police officers are human. It is certainly desirable for the police manager to avoid losing his temper, but if he does, he may be better off to withdraw from the situation. However, he must always be able to judge whether it is necessary for him to come back to the situation and try to achieve some solution with those involved.

Similarly, in dealing with others, the police manager must develop a tolerance of human reactions. He must realize that subordinates will become frustrated and, in many instances when they fail to understand the real issue, may also engage in withdrawal behavior. In summary, although it is generally undesirable to use defensive patterns of communication, in the following situations this may be the most appropriate form of behavior:

1. When there is a legal, moral, or ethical issue
2. When the individual is frustrated or does not fully understand the situation in which he or she is involved

## Developmental Pattern

In a majority of the situations faced by the police manager, he does not have all of the facts. There are usually differences of opinion and a need to develop understanding through personal two-way communication. The police manager needs the ideas of his subordinates, he needs their commitment, and he needs them to be self-motivated. It is almost impossible, in running any police agency today, for the police manager to be completely unilateral in his decision making.

If the police manager can answer yes to any of the following questions, then the developmental pattern would be the most appropriate pattern of communicative behavior for him to use:

1. Are there others who have additional facts, experience, or knowledge that can contribute to making a more effective decision?
2. Is joint commitment important?
3. Is there a difference of opinion among personnel who will be concerned with the implementation of this decision?
4. Is there a possibility of resistance to the decision?
5. Is there a need or opportunity for creativeness or innovation?

## Summary of Communication Patterns

The police manager must always realize that whenever he interacts with superiors and subordinates, his style of communication will fall into some behavior pattern. When speed is important, when he has the knowledge and experience to make effective decisions, the controlling pattern may be the most appropriate. The manager should use the controlling behavior pattern only when he is positive he is right and when there is no resistance on the part of the subordinates.

On the other hand, if someone else has more facts and knows and understands what is required, the manager should relinquish his influence by adopting the relinquishing pattern of behavior.

Situations in which the defensive pattern of behavior would be appropriate are rare, but the manager must realize that such behavior is normal, and he must be able to respond with understanding and guidance.

Finally, the developmental pattern has proven to be the most useful style of communicative behavior in situations where the decision makers are attempting to identify the causes of resistance to change, to work out some joint solutions to specific issues, where they want to produce high-quality results, and where they want to maintain a high degree of motivation among their personnel.

---

# NOTES

1. Jay Hall and Martha Williams, *Styles of Management Inventory*. Teleometrics Intl., Conroe, Texas.
2. Ibid; "Exposure-Feedback Tendencies."
3. From *Management Models—The Communication Process*, copyright © 1967 by Educational Systems & Designs, Inc., Westport, Connecticut. Reprinted with ESD's specific permission.
4. Ibid.

# CHAPTER 4

# *Organizational Environment and Hierarchy of Needs*

The study of organizational behavior is a search for answers to perplexing questions about human nature. What motivates people? How can the police manager make best use of the behavior patterns found within organizations? Recognizing the importance of the human element in organizational behavior, the attempt of this chapter will be to develop a framework for police managers that can help them to understand their employees better, enable them to determine the "whys" of past behavior patterns, and, if possible, allow them to predict, change, and control behavior patterns.

Police managers, having different types of personnel within their departments, must attempt to mold their people into productive units so that higher objectives may be set and reached. Only through the understanding of human behavior as it relates to the organization can managers make the most effective use of personnel within their departments.

A constant issue faced by police managers is that of motivation. Many managers believe it is part of their job to help motivate subordinates; indeed, the author's own studies show that there are three essential aspects to developing motivated, highly productive officers. First, assuming that the officer has the talent, he or she needs time to grow and develop; such time can be granted by the police manager. Second, officers need knowledge. This can be provided by the police manager through various kinds of individual and group training programs. The third and most important ingredient is desire or motivation. This must come from within the individual. Without such motivation, the employee cannot be expected to grow and develop.

How, then, does a manager promote motivation? Usually we attempt, as managers, to serve as examples to our subordinates. Police managers must be keenly aware that their performance is linked to the outcomes they seek. However, these outcomes are also controlled by the officers' performance. For example, if a police officer wishes to work in a certain patrol unit because this would give him extra time to continue his education, then his performance level may be high because he is strongly motivated to gain the potential reward. The manager, in turn, might be working closely with the officer, giving him additional responsibilities for the ultimate outcome of higher productivity within the patrol unit. Because the two outcomes—that of the officer and that of the manager—are consistent, the manager's goals will probably be met and the employee would be considered to be highly motivated. However, once the individual officer's goal ceases to be important—if, for example, he drops out of school, graduates, or possibly transfers to another shift where he cannot attend school—his performance level would probably drop. It is important for the manager to sit down with subordinates and discuss personal goals—that is, their reasons for working—and, whenever they are consistent with the manager's goals, help them to achieve these outcomes.

The officer's individual performance depends on ability as well as the drive or desire to succeed. It is also influenced by the officer's attitude, experience, and training. Assuming that an individual has ability, there will be a direct relationship between the manager's performance and outcomes and those of the individual officers. If motivation comes from within each individual, the police leader can play an important role in helping individual officers to achieve their ultimate goals.

In addressing the issue of motivation, the police manager must be careful not to attribute false motives to the behavior of others. Normally, when the new behavior is distinctive—that is, when the officer has performed well in the past but now suddenly changes her pattern of behavior—there is a tendency to attribute this change to factors within the officer. If, however, such a change in behavior is exhibited by several officers, the tendency would be to attribute this to external conditions and to institute special training programs. Although it is possible to make certain assumptions about motivation, it is important to test such assumptions by exploring them on a one-to-one basis. The police manager must understand that the greater the psychological difference between manager and subordinates, the more likely it is that motivational problems will be blamed on the officers. By being aware of individual differences, the police manager can check his or her assumptions and thus arrive at more effective final decisions.

## HIERARCHY OF NEEDS[1]

Dr. Abraham Maslow described human behavior in terms of human needs. He developed a five-step hierarchy outlining these and emphasized that this system is the source of all motivation. In essence, as the first need is satisfied, the person then moves on to the second, then to the third, to the fourth, and finally the fifth. If the manager wants to motivate his or her personnel, the manager's actions must fit the needs of the employee. According to Maslow, only the unsatisfied needs become sources of motivation. Furthermore, once having satisfied one level of need to some degree, an employee will advance to the next level. Certain conditions, however, may cause one to go back to his primary needs. For example, if an individual is satisfied with his present income, his basic and safety needs may be met. However, if that employee loses his job, then his basic needs become primary until a new job is found.

Maslow has suggested that people have five basic needs that account for most of their behavior (see Figure 4.1). He goes on to say that although the need may never receive total and complete satisfaction, there must be a degree of satisfaction before the need ceases to affect behavior. Once this minimum degree is reached, satisfaction is acquired and the person moves on to experience the potential associated with the next level.

## Basic Needs

The bottom level of the hierarchy refers to the need for food and shelter. These basic needs have, for the most part, been satisfied in our contemporary society. As they pertain to employees within a police department, these needs are sometimes reflected in the desire for added personal property and an increased salary—both directed toward increasing comfort. Once the officers receive adequate satisfaction of this basic need through wages sufficient to enable them to live comfortably, they begin to move upward in the hierarchy.

Most police departments today, especially those in and around major population areas, provide adequately for the basic needs of their officers. Many rural police agencies, however, are still seriously struggling with sixty- and seventy-hour work weeks as well as with salaries that place their officers in the poverty range. Until this problem is overcome, these agencies will have difficulty in progressing to professional standards.

## The Need for Safety

Once the officer has received adequate satisfaction of her basic needs, her awareness of the safety need is developed. She focuses on security, protection, and avoiding harm and risk. Within the police profession, the officer

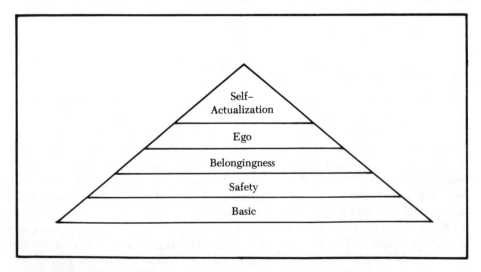

**Figure 4.1**  Maslow's Hierarchy of Needs
SOURCE: From Abraham H. Maslow, *Motivation and Personality* (New York: Harper & Row, Publishers, 1954).

begins to emphasize issues such as fringe benefits, hospitalization insurance, retirement and pension plans, and consistent performance standards. Officers concerned with safety needs are likely to be unimaginative, constantly complaining, and uncreative in their work activities. They generally exhibit little or no flexibility. A strict adherence to rules and regulations is important to these officers. The police department and police managers who overemphasize the upgrading of fringe benefits are, in essence, attempting to motivate the officers by satisfying their safety need. If, however, the safety need of the majority of the personnel is adequately satisfied, a different form of motivation is necessary. This is not to deemphasize the need or the necessity of satisfying it, but only to caution police managers not to devote all their motivation programs to the satisfaction of this need to the exclusion of the next three.

## The Need to Belong

The third level of the need hierarchy deals with the desire of the officer for membership within a department, for acceptance by fellow officers, and for the feeling of belonging to an organizational family. These needs are manifested in the officer's wish for friendly peers with whom he can develop personal relationships. The police manager is beginning to find that through the creation and implementation of team-type policing, this need to belong is satisfied in members of the department.

The officer will usually look first to the organization for satisfaction of this need. If, however, his need cannot be met within the department, he will then become involved with a formal or informal group established either inside or outside the agency. This belongingness or social need has often been satisfied through active participation in chapters of the Fraternal Order of Police or through other social groups closely related to the activities of the police department. By instituting activities designed to reach organizational goals, the police managers can often direct the enthusiasm and creativity of their personnel to benefit the department rather than losing these energies to outside interests.

## Ego Status Need

Once the officer has satisfied the belongingness need, she generally demonstrates interest in achieving some special recognition or status for her contribution to the department. Some police departments have attempted to satisfy this need through the creation of such systems as the "officer of the month," by special commendations and awards, or by giving the officer added responsibility. This ego status need usually drives the officer to find opportunities to show her competence, hoping that she will reap recognition from her peers as well as achieve some material reward. These factors motivate the officer to contribute as much as possible to the organization in order to be recognized by its members. Usually, the officer attempts to receive assignments that are recognized as the more challenging within the department. For example, some officers strive for assignment to specialized investigative units such as homicide or to administrative activities such as planning so that their contributions to the growth of the department will be immediately recognized.

## The Need to Self-Actualize

Although the ego status needs are difficult to meet and their satisfaction is not often enduring, there are cases where the fourth need has been adequately met and the individual moves to the highest level of the hierarchy. At this level, the officer is extremely concerned about improving his self-concept. He suddenly needs assignments that are challenging, meaningful, allowing him to be as creative as possible. He must be able to achieve a sense of growth and satisfaction through the performance of these activities. Self-actualization focuses on the personal satisfaction the officer receives from his work. At this stage he usually seeks out assignments that involve risk taking and experimentation. Behavior patterns on the self-actualization level generally foster innovative and creative projects and provide the officer with a higher degree of self-satisfaction. The behavior prompted by this need produces the mature and constructive contributions necessary for the accomplishment of the degree of professionalism sought by contemporary police departments.

In summary, the police manager's role is not simple. He must first assess his own motivating needs and then those of his subordinates. Only through these assessments can the police manager truly motivate and most effectively utilize the personnel assigned to him.

It is the police manager's role to assist his staff through the hierarchy of needs. Generally, when the police chief examines his officers and finds them fixed at one of the lower levels, a careful analysis of the reason for this fixation may indicate that the constraints or barriers to reaching the next level are imposed by the structure of the organization and not by the quality of the personnel.

In testing police employees, we found that there was a correlation between Maslow's hierarchy of needs and the needs expressed by some of the officers. The highest need expressed was usually that of the ego, with the second being safety or security. Self-actualization was usually placed third. The expression of such needs, however, depended a lot on the individual agencies tested. Where there were feelings of worthwhileness on the part of individual officers and managers, ego and self-actualization needs were higher. But where pay was higher than average, even though officers did not feel trusted or respected, the safety or security needs were rated highest.

## MOTIVATION-HYGIENE THEORY[2]

The more mature the individuals become, the more important become their ego and self-actualization needs. During the 1950s, Frederick Herzberg conducted a series of studies emphasizing the difference between maintenance factors and motivation factors. His studies further dramatized Maslow's findings. As a result of Herzberg's studies, a theory of organizational behavior and motivation was developed.

Herzberg collected data on job attitudes from which assumptions concerning human behavior could be made. The motivation-hygiene theory was the result of his studies. Over two hundred professional people were interviewed in an attempt to isolate the activities that gave them job satisfaction from those that brought about job dissatisfaction. From the information obtained by the studies, Herzberg defined two different categories of needs, independent of each other, that affect employee behavior in different ways. He found that if there was dissatisfaction, the employee emphasized the environment in which he or she worked. If, however, employees were satisfied with their jobs, they usually became more productive and had a stronger desire to help the organization grow. Herzberg titled the first category needs "Hygiene Factors" and the second category "Motivators," feeling that satisfaction of the second category of needs brought about superior performance.

Herzberg listed such issues as policies, procedures, administrative practices, techniques of supervision, working conditions, interpersonal relations, salaries, and security as hygiene factors. These may not be intrinsic parts of every police officer's job, but they are surely related to the conditions under which the officer must perform. Herzberg believed that hygiene factors do not produce growth in the individual or increase work output, but they do prevent losses in performance.

He defined as motivators the sense of achievement, challenge, professional growth, and recognition. Herzberg's use of the term "motivator" stresses that these factors have some positive effect upon the employee, resulting in increased job satisfaction as well as total output capacity (see Figure 4.2).

There is a close relationship between Herzberg's theory of motivation and the hierarchy of needs described and developed by Maslow. Maslow refers to needs and motives; Herzberg deals with the goals and incentives that tend to satisfy these needs.

Wages would satisfy these needs at the basic level, and fringe benefits would satisfy them at the security or safety level. Interpersonal relations tech-

| *Hygiene Factors* | *Motivators* |
|---|---|
| Salary | Challenging assignments |
| Fringe benefits | Increased responsibiliy |
| Security (civil service) | Recognition for work |
| Rules and regulations | Individual growth |
| Supervision | |

**Figure 4.2** Herzberg Motivation-Hygiene Theory

niques are examples of hygiene factors that lead to satisfaction of social needs, while increasing employees' responsibility and authority, assigning them challenging work, and helping them to grow and develop are motivators that bring about organizational behavior and satisfy needs at the ego and self-actualization levels.

The relationship between Herzberg's and Maslow's theories is shown in Figure 4.3.

The basic, safety, and social needs, as well as a part of the ego needs, are hygiene factors within an organization. The ego needs are divided because there is a difference between status and recognition for a job well done. Status may be defined as the position one occupies through seniority, by promotions, or as payment for a political debt. Therefore, the status position would not reflect the individual's personal achievements, or provide recognition for what he or she has earned. Recognition, as opposed to status, is gained only through the competence and achievement of the individual. It is earned by the individual and granted by others. Recognition is classified as an ego need and, along with the self-actualization needs, is defined and classified by Herzberg as a motivator.

Sometimes the police manager finds it difficult to recognize the difference between hygiene and motivating factors.

As an example, let us take the case of a police officer who is highly motivated and performing at 70 percent of his ability. He is satisfied with the existing police structure—the working conditions as well as the personal relationships with his supervisors. In fact, the officer has previously been involved in making important decisions affecting his job. Then the police manager transfers the officer's supervisor, and the new supervisor and the

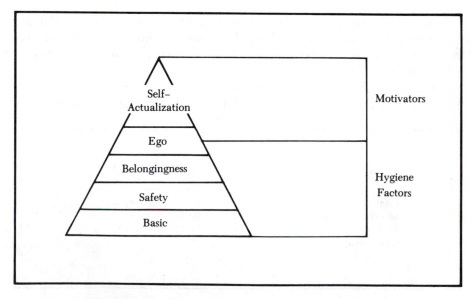

**Figure 4.3**   Comparison: Maslow and Herzberg

officer develop personality differences. In fact, the officer feels that he is better qualified to perform the supervisor's job, and he begins to resent the supervisor's larger salary—which actually covers a smaller workload. How, then, would this situation affect the police officer's behavior? The officer's performance and productivity depend on his ability, independence, and motivation. The unsatisfied hygiene needs for a supervisory position and the higher salary may restrict his output, resulting in a drop from a 70 percent capacity, for instance, to a 40 percent level. Even if the officer eventually finds a supervisor with whom he can work, and even if he receives a pay increase, his productivity would generally increase only to the original level of 70 percent. As a result, management has satisfied the hygiene factors for the officer but has succeeded only in restoring his productivity to its original level.

Conversely, if the same officer is still working at a 70 percent capacity, is satisfied with his working conditions, and the supervisor allows him the opportunity to mature and to satisfy his motivational needs and his ego and self-actualization needs, a growth in productivity will take place. If the officer is allowed to exercise some initiative and creativity in handling his own problems, in accepting responsibility and authority, and in making as many decisions as possible, the result is that he matures and increases his ability. Although still working at a 70 percent capacity, his productivity has greatly increased.

Therefore, if the police manager is careful to see that the hygiene factors and the basic safety and social needs of the employees are satisfied, he can then take the time and effort to stress the motivating factors to satisfy the ego and self-actualization needs. Although the officer may still only perform at 70 percent capacity, his productivity will increase due to the encouragement and challenge offered by the manager.

Police managers will find that when the hygiene needs are satisfied, dissatisfaction and work restriction will also be reduced but the individual will have little desire for achieving a superior performance. If, however, the police manager emphasizes satisfaction of the motivating factors and allows the individual officer to grow and develop, then he will witness an improvement in the officer's productivity as well as in the quality of his work.

Prior to Herzberg, most behavioral scientists dealing with worker motivation emphasized what is termed "job enlargement." The theory of job enlargement assumes that if the employees are given an increase in the number of tasks similar to or identical to those they are presently doing, they will gain more satisfaction from their jobs.

Herzberg disagreed with the job enlargement theory. He argued that in order to satisfy the worker's motivation factors, management must take the responsibility of enriching the job as well as expanding it. If the officer writes crime and traffic reports and then is allowed to write juvenile, property, and missing persons reports, she will be no more satisfied than if she had remained restricted to writing only one or two types of reports. Job enrichment, on the other hand, implies that the officer is given the challenge of added responsibilities in all of her activities.

It is important to note that the attempt to implement motivating factors to enrich the officer's job does not always succeed in completely satisfying ego and self-actualization needs. If the police department hires an officer whose ability exceeds the demands of the police job, then job enrichment would have no effect in satisfying ego or self-actualization needs. Therefore, the job enrichment must be equal to the ability of the police officer. If, for example, the officer is selected, trained, and prepared to deal with problems on a day-to-day basis and then is assigned to push the button to open the jail for eight hours a day, even the further step of enriching the job by adding the responsibility of walking the floors once an hour will not serve as a motivating factor.

Herzberg's studies of motivation produced interesting observations, which in some ways support Maslow's position and in other ways suggest that the satisfaction of lower-level needs may have different results than will the satisfaction of higher-level needs.

Herzberg asked thousands of employees to describe situations that resulted in their feeling exceptionally good about their jobs. They were asked if the feelings of satisfaction in their work had affected their performance, their personal relationships, and their well-being. Finally, the nature of the sequence of events that served to return the workers' attitudes to normal were elicited. Following this sequence, the interview was repeated, asking respondents to describe events that made them feel exceptionally bad about their jobs.

Events were evaluated in terms of those situations that led to feelings of dissatisfaction. They were defined in terms of whether the effect was long or short. "Long-term" was defined as two weeks or longer.

They identified five major factors that helped produce satisfaction. These included achievement, recognition, the work itself, responsibility, and advancement. They identified the five major factors that led to dissatisfaction. These included policies, supervision, salary levels, interpersonal relationships, and working conditions. Salary, however, was generally considered to be both a satisfier and a dissatisfier, depending on the way the money itself was used. For example, a 10 percent pay raise that keeps officers more or less at their present level both in terms of their work and of living standards tends to be seen as not bringing about dissatisfaction. However, a large pay increase—as might result from taking another job—is sometimes viewed as a satisfier because it allows the recipient to use the money for some specific growth goals such as furthering a child's education.

In studies of police personnel at the supervisory, middle-management, and management levels, the following results were noticed. Personnel at the lower levels of the department have a tendency to rank the following five factors as strong motivators: (1) feeling of achievement from doing a challenging job, (2) the inner need to do a good job, (3) doing work that they felt was important, (4) having personal work-related goals, and (5) doing interesting work. Managers, on the other hand, ranked the following as the factors that they believed to be most motivating to subordinates: (1) doing work that they felt was important, (2) recognition and appreciation from supervisors and managers (the item ranked tenth by police officers), and (3) recognition from peers (ranked twelfth by subordinates). The possibility of promotion was ranked fourth by managers and sixth by officers. Finally, having personal work-related goals was rated fifth by managers. There is a slight difference, although recognition seems to play an important role in the eyes of both managers and police officers. The nature of the job itself is a motivating force for police officers, although such work-related motivation is not viewed as highly significant by police managers.

## THEORY X AND THEORY Y[3]

Theory X and Theory Y were developed by Douglas McGregor during the 1950s. According to McGregor, the traditional organization is one that emphasizes centralized decision making and reflects the pyramid structure typical of most law-enforcement agencies. It was McGregor's belief that traditional managers share certain basic assumptions, which he labeled Theory X. He has defined these assumptions in the following way:

1. It is management's role to organize resources—money, equipment, personnel—in a structure that requires close supervision of all employees and brings about maximum control. (The recommendation of one police sergeant for every eight police officers, without any regard to the ability of the officers or the sergeant, is an example of the Theory X type of control.)
2. It is management's responsibility to direct the efforts of the personnel of the agency, keeping them motivated, controlling all their actions, and modifying their behavior to fit the needs of the organization.
3. If management's staff does not take an active part in controlling the behavior of the employees, the employees will be passive, even resistant, to the needs of the organization.
4. The average employee is, by nature, lazy and will work as little as possible, as work is inherently distasteful to him or her.
5. The average employee lacks ambition, dislikes responsibility and authority, and prefers taking orders to being independent.
6. The employee is basically self-centered, has no feeling for organizational needs, and must be closely controlled and even coerced in order to achieve organizational objectives.
7. By nature, the average employee resists change.
8. The average employee does not have the ability to solve problems creatively.

Most police departments, in developing rules and regulations, use these assumptions as a basis. Police departments occasionally develop organizational structures in which a superior closely supervises each subordinate. Furthermore, most of the police manager's time is spent checking and rechecking the daily activities of immediate subordinates. The widespread practice of allowing patrol officers to perform only menial duties and of assigning any tasks that require intelligence to the detectives or so-called specialized units is often viewed by personnel in the agencies as the practice of Theory X.

One of the first questions that police managers must ask themselves is whether or not the assumptions of Theory X are appropriate for use in running police agencies today. Educational and living standards in our country have risen immensely in the past decade. Among police officers today, the motivation for pay increases has greatly decreased.

Theory X assumptions about police officers are, for the most part, inaccurate. Many police agencies, in implementing such theories and assumptions, create serious management trouble, generally resulting in their failure, to motivate personnel toward the achievement of departmental goals. Management by strong, centralized control will not usually succeed in our society. Theory X managers motivate people by attempting to satisfy basic and safety needs. Most people today, however, have reasonably satisfied these needs and seek motivation directed toward fulfilling belongingness, ego, and self-actualization needs.

Douglas McGregor also developed a second theory of human behavior called Theory Y. It is based on the assumption that it is management's role to unleash the potential of every member of the organization. If the individual can be properly motivated to obtain his or her own goals through the achievement of organizational goals, then the agency can be extremely effective.

McGregor's assumptions regarding Theory Y managers are:

1. It is management's role to organize resources—money, material, equipment, personnel—to reach organizational goals.
2. Work can be an enjoyable part of one's life if the conditions are favorable.
3. People are not by nature lazy, passive, or resistant to the needs of the organization but have become so as a result of their experience working within the organization.
4. Management does not place the potential for development within the employee. Motivation, capacity for accepting responsibility, and willingness to work toward organizational goals are present within the individual. It is then the management's responsibility to recognize this potential and allow the individual the freedom to develop his or her abilities.
5. People possess creativity and can solve organizational problems if encouraged by the management.
6. The essential task of management is to develop organizational conditions and operational procedures that will encourage individuals to attain their goals by directing their efforts toward organizational goals and objectives.

Police managers who accept Theory Y assumptions usually have (1) fewer levels in their departmental hierarchies, (2) controls with broad guidelines, and (3) minimal first-line supervision of police activities. The Theory Y police agency gives increased autonomy to middle management, first-line supervisors, and police officers. By allowing them to develop the projects and programs, it involves the personnel in identifying and overcoming obstacles to their goals. Police officers under a Theory Y organization achieve satisfaction for their ego and self-actualization needs.

Some police departments allow individual police officers to become involved in activities such as planning and problem resolution on a daily basis. For example, the agencies implementing "management by objectives"—where top management has clearly defined the major objectives of the department for the coming year and has advised middle management and first-line supervisors of these objectives—then assign the individual projects to the squads for development. Departments implementing Theory Y involve officers in many management functions such as developing training programs, hiring personnel, and even assisting in the preparation of budgets. Some police agencies are finding that police officers are as satisfied by their jobs as they are by their hobbies and recreation. As a result, officers are spending off-duty hours in preparing for the implementation of projects within their agencies. The police role begins to take on a different meaning to the officers and they, in turn, lighten the load of management.

## IMMATURITY–MATURITY THEORY[4]

As a result of the outdated management practices of many police departments and their emphasis upon Theory X assumptions, the law-enforcement profession still treats many police officers as immature.

During the 1950s, Chris Argyris conducted extensive studies of industrial organizations to determine the effect of management practices on the personal growth of the employees within the organization. Argyris listed seven changes that should occur in the employee's personality if he or she is to develop into a mature person and be an asset to the organization (see Figure 4.4).

Individuals move from a passive state as infants to increased activity as adults. Second, as mature, thinking adults, they develop from a state of dependence on others to one of independence. Third, they increase their number of behavior patterns. Fourth, they move from erratic, casual, and shallow interests to deeper and stronger interests in specific directions. Fifth, the mature adult develops a time frame that includes the past, present, and future, as opposed to the child's frame, which emphasizes only the present.

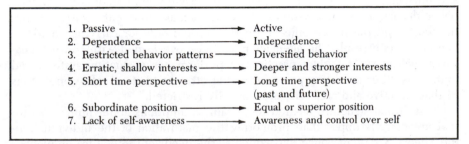

1. Passive ⟶ Active
2. Dependence ⟶ Independence
3. Restricted behavior patterns ⟶ Diversified behavior
4. Erratic, shallow interests ⟶ Deeper and stronger interests
5. Short time perspective ⟶ Long time perspective (past and future)
6. Subordinate position ⟶ Equal or superior position
7. Lack of self-awareness ⟶ Awareness and control over self

**Figure 4.4** Seven Changes in Employees

Sixth, as children they are subordinate to almost everyone, but as adults they assume equal or superior status to others. Finally, as children they lack self-awareness, but as adults they understand and are able to control themselves. Argyris postulated that these changes are normal, healthy, and bring the individual from immaturity to maturity.

The major point is that although people rarely develop to the state of full maturity, as they grow older and learn from their experiences, they constantly move toward the maturity end of the continuum.

In many police departments, managers sometimes question the personnel's maturity or even their desire to become mature. Apathy begins to spread through the department, and management immediately accuses the workers of being lazy and of having no interest in their jobs. Generally when individuals come to work for an organization such as a government bureaucracy, the management practices utilized by the agency actually prohibit the employees from obtaining maturity. In many police departments, the individual police officers are given minimal control over their respective job assignments and, in fact, are encouraged to be dependent upon and subordinate to the first-line supervisors and middle managers. As a result, these adults begin to behave immaturely, which, according to the assumptions of Theory X, is how many police agencies expect them to act.

The formal organizational structure of many police bureaucracies often forces the employee to remain immature. The emphasis of the organizational structure is toward fitting the individual to the job. The design for the organization always comes first, and this design is usually based on the concepts of scientific management—task specialization, chain of command, and span of control. Many police agencies attempt to increase the efficiency of the organization by using the police officers as interchangeable parts within the total structure.

Basic to these concepts is the fact that the authority and power to run the department rests in the hands of a very few individuals who are at the top of the organization and who make all major and most minor decisions. And these decisions are usually made with little input from middle management and no input from the lower links in the chain of command. In fact, those at the bottom of the chain are strictly controlled by their superiors and by the rigidity of the system itself. Specialization of many police activities has resulted in the oversimplification of the duties, which soon become repetitive, routine, and unchallenging. This implies that in the task-oriented leadership of many police departments, supervisors and managers make frequent decisions about the work, and the police officers are responsible only for carrying out these decisions. As a result, the agencies have been overloaded with control measures such as strict budget practices, a performance evaluation system, and numerous other operating procedures that attempt to standardize operations so that initiative and creativity are carefully restricted.

This formal structure has led to certain assumptions about human nature that are directly opposed to promoting the maturation of the individual. In the Theory X type of police departments, the needs of the mature employees cannot be satisfied due to the inflexibility of the formal organizational structure within which they must work. New police officers soon recognize that Theory X assumptions prevail and that management has designated childlike roles for them, thus frustrating their natural development. The officers are forced either to turn to outside activities for fulfillment, to leave the department, or to change their profession.

The present challenge to police managers is to provide a work climate in which every employee has the opportunity to mature, both as an individual and as a member of the department. However, the police manager must believe that individuals can be essentially self-directed and creative in their work environments if they are motivated by the management. Implicit here is the manager's acceptance of Theory Y and the Argyris theory, which allow the individual to grow from immaturity to maturity.

## MANAGEMENT SYSTEMS[5]

As a result of behavioral research studies of numerous industrial organizational structures, Rensis Likert developed a definition of management styles on a continuum ranging from System 1 through System 4.

### System 1

Under this system, management is seen as having no confidence or trust in its personnel and seldom involving them in any part of the decision-making process. Top management makes a large majority of the decisions, sets the goals, and then issues rules, regulations, and orders through the chain of command. Subordinates are kept in line by the use of fear, threats, or occasionally by a reward, such as a letter of commendation. The emphasis within this system is on satisfying basic and safety needs. Usually any contact between the superior and the subordinate is brought about through the alleged mistakes or misconduct of the subordinate. The relationship between the first-line supervisor and the workers is usually one of fear and mistrust.

The trend in police departments today is to move away from System 1 and toward the other end of the continuum. However, some police organizations still place the control process in the hands of top management. This has affected the development of strong informal organizations within the agency, which, in many instances, oppose the goals of the formal structure. Most of the manager's time within System 1 police departments is spent in preventing conflict between the formal and informal structures.

### System 2

This type of management places some confidence and trust in the lower-level police officers, but the structure still retains many qualities of a master-servant relationship. Most of the decision making and goal setting occurs at the top of the organization. But at least management has a structure through which input can be received from the lower levels, and it even allows the lower levels to make some of the less important decisions. Rewards and actual or potential punishments are the tools used to motivate employees. Usually the manager's relationship to the police officer is viewed as distrustful. Police departments with System 2 characteristics will usually have some communication between the top, middle, and lower levels, but generally the upward communication is carefully screened to feed information to middle and upper management that the lower level thinks they want to hear. The superiors still inject a large amount of fear and caution in their subordinates. Under System 2, the police department's control process begins to be delegated to the middle and lower levels. The informal organization existing in System 1 police agencies is still present, but it is not usually in direct conflict with the formal organizational goals.

## System 3

Police departments under System 3 demonstrate substantial but not complete trust between the management and subordinates. More decisions are made at the lower levels, but policies and high-level decisions still remain in the hands of those at the top. Communication flows both upward and downward, and rewards and occasional punishment are used to generate in the officer a greater interest in department goals. Since the amount of interaction between superior and subordinate broadens under System 3, confidence and trust begin to develop. Both the higher and lower levels feel responsible for controlling the organizational activities. If informal organizations do develop within System 3 police agencies, they will either support them or give only a partial resistance to their goals.

## System 4

Under System 4, the management practices of the police department clearly indicate complete confidence and trust in the subordinates on the part of the top management and middle management personnel. Decision making, although well integrated, is widely dispersed and made throughout the department. Communication flows not only up and down the structure but also horizontally among the peers. There is much participation and involvement in establishing goals; in improving techniques, methods, and operations; and in evaluating the success of the organization. There are extensive friendly relations between supervisors and subordinates at all levels of the organization. The control process flows from the lower units to the top, and all levels are as fully involved as possible in decision making. The informal structure, if one develops, usually supports the formal organizational structure. As a result, the social forces that develop within the department support the efforts to achieve its goals and objectives.

In summary, System I may be defined as a highly structured, autocratic type of management, while System 4 is based upon more participation, teamwork, and mutual trust within the hierarchy. Systems 2 and 3 are the intermediate stages between the two extremes which closely approximate the assumptions of Theory X and Theory Y.

## SUMMARY AND CONCLUSIONS

This chapter has attempted to examine organizational behavior and the theories of motivation prevalent in contemporary management. Examples have been cited to provide a framework against which police managers may analyze and understand their own organizational behavior. Analyzing and understanding organizational behavior is a necessary start; but only if managers implement decisions and develop their own style of leadership, utilizing the positive side of each theory, will they be able to advance the profession of law enforcement.

---

## NOTES

1. Abraham H. Maslow, *Motivation and Personality* (New York: Harper & Row, Publishers, 1954)
2. Frederick Herzberg, *Work and the Nature of Man* (New York: World Publishing Company, 1966)
3. Douglas McGregor, *The Human Side of Enterprise* (New York: McGraw-Hill Book Company, 1960)
4. Chris Argyris, *Personality and Organization* (New York: Harper & Row, Publishers, 1957)
5. Rensis Likert, *The Human Organization* (New York: McGraw-Hill Book Company, 1967)

# CHAPTER 5

# *Transactional Analysis*

## BEHAVIORAL MODELS AND THE CHANGE PROCESS

Throughout this book, there has been a strong emphasis on behavioral models regarding communication, leadership, motivation, and planning. Each of the models can assist the police manager in conceptualizing approaches to organizational problems. In addition, these models provide managers with a variety of approaches for making judgments as to needed changes in policy, procedure, personnel, and their own behavior. All models, however, are only approximations of reality. They are only useful when police managers can adapt the model to assist their understanding of the realities of the organizational environment.

Each of the models presented emphasizes the fact that the outcomes, in terms of results and side effects, show wide variance depending on the approach used in a given organizational situation. This emphasis on the dynamic character of organizational behavior highlights the complexity and importance of organizational development approaches to change. Thus, a change in leadership style may affect morale and relationships without having a major impact on production. Effective change comes only through the careful development of all aspects of the organization that influence the outcomes important to the manager. There are many excellent expositions of organizational development approaches. This chapter focuses on the police manager as an object of change and provides a model for conceptualizing this change process.

In most change approaches, the role of top management is singled out as the major force in the change process. Fortunately most police managers are keenly aware of the importance of their leadership in change efforts. What is often absent, however, is the awareness of how their own personalities and established approaches to interaction with others interfere with their intentions. In many instances, the first change that must occur in the change effort is a change in the behavior of the police manager.

There are few people who believe that significant changes in personalities or behavior can be accomplished by simply "willing" this change. However, most individuals who reach police management positions are reasonably competent, mature individuals capable of effecting behavioral changes in the interest of becoming more effective as managers. Often such changes occur as managers become more observant of their own behavior and more sensitive to the impact of their behavior on others.

This chapter provides a brief overview of a model that offers significant assistance to police managers in understanding their personal reactions and the nature of their interactions with others. With a little effort and study, this approach can provide a conceptual or "thinking" approach to managing personal change. The approach is called *transactional analysis*.

Since the publication of his best-seller *Games People Play*,[1] Eric Berne's psychological approach to human behavior has become more and more influential in a variety of settings where behavioral change is deemed important. Transactional analysis (TA) as it is presented in this chapter is a conceptual tool that may assist police managers in developing considerable insight into their own behavior. As a general model, it can assist them in determining the extent to which their behavior and attitudes are consistent with their managerial intent. The terminology used is simple and easily learned. Its effect can be powerful and not easily avoided. Most of what Eric Berne says is not new; what is new is that he has taken much of the mystery out of human behavior through a language system to which most people can relate.

## EGO STATES

As a result of broad experiences with both individuals and groups in a variety of treatment settings, Berne became more and more convinced of the importance of analyzing the interactions of individuals in terms of the way they go about obtaining satisfaction of their needs. He was particularly impressed by the fact that individuals in their interactions with others exhibit behavior that is, at times, reminiscent of childlike behaviors, at other times like behaviors one might expect from one's parents, and at other times rational and mature behaviors. Berne saw all of these behaviors as psychological realities representing different states of the *self* or *ego*. Basically the ego states are thought to be much like the sound tracks on a tape, and depending on which track is activated by the situation, the police manager responds accordingly. Managers have learned to relate various behaviors to feelings and experiences that they have had previously. When these feeling tapes are turned on, they respond with the behaviors they have used to deal with these feelings in the past.

As a result of a person's unique personal development, her feelings, reactions, attitudes, and experiences become organized into three major influence systems or ego states. These ego states are referred to as "parent," "adult," and "child" to call attention to the fact that the origins of their development come from different life experiences. If we know the nature of the experiences and feelings that make up each of these ego states, we can describe a given personality.

Transactional analysis is based on the belief that the ego states are consistent patterns of feelings and experiences faithfully recorded in the nervous system and evoked by stimulus situations we experience. It is the analysis of how the manager interacts with others in relation to these ego states that is important in the understanding of human behavior. Most managers have the capacity to identify many of the feelings and behaviors associated with each of the ego states. Through such analysis, police managers can develop the capacity to monitor these behaviors and work toward more effective performance.

These ego states are shown in Figure 5.1.

## Parent Ego State

The parent ego state contains all the attitudes, ideas, postures, gestures, habits, and reaction tendencies that were learned from parents, grandparents, older siblings, or other influential figures in the individual's life. Many of the assumptions, attitudes, ideas, and behaviors that are characteristic of the parent ego state were learned through modeling and were incorporated into behavior patterns without critical examination.

The characteristics of a police manager's parent ego state are entirely determined by the characteristics of his or her own parents and by those of other significant influential figures. Therefore, in acting out the parental ego

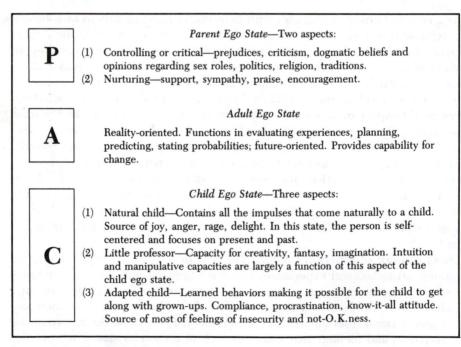

**Figure 5.1** Ego State Diagram

state, the manager is interacting with behaviors observed in his or her own parents or other authority figures.

The parent ego state tends to be filled with opinions and prejudices about religion, politics, traditions, sexual roles, life-styles, role of authority, proper dress, ways of speech, and so on. The critical or controlling aspect of the parent ego state is expressed in a domineering and judgmental fashion. What is right is right, and there is no room for compromise.

The parent ego state, however, includes those feelings and behaviors that make it possible for the police manager to give support, praise, encouragement, or compliments to subordinates. This nurturing side of the parent ego state is particularly important in working with peers or subordinates or in relating to individuals in difficulty. Some police managers have parent ego states that include very little capacity to nurture others; consequently they have difficulty in relating to situations calling for this kind of behavior.

The parent ego state is particularly useful in helping to determine appropriate behavior when the manager has no other data available in providing support to subordinates. Managers who have had good "parental" guidance and nurturing behavior have many attitudes and actions that serve to make their interactions with others pleasant and effective. Other police managers have incorporated attitudes and behaviors that interfere with their effectiveness in dealing with conflict and change.

The content of each manager's parent ego state is unique. It is only through personal awareness of his own reaction tendencies that he can begin to change those behaviors that interfere with his effective functioning. The nature of the parent ego state and the manner in which he expresses parent behavior can be modified through careful monitoring of gestures, feelings, and behavior. Thus, even though he cannot erase the parent tapes, he can gain control through using his capacity to analyze situations objectively and test the effects of his interactions with others.

## Adult Ego State

The adult ego state comprises the capacity to reason, to evaluate situations, gather information, and store this information for future reference. It is not related to a person's age, even though the content of the adult ego state changes with age. When a police manager is operating in her adult state, she is oriented toward present reality and the objective gathering of information. This aspect of her personality is well organized, adaptable, and provides her with the capacity to monitor her thought processes. Consequently, the adult ego state is indispensable in changing her own behavior. In the adult ego state, the police manager is detached from her own emotional and other internal processes. While in the adult state, the manager may be unemotional, although she may be able to appraise child and parent feelings. In the adult ego state the manager considers past, present, and future. Thus, this ego state is essential for effective planning and overall management.

## Child Ego State

The child ego state is essentially childhood preserved in its entirety. It contains the impulses that come naturally to the infant. It contains the recordings
of early experiences, how the one responded to them, and the positions he
took about himself and other people. When a person responds in an inquisi-
tive, affectionate, selfish, mean, playful, whining, or manipulative manner,
he is responding from the child ego state. There are three discernible parts
of the child ego state.

The *natural child* is the part that is very young, impulsive, untrained, and
expressive. When his needs are met, the manager responds out of the child
state with affection. Angry rebellion at having his needs frustrated is also a
reaction of the child state.

The *little professor* refers to the unschooled wisdom that we observe in
children. It is the part of the child ego state that is able to influence the
motivations and feelings of other people. It is through this aspect of the child
ego state that the infant figures things out—when to cry, when to be quiet,
and how to manipulate his or her parents. This aspect can be indicative of a
highly creative mind, even though many of the child ego state creations might
be impractical if not developed by the adult ego state. The police manager's
capacity to create and fantasize is directly related to the degree to which he
is able to permit the little professor in himself to work.

The third aspect of the child ego state is the *adapted child*. This is the
part of the child ego state that exhibits modifications of the natural child's
inclinations. These adaptations of natural impulses occur in response to parental training and demands from significant authority figures. When the
manager complies, procrastinates, acts like a bully, withdraws, or in other
ways behaves as he did in response to the demands of his parents, he is acting
from his adapted child state.

Each of the ego states is important to the manager's being effective in
daily interactions with others. Effective decision making requires that the
police manager be able to process data through the adult state without undue
influence from the child and parent ego states. However, in order to have
fun, he must be able to indulge in his child ego state. To give support to
others or to exercise control of situations, he must be able to rely on his
parent ego state. Good adjustment comes when he is able to use the ego state
that is appropriate to the situation.

The police manager can diagnose ego states in himself and others by observing people's visible and audible characteristics (see Figure 5.2). Certain
words, gestures, postures, mannerisms, and facial expressions are typically
associated with each of the three ego states. In addition to what he sees in
the person being observed, the manager can use his own emotional reactions
and thoughts to help interpret the ego state that he has observed. A parental
reaction in the manager may mean that a child ego state is being observed in
the subordinate.

Feelings of inferiority or rebelliousness in the subordinate may mean that
the ego state being observed in the manager is that of the parent. These clues

|  | *Parent Ego State* | *Adult Ego State* | *Child Ego State* |
|---|---|---|---|
| *Voice tones* | Condescending, putting down, criticizing, or accusing | Matter-of-fact | Full of feeling; high-pitched, whining voice |
| *Words used* | Everyone knows that . . . You should never . . . You should always . . . I can't understand why in the world you would ever . . . I'll put a stop to that once and for all . . . If I were you . . . Stupid . . . naughty . . . ridiculous . . . shocking . . . poor thing . . . good girl . . . good boy | How . . . What . . . When . . . Where . . . Why . . . Who . . . Probable . . . In what way . . . I think . . . I seem . . . It is my opinion | I'm mad at you . . . Wow, terrific! (or any words that have a high feeling level) . . . I wish . . . I want . . . I dunno . . . I guess . . . Bigger . . . Better . . . Best |
| *Postures* | Puffed-up with pride, super-correct, very proper | Attentive, eye-to-eye contact, listening and looking for maximum data, continual action | Slouching, playful, beaten down, burdened, self-conscious |
| *Facial expressions* | Frowning, worried or disapproving looks, chin jutted out, furrowed brow, pursed lips | Alert eyes, maximum attention given | Excited, surprised, downcast eyes, quivering lip or chin, moist eyes, rolling eyes |
| *Body gestures* | Hands on hips, pointing finger in accusation, arms folded across chest, patting on head, deep sigh | Leaning forward in chair toward other person, moving closer to hear and see better | Spontaneous activity, wringing hands, pacing, withdrawing into corner or moving away from laughter, raising hand for per-mission, shrug-ging shoulders |

**Figure 5.2**   Clues to Ego States

assist in determining the effect of behavior on others and the appropriateness of interaction. Awareness of these clues can be of assistance to the manager in understanding differences in approaches to various situations and may provide a basis for determining changes that may be necessary in his interactions with others.

Any one of the ego states discussed can serve as the determinant of the police manager's personality at any given time. In order for him to be well-adjusted, he must be able to move from one ego state to another using the proper ego state for a given situation. People normally develop some form of control that helps them in their movement from one ego state to another. This control may be lax, that is, there may be very little control from the adult ego state and therefore the manager may move very rapidly from one ego state to another: from child to parent or from parent to child. The other extreme is a manager who has a very rigid ego state boundary. In this case, there is very little free movement between the ego states.

The manager who has a rigid or constant parent ego state tends to treat subordinates as if they were children, refusing to accept their abilities or ideas. As a police manager, he might go about constantly trying to help the officers carry their everyday responsibilities. The manager who is constantly using his adult ego state has developed little in his personal relationships with people. He is extremely logical and requires hard-core data before making any kind of decision. This type of manager, although quite effective in such fields as research, might be ineffective as a commander of personnel within the police department.

The constant child is one who refuses to accept responsibility and refuses to make decisions. This kind of an individual rarely climbs the ladder of promotions within the police department and is satisfied with staying at the entrance level for his entire career. This is not, however, to imply that all people who remain at the entrance level are doing so because of their reliance upon their child ego state. The constant child uses devices such as seeking direction for minor tasks for which he has been well trained, or he may constantly ask for reassurance before making any decision.

Police managers must also be aware of problems of *contamination* and *isolation*. By contamination is meant that the adult ego state is contaminated by either the child or the parent ego state. A typical example might be that of the police manager who refuses to have women under his command. He uses strong rationalization and attempts to prove his point by citing the possibility of injuries and even finds data to help to reinforce his position. The action may appear to be adult; however, careful examination may reveal that this police manager is highly prejudiced in his attitudes toward women. It is this prejudice rather than the facts he has gathered that governs his behavior. This can be tested by providing counterexamples to determine whether or not the individual manager is able to deal with the new data from his adult ego state. If he refuses to accept its importance, totally rejects it, and makes a judgmental decision strictly from his parent ego state, then there is contamination.

Isolation means the complete blocking out of an ego state. If the child ego state is blocked out, the manager is also blocking out the spontaneous, fun-loving side of his nature. Managers who are ony fact-seeking and are never able to laugh at life or accept humor within the daily operations of their legal responsibilities might have blocked out their child ego state. If the parent ego state is blocked out, there is no conscience involved in the manager's decision. These managers show little remorse or shame. In many instances, they become criminal in their actions and may eventually be arrested for dishonesty or unethical conduct. If the manager isolates the adult, he is usually in conflict with the world of reality and may even have mental disorders severe enough to require hospitalization.

Of the three ego states, the adult state is usually the last to be effectively developed. Assuming that the police manager was attempting to build a stronger adult ego state, he could follow some of the following principles from *I'm O.K.—You're O.K.*"[2]

1. Learn to recognize his child ego state, its vulnerabilities, its fears, its principal methods of expressing feelings.
2. Learn to recognize his parent ego state, its admonitions, injunctions, and positions.
3. Be sensitive to the parent, adult, and child ego states in himself and in others.
4. Count to ten if necessary in order to give the adult ego state time to process the data coming into the human computer of the brain and to sort out the parent ego and child ego realities.
5. Work out and develop a system of values.

Once this system of values has been established, decisions can be made within its ethical framework.


# TRANSACTIONS AND COMMUNICATION

It is important that the police manager understand his own ego states if he is to make transactional analysis (TA) work for him. However, it is the application of this knowledge in his daily interactions that is most useful. In TA, an interaction with another person is called a *transaction*. In all transactions, the person's ego state will determine his response to others. Three major patterns of interaction can be identified.


## Complementary Transactions

In many transactions, the police manager will find communication going smoothly; he will feel comfortable in the relationships and find it easy to continue the conversation. These transactions are most frequently referred to as *complementary transactions*. In such transactions, both parties in the interaction are responding from ego states that are appropriate to maintaining the communication. In the example below, the manager tells a subordinate to have a report in on Friday, and the subordinate dutifully confirms that he will have the report in on that day.

MANAGER: John, I want that report by Friday, and you had better not be late. (The parent ego state is dominant, and the expectation is compliance from the child ego state in the other person.)
JOHN: Yes, Sir. No problem. (Child compliance back to the parent in the manager.)

The manager's order is made in a demanding, uncompromising tone indicating that he is coming out of his controlling parent ego state. The response of the subordinate indicates that he will comply without question. This response—from the child ego state—is the one the manager expected, and no apparent problem exists. Such transactions are referred to as complementary because the person who initiates the transaction communicates from a particular ego state and receives a response from the other person that meets his expectations. Following are examples of complementary transactions:

1ST SGT.: These new recruits just don't have any guts.   (parent to parent—judgmental)
2ND SGT.: You're right. I don't know how they expect us to do anything with these jerks.   (parent back to parent)

OFFICER: Let's knock off early and get in a few games of bowling.   (child to child)
2ND SGT.: That's a good idea, where do you want to go?   (child to child)

1ST SGT.: How many men do you think we will need during the 4 to 8 period this Saturday?   (adult to adult)
2ND SGT.: From the data we have, I would say we need at least twelve additional officers.   (adult to adult)

OFFICER: Sgt. Brown, I really screwed up this report, can you help me?   (child to parent)
SGT.: Certainly, son, I used to have a little trouble with those reports myself.   (nurturing parent to child)

In each of the transactions illustrated above, the person initiating the transaction received a response that was consistent with the stimulus message. Such transactions set the stage for continuing communication between the two persons.

## Crossed Transactions

In some transactions with others, the manager may immediately be aware that something has happened to disrupt the relationship. For example, after an initial exchange, he and the subordinate may stand glaring at each other, turn their backs on each other, change the topic abruptly, or show puzzlement at what has just occurred. The behaviors suggest that the transaction has resulted in a disruption of communication. In most instances, the manager initiating the transaction has received a response that was inconsistent with his expectations. Such transactions are referred to as *crossed transactions*. A crossed transaction occurs any time the person initiating the transaction receives a response that is perceived as inappropriate or unexpected. As an example:

CAPT.: Have you spoken to the chief about the court schedule? (adult to adult)
LT.: No, and I'm not about to. He can go jump in the lake. (child to parent)

In the example above, the captain is communicating from his adult ego state, expecting a reasonable, adult reply. The lieutenant, however, responds out of his child ego state in an angry, rebellious manner. The lieutenant's response is directed to the parent in the captain. The subsequent conversation will largely be determined by the captain's response. He may choose to stay in the adult ego state and try to find out why the lieutenant is annoyed with the chief. If he moves to his parent ego state, he may either berate the lieutenant for his poor attitude or be sympathetic. In either case, the crossed transaction results in a change in the level of communication between the two. Other examples of crossed transactions are illustrated below:

CAPT.: George, you are changing shifts with Harold next week. (parent to child)
LT.: You're crazy. How did you make captain anyway? (parent to child)

LT.: Let's organize a card game this week. (child to child)
CAPT.: If you would quit trying to figure out ways to avoid work, we might get something done around here. (parent to child)

In the first example, the captain changes the shifts of one of his lieutenants and directs that the change be made. George responds from his parent state by making derogatory remarks about the captain. This transaction will probably lead to disciplinary action, which could have been avoided by an adult-to-adult discussion about the change of shift.

In the second example, the lieutenant expresses his wish to organize a card game and the captain responds in a critical, judgmental fashion. The lieutenant may not mention cards again, but he will also carry around a lot of hard feelings toward the captain. The captain could have avoided this by crossing the transaction to his adult state and saying something like: "I wouldn't mind discussing that later, but right now I have a lot of work to do."

In both examples, the crossed transaction results in consequences that are not productive as far as the police department is concerned. By paying more attention to their communications, the commanders in each instance could have avoided costly reactions on the part of their subordinates.

However, crossed transactions are sometimes useful and necessary in order to gain control of situations or to bring about a change in behavior that is inappropriate to the situation. The general rule is that a cross over to the adult state is likely to be the most productive. For example:

LT.: That stupid lieutenant couldn't supervise if he had a seeing-eye dog.
    (parent to parent)
CAPT.: What has he done to make you so angry? (adult to adult)

In this cross, the captain avoids getting into a parent-to-parent criticism of the lieutenant and begins to explore the problem between the two lieutenants. While such a cross does not always lead to problem-solving behavior on the part of the responder, it provides a better chance than a parent-to-child cross or a child-to-child interaction.

Crossed transactions leading to ill feelings, unproductive use of time, and organizational conflict can be avoided if police managers are aware of their tendencies and become more proficient in determining the appropriateness of the adult-to-adult pattern of communication.

## Ulterior Transactions

The third type of transaction is referred to as an *ulterior transaction*. Here there are two messages. One, the overt message, is communicated at the verbal level. At the same time, the second or covert message is communicated subliminally. This second message is intended to elicit a response different from that called for by the first message. Managers may use ulterior transactions in attempting to sell a project. For example, the following, which on the surface sounds like an adult-to-adult transaction, may take place between a chief and his command staff:

CHIEF: This is a really good project I have developed, and I would like you to see if there is anything wrong with it.

The verbal message appears to be a straightforward request for constructive criticism. However, the implication is that the chief thinks highly of the project and is already committed to it; he is therefore probably *not* really interested in seeing the staff come up with alternative plans. These implications stem from the manager's parent ego state and are addressed to the staff's child ego state. If the staff accept the ulterior message, they will respond from their child ego state and say "Yes, chief, that project sounds good." If the staff do not read the ulterior message and question the chief, they may get a parent-to-child response from the chief, such as "You don't really understand the problem."

When a subordinate, overworked and looking discouraged, comes in with a report, her verbal comment "Here is the report" is on its face an adult-to-adult transaction. However, her demeanor may provoke the manager to say: "You look down, what's wrong?" The subordinate's physical appearance communicates a message from her child state that she wants encouragement and support from the manager's parent state. The manager, in acknowledging the report in his adult state, may or may not respond to the child needs of the subordinate.

An ulterior message is often involved when a person announces, seemingly from his adult state, that he has done something wrong or is having difficulty. For example:

LT. TO CAPT.: I've read this statute two or three times, but I just don't understand
   it.

On the surface, this is an adult-to-adult description of the lieutenant's state of
mind. However, the child message asks for either a put-down for being stupid
or for support from the captain.

Ulterior transactions are sometimes used to communicate feelings or ideas
when the individual wants to avoid a direct statement, being uncertain of the
response he or she might otherwise receive. However, ulterior transactions
are a poor substitute for honest ones and are the basis for psychological
games, which will be discussed later in the chapter.

The police manager, in dealing with ulterior transactions, must be aware
of the following:

1. What ulterior transactions he deliberately engages in
2. Which of his honest transactions may be interpreted as ulterior messages
3. What ulterior transactions others are initiating

Ulterior transactions can cause major obstacles in the way of effective
communications in a police department; they prevent the agency from becoming as effective as it could be if honest transactions were more common.

## BASIC LIFE POSITIONS AND ORGANIZATIONAL SANCTIONS

The police manager's ego states and the nature of the transactions that he or
she customarily engages in are to a large extent determined by the manager's
early life experiences. In all probability, one of the most important determinants of how we interact with others is how we view ourselves and other
people. How we view our adult selves is very much a function of the view
we held of ourselves as children. Likewise, the degree of trust we place in
other people and our general beliefs about them are established on the basis
of our early life experiences. In one way or another, at some time early in
our life, we make decisions about ourselves and others that determine the
nature of our future interactions. These decisions are referred to in transactional analysis as *basic life positions*.

There are four basic life positions, which are determined by whether one
has made positive or negative decisions about oneself and others. People
whose life experiences have been rewarding and who have had a sufficient
amount of praise and encouragement will probably see themselves in a very
positive light. That is, they are "O.K." If, on the other hand, they were
constantly ridiculed, called dumb, or rejected by their peers, they will likely
see themselves in a negative light, or as "not O.K." How other people be-
haved toward us determines whether we see others as "O.K." or "not O.K."
All combinations of decisions are possible, which lead, in turn, to one of four
basic positions.

*First Position: "I'm O.K., You're O.K."* If realistic, this is the position of managers who are psychologically healthy, mature, and able to develop open, trusting relationships with other people. They see others as having potential for development and assume responsibility for their own behavior. While they may occasionally experience depression, they recognize that it is temporary and take steps to overcome their negative feelings.

*Second Position: "I'm O.K., You're Not O.K."* This is the position of the manager who feels that others are out to degrade and persecute him. He blames others for his miseries and is unwilling to take responsibility for his shortcomings and mistakes. His relationships are marked by a strong distrust of other people and a need to be in control of others and of all situations.

*Third Position: "I'm Not O.K., You're O.K."* Police managers in this position feel powerless. When they compare themselves to others, they come up short. Managers in this position are self-critical and overly concerned about their shortcomings and mistakes. They have a tendency to become easily depressed and are at times irrational in their decisions.

*Fourth Position: "I'm Not O.K., You're Not O.K."* Individuals in this position have given up on life. They see little good in themselves or in other people. They may be withdrawn, moody, and pessimistic, and it may be very difficult to develop any kind of effective working relationship with them. Usually they are not involved in steady employment at management positions in law enforcement due to the necessity of decision making in police departments.

The concept of the basic life positions is useful in understanding individual differences in response to organizational sanctions and the differences in the use of sanctions by police managers. Most police departments have some form of positive and negative sanctions in order to reward good performance and punish poor performance. However, people differ in their reaction to advancements, awards, and praise as well as to negative sanctions such as suspensions, criticism, demotions, and transfers.

Managers who feel "O.K." about themselves and others seek and give as many forms as possible of positive recognition. Others who feel "not O.K." about themselves are more frequently in a position to receive negative sanctions than positive sanctions. Similarly, managers who take life positions that emphasize the "not O.K.ness" of other people have a tendency to impose as many negative sanctions as possible. In all probability, the difference between police managers who constantly look for opportunities to criticize, suspend, or demote and police managers who are conscientious in their efforts to provide positive sanctions has a great deal to do with their life positions regarding other people.

Both positive and negative sanctions are acts that recognize the behavior of other people. In TA, such acts are referred to as *strokes*. Everybody needs a certain amount of stroking, or recognition, to survive. Infants need physical stroking if they are to develop properly. After infancy, the need for physical stroking diminishes, and a need for recognition from other people becomes essential to psychological development. Whether the manager praises or punishes a person, her acts recognize the other person, which is the basis of a stroke.

In order to be psychologically sound and to relate meaningfully to others, people need positive strokes such as praise, compliments, appreciation, and attention to their ideas and feelings. Positive strokes make subordinates feel stronger, more competent, and more effective. Negative strokes such as criticism, being ignored, or having ideas and feelings discounted make subordinates feel weaker, less effective, and less competent. The police work situation can be a major source of strokes. Unfortunately, some police departments give many more negative than positive strokes, and their officers are angry, unhappy, and less effective on the job.

Positive strokes can take many forms. Simple acts of recognition such as a friendly "good morning" or a welcoming handshake are important in maintaining a sense of "O.K.ness." However, subordinates also need the more lasting strokes that come from having good work recognized, being given a chance to use their skills, and being rewarded for their service and hard work. At the deepest level, subordinates need the strokes that come from having an intimate, caring relationship with a manager they respect and trust.

Within police departments, managers and supervisors should be a major source of positive strokes. Many departmental change efforts result in different patterns of stroking. For example, placing decision-making responsibility in the hands of officers at lower levels in the hierarchy is a way of recognizing their competence and importance and becomes a powerful positive stroke. Likewise, moving to team decision making gives every officer a chance to be heard, which for most is an important stroke in their relationship with others.

As a police manager becomes more aware of her own stroking tendencies, she often finds that she too frequently fails to give positive strokes in appropriate situations. On the other hand, she may ignore the negative stroking situations that she finds during the course of a day. Such stroking patterns often create cautious, unhappy subordinates who may begin to feel themselves incapable of making sound decisions. In addition, the officers and supervisors working in police departments where there is a deficit of positive strokes will frequently do only that which is required of them and use their energies and skills to obtain strokes in their time off or through sabotaging the efforts of the police command structure.

It is essential to recognize that everyone needs a certain amount of stroking and that they will find some way to obtain the strokes they need. For the "I'm not O.K." individuals, negative strokes may be more important than positive strokes. However, most officers who make contributions to the police mission feel "O.K." about themselves and need positive strokes to maintain this "O.K." feeling.

## Time Structuring

In order to obtain the strokes they need, subordinates structure their time in a variety of ways. The six ways that have been identified as providing opportunities for obtaining strokes are described below:

One way to structure time is to *withdraw.* The manager can withdraw through fantasy, by ignoring others and watching TV, or by going off by himself to a favorite thinking place. He may withdraw when he is uncomfortable, bored, or feeling "not O.K." In moderation, withdrawal is a healthy way to obtain vicarious strokes. The overuse of withdrawal may suggest that the manager is not getting enough strokes in his relationships with other people.

A second way to structure time is through *rituals.* Some rituals are social exchanges that we have learned from our parents, such as the proper ways to greet and introduce people, polite table manners, and so forth. Other rituals are unique to the culture or organizations to which we belong. There are many rituals in the typical police department. Some examples are the way subordinates address ranking officers, how seating is arranged at staff meetings, and how communication is formalized within the hierarchy. These are ritualistic in that they provide the structure for individuals in the various ranks to be recognized and respected by those below them in the rank structure. Observation suggests that the fewer opportunities for obtaining positive strokes in normal exchanges at work with the police department, the more important these ritual behaviors become. To be effective, a police manager must be aware of the importance of rituals within the department and within the community in which he works. He also needs to be wary when rituals become more important than results.

A third way to structure time is through *pastimes.* Pastimes include the general discussion between people of interests, values, and events. Pastimes are a rich source of strokes in the absence of other types of time structuring. Between casual friends, this is a major form of time structuring. An exchange of their latest "war stories" is a favorite pastime among officers. Managers can spend hours talking about the "new breed" of officer or "how it was in the good old days."

Being able to engage in pastimes is an important social skill in making new acquaintances, enjoying a luncheon, or relaxing with associates. Pastimes are also useful departmentally when there is informal discussion of issues relevant to the police organization. However, they can also be harmful, as when supervisors get together over coffee and "knock" the police department—an example of a parent-to-parent pastime. Too much use of pastimes during work hours suggests there is a lack of sufficient stroking for good police work habits.

The fourth time structuring approach is *activity.* Activities comprise all manner of time usage related to recreation and work. Home improvement projects, golf, tennis, or any other occupation in which an individual spends time actively is an activity. Activities are a primary source of gaining strokes. When the police department fails to provide enough strokes for the activity of police work within the department, many officers find activities outside of police work to gain the strokes they are missing. For instance, they take on second jobs. The dramatic increase in recreational activities in our culture suggests that police employees are highly motivated to gain strokes and use their work not as a primary source of strokes but as a way of earning the necessary income to engage in those activities where they may obtain the strokes they need. The test of management is in the creation of a police department where police activities are a rich source of strokes.

Psychological *games* are the fifth way of structuring time. Psychological games are a devious way of obtaining or giving strokes. All have certain basic elements:

1. There is a series of complementary transactions that on the surface seem reasonable.
2. There is an ulterior transaction that is the hidden agenda or reason for the interaction.
3. There is a negative outcome or payoff that concludes the game and is the real purpose for playing it.

Structuring time through games decreases the problem-solving capacities of the police department. While games appear to have advantages, they are all to some degree destructive to effective work relationships. In departments where officers are bored with their jobs or where the work environment is void of positive strokes, the officers have more need to play games. The next section of this chapter will describe some typical police department games.

The sixth way to structure time is through *intimate relationships*. Intimate relationships are free of games and free of exploitation. The relationship is straightforward and honest, arousing feelings of tenderness, empathy, and affection. It involves a genuine caring for another person. Intimate relationships require a sense of "O.K.ness" regarding oneself and others. The intimate relationship is a source of some of the most lasting and enriching strokes, but it is not the most typical form of structuring time in police departments.

Intimacy cannot be created or engineered by the manager. It must occur spontaneously. It occurs between people who may not even be expecting it, and it seldom occurs when the manager goes out in deliberate search of it. The experience of intimacy is the experience of feeling a massive dose of positive stroking. In an intimate relationship, people feel unconditionally stroked and accepted for who they are, not for what they can do, how they dress, how they look, or how important a position they hold.

Certain conditions must exist in order for intimacy to occur. These conditions are:

*First,* all defenses must be down. This means the manager must give up some personal gains, ceasing to emphasize rituals and pastimes.

*Second,* the manager must take the risk of being vulnerable. If he lets down his defenses, he may get hurt, and this is what the adapted child in him may fear.

*Third,* he has to feel positively, not negatively, toward the other person. His nurturing parent and natural child must feel "O.K." about the other person. He has to be in a state where he moves toward the other person and not against him.

*Fourth,* he must accept the other person unconditionally. If he places demands or sets up rules that control how close others can come, then he blocks intimacy.

The time-structuring characteristics of managers in a police department provide important clues as to the changes needed in the work environment. Where withdrawal, rituals, pastimes, and games make up the major stroke-acquiring transactions, the department's effectiveness will be seriously curtailed. Most change efforts focus on making the activities of police work more meaningful sources of strokes.

The police manager's own time-structuring characteristics are important determinants in the effectiveness of such change efforts.

## ORGANIZATIONAL GAMES

Psychological games are played by individuals who have a need to receive or give negative feelings, which are the payoff in the games. A fairly typical game played in police departments begins by a supervisor asking his subordinates for suggestions:

CHIEF: We're in a real pinch. Headquarters wants us to develop a better relationship with the community; any suggestions?

1ST CAPT.: Why don't we approach all the business leaders on a personal basis and give them information about our department and have them submit their ideas and complaints?

CHIEF: That's O.K., but it would take too much time.

2ND CAPT.: I think we should start with the schools and increase our contact with teachers, kids, and parents.

CHIEF: That would be all right, but it doesn't relate to stopping crime.

Other commanders offer suggestions, only to be told that their ideas are "all right, but. . . ." The chief finally leaves with the comment that "I guess you can't help me with this problem." This leaves the commanders feeling that they have wasted their time and couldn't help. The chief leaves feeling that "These guys can't help with anything." The bad feelings the commanders have and the bad feelings the chief has toward them is the payoff for the game of "Yes, but." The "Yes, but" player can be distinguished from one who genuinely requests help by the fact that the "Yes, but" player is often asking for input but never accepts any ideas. The player will continue to play this game until his subordinates cease to offer suggestions.

Psychological games reinforce or confirm a person's basic life position about himself and others. Thus, the police manager who is successful in playing "Yes, but" with his staff confirms his "O.K.ness" and the "not O.K.ness" of other members of his staff. Games played from the "I'm O.K., you're not O.K." position are attacks on subordinates and are designed to reinforce feelings that others are "not O.K." Other games are played from the "I'm not O.K., you're O.K." position and reinforce negative feelings the police manager has about himself.

Some of the common games played by people in law enforcement are briefly described below.

*If It Weren't for Him (Them)*.   This is a game designed to blame someone else for one's own poor performance or production. The "him" or "them" usually represents a person higher in the department. The chief may point to the city council. The payoff is that the player takes himself off the hook and places responsibility for his failure to perform on someone else. Basically, this game allows an individual to maintain his own sense of "O.K.ness" by placing others in a "not O.K." position.

*Now I've Got You, You SOB (NIGYYSOB)*.   This is a game in which the player attempts to catch another individual or group in a mistake, a lie, or a violation of rules and orders so that he can discipline the person in violation. This might be played by anyone in the police department. For example, a lieutenant, knowing of the tendency for officers under his command to sleep on the midnight shift, might make a surprise check to catch sleepers. He then imposes disciplinary measures on both the officers and their sergeant. The game permits the lieutenant to get rid of his angry feelings toward others and puts the sergeant in his place. He is also confirming in his own mind that he is "O.K." but that the others are "not O.K." This game tends to destroy the lieutenant's chances of ever developing trusting relationships with these officers in the future.

*Blemish*.   In this game, the player may review a report or performance evaluation and pick out minor flaws in an otherwise good report. He is the "nit-picker" who always has to find something wrong and seldom comments on the good parts of the report. The payoff for the blemish player is the bad feelings he gives to others.

*Corner*.   The players of this game put people into impossible binds. The corner player may ask for a report with a tight deadline. When the report comes back with understandable omissions, the player returns the report with a reprimand. If the report writer turns the report in late in order to make sure it is complete and accurate, he is reprimanded for being late. The payoff is the reprimand the player gives to the report writer.

In addition to the games played for the purpose of punishing others or of proving their "not O.K.ness," there are a number of games that result in the player being put down or criticized or that are designed to provoke sympathy. Players of these games experience a keen sense of "not O.K.ness" or inadequacy.

*Poor Me*.   In this game, the player finds herself in a situation she doesn't like and spends hours of time griping to anyone who will listen. Usually this gets the player a lot of sympathy from the listeners. Players of "poor me" refuse to do anything constructive to remove themselves from the situation; if the conditions they gripe about were changed, they would find something else to make their lives miserable. "Poor me" players see themselves as "not O.K." and constantly find situations that confirm their dismal feelings.

*Kick Me.* Players of "kick me" are constantly getting into situations that provoke their managers or supervisors into taking some form of negative action against them. Some "kick me" players are chronically late for important assignments or turn in reports with errors on them. Even after close instruction as to what is required, they continue to make important mistakes. Hard-core players ultimately end up getting "kicked out" of the police department by being fired. Others receive enough "kick" to prevent them from ever being considered for promotion and use this circumstance to play "poor me."

*Stupid.* This is a variation of the "kick me" game. In this instance, the player is constantly doing "stupid" things that provoke the supervisor or colleagues into commenting on his stupidity. Stupid players are usually bright enough to perform but are constantly making dumb mistakes or placing themselves in jeopardy by their poor judgment. Stupid players may fail a sergeant's exam for years despite their intelligence. They usually comment that they are probably too dumb to pass the exam.

*Wooden Leg.* In "wooden leg," the player finds some excuse to avoid success or accomplishment. It is a cop-out game where a person uses a physical or social handicap to avoid being successful. A long-term officer who has failed to advance may say that he would try something else but that he is too old. The middle-aged sergeant might use the excuse of age not to attend college classes even though they may be necessary for him to advance any further. Any number of excuses can be used as a "wooden leg," such as family background, lack of education, age, or lack of physical capabilities. By using excuses, people escape from the challenge to grow and get ahead; thus they are able to maintain their "not O.K." life position.

While all the behaviors involved in these games can be exhibited by non-game-playing individuals, games can be recognized by the fact that they occur over and over again and that the outcomes are predictable for the individuals involved. The kind of games a person plays seldom change. The "kick me" player and the "Yes, but" player continue as long as there are people who allow them to get away with their games. The player of games from the "I'm O.K., you're not O.K." position needs individuals in the "I'm not O.K., you're O.K." position to make his games work. As in every game, certain players are necessary. The breaking up of games requires straight adult-to-adult transactions. By pointing out organizational games and being unwilling to support them, it is possible to discourage their players. The police manager's task is to recognize the time-wasting games played in the department and to begin developing an atmosphere that discourages games and encourages straight, honest, problem-solving behavior.

## SUMMARY

This chapter has attempted to summarize the basic concepts of transactional analysis and to provide a limited number of illustrations as to the implications of TA concepts in organizational and personal change efforts. The material presented does little more than introduce the basic concepts. For interested police managers, further study and training are essential for these concepts to be of value in their management practice.

There has developed a substantial body of literature that covers in detail the theory and implications of TA to management practice. In addition, there are many consulting firms ready and able to provide training and consultation to police managers interested in implementing these concepts in their police departments.

There may be many who criticize TA on theoretical and practical grounds. However, the model has wide applicability, its major concepts are easily understood, and it provides an excellent set of concepts for giving direction to personal change. These comments in no way suggest that personal or organizational change is easy or that TA will solve all the problems for a police manager. Like all other models, it is a tool that can prove effective in the hands of those police managers who understand and believe in the approach.

## NOTES

1. Eric Berne, *Games People Play* (New York: Grove Press, 1964)
2. Thomas H. Harris, *I'm O.K.—You're O.K.* (New York: Avon Books, 1967)

## BIBLIOGRAPHY

Berne, Eric. *Games People Play*. New York: Grove Press, 1964.
———. *Principles of Group Treatment*. New York: Grove Press, 1966.
———. *The Structure and Dynamics of Organizations and Groups,* New York: Grove Press, 1963.
———. *Transactional Analysis in Psychotherapy*. New York: Evergreen Original, 1961.
———. *What Do You Say after You Say Hello?* New York: Bantam Books, 1972.
Harris, Thomas H. *I'm O.K., You're O.K.* New York: Avon Books, 1967.
James, Muriel. *The O.K. Boss*. Reading, Mass.: Addison-Wesley, 1976.
James, Muriel, and Jongeward, Dorothy. *Born to Win*. Reading, Mass.: Addison-Wesley, 1971.
Jongeward, Dorothy, and contributors. *Everybody Win, Transactional Analysis Applied to Organizations*. Reading, Mass.: Addison-Wesley, 1974.
Jongeward, Dorothy, and James, Muriel. *Winning with People: Group Exercises in Transactional Analysis*. Reading, Mass.: Addison-Wesley, 1973.
Meininger, Jut. *Success through Transactional Analysis*. Signet Book, 1973.
Steiner, Claude. *Games Alcoholics Play*. New York: Ballantine Books, 1971.
———. *Scripts People Live*. New York: Bantam Books, 1974.

# CHAPTER 6

# Understanding Personnel Through MBTI

## OVERVIEW

How do the people in your police department get along? How do they feel about their superiors or their colleagues across the hall? Do they agree on how decisions are made and who should do what jobs? Probably not. Conflicts are inevitable in human organizations. These conflicts are believed to arise from personality differences, and they can be major obstacles to efficient operation. This chapter will describe a method of helping police managers recognize these differences and use them to strengthen their agencies.

"Personality," as used here, refers to the complex array of personal characteristics (needs, motivations, values, morals, etc.) that make people different. But these general terms do not describe the individual's basic attitude—or approach to life—that guides behavior and is reflected in personality (and sometimes conflicts with other approaches). As a result, psychologists have sought ways to identify what it is that makes up each person's preferred way of dealing with the world.

The Myers-Briggs Type Indicator (MBTI)[1] does just that; it is an instrument that specifically reveals one's personal traits and makes it possible to compare differences in fundamental approaches among individuals. The MBTI is used for management training and consultation. The police managers who have used it find that it helps them to recognize both compatible and incompatible styles. By understanding the differences in approach, managers can see how these differences affect relationships; thus they are better able to avert unproductive conflicts and improve the department's overall performance.

## FUNCTIONAL BEHAVIOR

The MBTI instrument identifies four basic preferences that relate to (1) the way people become aware of the outside world; (2) the way they come to conclusions about what they become aware of—that is, how they make decisions; (3) their degree of flexibility; and (4) their orientation toward the external world. The theoretical direction for the MBTI came from Carl Jung's theory of types.[2]

Jung believed that when we become aware of the world around us and make decisions on the basis of that awareness, we use a combination of mental processes:

- Sensory (through the five senses), symbolized by the letter S
- Intuitive (indirectly—through the subconscious, what is learned through the senses, and by pursuing the possibilities of the situation), symbolized by N
- Thinking (rational), symbolized by T
- Feeling (on the basis of a value system), symbolized by F

Ideally, the individual develops a command of all of these processes and uses them throughout life. But because of differences in life experiences, people vary in the degree of their development of these processes and have different preferences and approaches to the situations that life presents.

Let's begin with awareness. How do people get their fundamental view of the world? By using the sensory process, the intuitive process, or a combination of the two. The degree to which a person prefers one over the other can be visualized on a continuum that places total reliance on understanding through the senses at one end of the scale and total reliance on intuition at the other.

SENSORY                           INTUITIVE

Most of us fall somewhere between the two extremes. Those who find themselves on the sensory side of the scale prefer gathering the observable facts of a situation; they tend to be "realistic, practical, observant . . . and good at remembering a great number of facts and working with them."[3] Those who rest on the intuitive side tend to value imagination and inspiration, are good at producing new ideas and projects, and like to solve problems.

What about decision making? When a person comes to settling, closing, or completing an issue, he or she primarily uses one of two processes: thinking or feeling. The person in whom the thinking (rational) process dominates tends to be logical, objective, and consistent, making decisions by analyzing and weighing the data. Those who rely mostly on the feeling process tend to make decisions on the basis of values, or "because it feels right." They also tend to be sympathetic, appreciative, and tactful in dealing with others. These processes can also be visualized on a continuum:

THINKING                           FEELING

The processes of becoming aware and reaching conclusions develop independently. Thus the processes of becoming aware and the processes of making decisions can be joined in the following combinations:

**ST** (sensory plus thinking). People with this combination are mainly interested in facts; they make decisions by impersonal analysis. As individuals they tend to be practical and matter of fact.

**SF** (sensory plus feeling). People with this combination are interested in facts but are also in tune with feelings in themselves and others. They are sociable and friendly.

    **NF** (intuitive plus feeling). People with this combination are interested not in
facts but in possibilities for the future—they base their decisions on personal
feelings. They are enthusiastic and insightful.

    **NT** (intuitive plus thinking). People with this combination are interested in pos-
sibilities but approach them with impersonal analysis. In decision making,
they more or less ignore the human element.

    Which combination of preferences an individual has developed makes a
difference in the types of work he or she will enjoy. An ST (sensory–thinking)
person would prefer a job that requires data gathering and the making of
logical, calculated decisions based on the data (a good example would be patrol). An SF (sensory–feeling) person would probably prefer a project that
requires extensive dealings with people (working with juveniles), while an
NT (intuitive–thinking) might prefer abstract concepts or ideas (homicide investigation). An NF (intuitive–feeling) person would enjoy a job that deals
with people and requires creativity and originality (training, community
relations).

    Another aspect of personality type identified by the MBTI is whether a
person prefers closure and having things settled or prefers to keep options
open. People who choose closure over keeping their options open are referred to as judgers (J's); those who prefer to keep things open and fluid are
perceivers (P's). Judgers like to decide matters quickly. They live in a
planned, decided, orderly way, wanting to regulate life and control it. Perceivers, on the other hand, like to keep their options open; they are not
dependent on order and stability. They are flexible and enjoy seeking alternatives, being spontaneously able to understand life and adapt to it.

    The final trait measured by the MBTI centers on relative interest in the
outer or inner worlds—that is, on whether an individual is an introvert or an
extrovert. Introverts concentrate on their inner world, more content in dealing with ideas and concepts. Extroverts enjoy focusing on the world around
them and are more comfortable in action than in contemplation. Sometimes
these words are given positive or negative connotations; in this context they
merely describe individual preferences.

    In terms of these four traits—preferred method of becoming aware, pre-
ferred method of reaching conclusions, preferred degree of closure, and preferred orientation toward the outer world—a person can be predominately:

1. S (sensing) or N (intuitive)
2. T (thinking) or F (feeling)
3. J (judging) or P (perceiving)
4. I (introverted) or E (extroverted)

Figure 6.1 shows (a) the possible combinations of these four preferences into
the sixteen types described by the MBTI and (b) some characteristics of people who have each combination.

    Each preference contributes unique characteristics that help to shape the
individual. People tend naturally to act and react in ways that are most com-

| **ISTJ** | **ISFJ** | **INFJ** | **INTJ** |
|---|---|---|---|
| —Dependable | —Service-oriented | —Highly sensitive to others | —Self-confident |
| —Decisive | —Willing to work long hours | —Perseverant in his work | —Is natural decision-maker |
| —Quiet, serious | —Respects tradition | —Enjoys problem-solving | —Extremely theoretical |
| —Interested in thoroughness, detail | —Extremely dependable | —Has strong drive to help others | —Single-minded |
| | —Devoted, loyal | | |

| **ISTP** | **ISFP** | **INFP** | **INTP** |
|---|---|---|---|
| —Impulsive | —Sensitive | —Deeply caring | —Very precise in thought and language |
| —Free spirit | —Shuns leadership | —Enthusiastic | —Has intense concentration |
| —Risk taker | —Experiences intensely | —Independent | —Curious, searching |
| —Thrives on excitement | | —Adaptable | —Quiet, reserved |
| | | —Welcomes new ideas and information | |

| **ESTP** | **ESFP** | **ENFP** | **ENTP** |
|---|---|---|---|
| —Person of action | —Warm, optimistic | —Enthusiastic, imaginative | —Deals imaginatively with others |
| —Negotiator, diplomat | —Charming, clever | —Independent | —Good analyst |
| —Theatrical, exciting | —Sociable | —Keen and penetrating observer | —Open-minded attitude |
| —Witty, clever | —Outstanding conversationalist | | —Fascinating conversationalist |
| | —Prefers active jobs | | —Versatile |

| **ESTJ** | **ESFJ** | **ENFJ** | **ENTJ** |
|---|---|---|---|
| —In touch with external environs | —The most sociable | —Person-oriented | —Strong leader |
| —Good organizer | —Promotes harmony | —Willing to be involved | —Searches for policy, goals |
| —Adheres to standard operating procedures | —Outstanding salesperson | —Sociable, popular | —Natural organization builder |
| —Traditional, feels that rituals are important | —Duty- and service-oriented | —Settled and organized | —Devoted to job |
| | —Emotional | | |

| | |
|---|---|
| S = sensor | N = intuitor |
| T = thinker | F = feeler |
| J = judger | P = perceiver |
| E = extrovert | I = introvert |

**Figure 6.1** The Myers-Briggs Type Indicator Combinations
SOURCE: *Myers-Briggs Type Indicator* (Palo Alto, Calif.: Consulting Psychologists Press, 1982).

fortable for them. But one's preferred approach may not be the most appropriate for dealing with the situation at hand—or it may conflict with the approach preferred by a fellow officer. When this happens, knowing about and accepting the psychological preferences of both ourselves and those with whom we work can help to maintain healthy, productive relationships.

Generally, it is easier for police officers to develop the traits that are strongest in them. According to Jung, in becoming aware and in reaching decisions, most people rely on their dominant process instead of using their sensory, intuitive, thinking, and feeling capacities equally.[4] But people usually have at least some overlapping characteristics. For instance, the dominant preference in extroverts pertains to the outer world, but the extrovert also has an auxiliary quality that provides a reasonable balance. Without the inner life, extroverts would become extreme in their extroversion and thus appear to be superficial to better-balanced officers.[5]

Introverts rely on their auxiliary as a connection with the outer world. If it is undeveloped, they will seem awkward and uncomfortable. Therefore, introverts who lack an adequate auxiliary tend to be at a greater disadvantage than extroverts who lack such a modifying quality.[6]

To extroverted officers, introverts may seem aloof, but the introverts' reserve may stem from the fact that their energies are fueled by ideas and not by social contact.[7] In ordinary dealings, introverts do not necessarily say how they really feel about an issue. Only when they feel strongly enough about something will they reveal their thoughts. Through understanding and a developed auxiliary, introverts can learn to deal effectively with the outside world without becoming full-fledged members of it.[8]

## Data Experience

Through a variety of programs, the Myers-Briggs Type Indicator has been given to 707 law-enforcement personnel from the ranks of sergeant through chief. While a majority of these participants came from North Carolina, about 200 came from other areas of the country. Of the 707 officers, 23 were women. An analysis of the MBTI data (Figure 6.2) provides a realistic profile of types of people in law enforcement.

A slight majority (53 percent) of those tested were introverts. That figure seems to carry no significance until it is compared with MBTI figures for the general population. Across the country, approximately 76 percent of those tested were extroverted and only 24 percent introverted. In other words, law enforcement seems to attract more basically introverted (that is, inner-directed) people than people who are basically outer-directed and prefer to interact with others. In regard to preferred method of becoming aware, through the senses or through intuition, ratios among police officers ran about the same as among people in general. Seventy-five percent of people tested, regardless of their occupation, prefer the sensory mode; 77 percent of law enforcement officers have this preference. The general population is about equally divided between those who reach decisions on a rational basis (think-

| SENSING TYPES | | INTUITIVE TYPES | | | | NUMBER | PERCENT |
|---|---|---|---|---|---|---|---|
| with THINKING | with FEELING | with FEELING | with THINKING | | | | |
| **ISTJ** | **ISFJ** | **INFJ** | **INTJ** | | E | 329 | 46.53 |
| N = 240 | N = 32 | N = 6 | N = 30 | | I | 378 | 53.47 |
| % = 33.95 | % = 4.53 | % = 0.85 | % = 4.24 | | | | |
| | | | | | S | 548 | 77.51 |
| | | | | | N | 159 | 22.49 |
| | | | | | T | 600 | 84.87 |
| | | | | | F | 107 | 15.13 |
| **ISTP** | **ISFP** | **INFP** | **INTP** | | J | 579 | 81.90 |
| N = 39 | N = 10 | N = 3 | N = 18 | | P | 128 | 18.10 |
| % = 5.52 | % = 1.41 | % = 0.42 | % = 2.55 | | | | |
| | | | | | I J | 308 | 43.56 |
| | | | | | I P | 70 | 9.90 |
| | | | | | E P | 58 | 8.20 |
| | | | | | E J | 271 | 38.33 |
| | | | | | S T | 476 | 67.33 |
| **ESTP** | **ESFP** | **ENFP** | **ENTP** | | S F | 72 | 10.18 |
| N = 17 | N = 8 | N = 13 | N = 20 | | N F | 35 | 4.95 |
| % = 2.40 | % = 1.13 | % = 1.34 | % = 2.83 | | N T | 124 | 17.54 |
| | | | | | S J | 474 | 67.04 |
| | | | | | S P | 74 | 10.47 |
| | | | | | N P | 54 | 7.64 |
| | | | | | N J | 105 | 14.85 |
| **ESTJ** | **ESFJ** | **ENFJ** | **ENTJ** | | T J | 506 | 71.57 |
| N = 180 | N = 22 | N = 13 | N = 56 | | T P | 94 | 13.30 |
| % = 25.46 | % = 3.11 | % = 1.84 | % = 7.92 | | F P | 34 | 4.81 |
| | | | | | F J | 73 | 10.33 |
| | | | | | I N | 57 | 8.06 |
| | | | | | E N | 102 | 14.43 |
| | | | | | I S | 321 | 45.40 |
| | | | | | E S | 227 | 32.11 |

Note: ◙ = 1% of sample.

**Figure 6.2** MBTI Data Analysis for 707 Police Managers
Data collected by Ronald Lynch, Institute of Government, University of North Carolina, Chapel Hill, NC 27514, between 1980 and 1983. Samples includes managers in police departments.

ers) and those who decide on the basis of feelings (feelers). In this study, 85 percent of law-enforcement personnel preferred thinking over feeling. About the same ratio existed in police preferences for judging (82 percent) over perceiving. The general population divides about 50:50.

The implication, then, is that the majority of law-enforcement personnel are STJs—that is, they are logical in nature, designing their environment to close out issues as quickly as possible. They examine and direct issues on the basis of past and present experience, without much consideration of the future. Of the sixteen types, two styles are common among police personnel: 34 percent of those tested are ISTJs and 25 percent are ESTJs; 59 percent of the total show a strong preference for one of these two related styles. Law-enforcement managers must therefore consider how best to deal with these styles.

ESTJs are described as follows:

> Extroverted thinkers tend to use their thinking to run as much of the world as may be theirs to run. . . . Ordinarily they enjoy deciding what ought to be done and giving the appropriate orders to ensure that it will be done. They abhor confusion, inefficiency, half measures, anything that is aimless and ineffective. Often they are crisp disciplinarians, who know how to be tough when the situation calls for toughness. . . . They act forcefully upon the basis of their judgment, whether well-founded or not.[9]

On the other hand, ISTJs possess

> a complete, realistic, practical respect both for the facts and for whatever responsibilities these facts create. . . . The interaction of introversion, sensing and the judging attitude gives them extreme stability. . . . ISTJs emphasize logic, analysis, and decisiveness.[10]

While these traits serve most decision makers very well, their high representation among police managers can account for some underlying problems in these officials' respective functions. Conflict can arise in working with citizens and fellow agency members who see the advisability of change. ST commanders may not always be responsive, when dealing with a problem, to other points of view or sensitive to the emotional needs of others.

ESTJs are so in tune with the established, time-honored institutions that they may not understand those who might wish to abandon or radically change those institutions.[11]

ISTJs also rely on time-honored institutions and base their decisions on the facts before them. On a day-to-day basis, this approach probably proves very useful, but over the long run it can produce a police department that resists adapting to new law-enforcement techniques.

Some police managers' impersonal analysis of situations and lack of feeling can make them less aware, in reaching a decision, of others' personal needs. Since they may rely on the past in decision making, they may not be inclined to take risks or engage in creative or intuitive thinking. Consequently their organization may tend to resist change. The police chief who fits this description may find an obstacle in an intuitive city manager; he may look for stability while the city manager inclines toward being more experimental.

## Temperament

Divergent types become departmental assets when the differences are recognized and put to use in problem solving. Even though there are some people who consistently fall in the middle of the continuum, nearly everyone has an enduring set of characteristics that give special quality to his or her behavior and relationships. This personal makeup is sometimes referred to as one's "temperament." It is this underlying quality that may determine one's leadership skills, teaching ability, and degree of successful participation in the departmental structure.

Specific temperaments have been associated with the four categories of Jung's typology.[12] The SPs (ISTP, ESTP, ISFP, ESFP), who share the first type of temperament, are called "negotiators." For the most part, SPs do not like to be tied down or obligated. They feel a sense of joy, living for today and barely glancing at tomorrow. SPs are impulsive—they do things because they want to. Of all temperamental types, they are the most likely to "share and share alike." Resources are to be used; machinery is to be operated; people are to be enjoyed. SPs may have a flair for the dramatic and a disdain for detail. Frequently these people are described as exciting, optimistic, cheerful, and full of fun.

SJs (ISTJ, ESTJ, ISFJ, ESFJ) represent the second type of temperament. SJs are labeled as the "stabilizers." They feel a sense of duty and a need to belong. But this belonging must be earned. SJs do what they are required to do, and they want to be useful. As a type, they feel obligated, responsible, and burdened. SJs are also known as the stabilizers of society. They are the ones who are most inclined to save for future emergencies because they believe firmly in "Murphy's law"—whatever *can* go wrong *will*. SJs and SPs make up over 70 percent of our population.

The third temperament group comprises all the NTs (INTP, ENTP, INTJ, ENTJ). They are referred to as "visionaries." NTs have a sense of power and an urge to understand, control, predict, and explain realities. NTs want to be competent and make a fetish of intelligence. They are the most self-critical of all the types and are very sensitive to the credentials of their critics. To others, NTs may seem cold, remote, and sometimes arrogant. For the NT, work is work and play is work. NTs find SPs hard to understand.

The fourth type of temperament is represented by the NFs (INFJ, ENFJ, INFP, ENFP). NFs are called "catalysts." They have a sense of spirit, being basically involved in the search for self. NFs hunger to become better people, and their purpose in life is to have a bigger purpose in life. NFs feel they must have integrity: there must be no facade, no mask, no playing of roles—only one's genuine self. NFs also bring meaning and a heightened sense of drama to their relationships, which often become intense. The other types have trouble understanding the NF, and the NF, in turn, cannot really grasp the others' commitment to what seem to him to be false goals.

If we can identify the respective personality types to be found within a police department and then determine the behavioral characteristics associated with each, we may learn something about the climate within that agency. For instance, NT commanders may direct an agency that runs like clockwork, but in doing so they may demand too much of themselves and others. NT officers maybe insensitive to the needs of others—namely, their peers and the community's citizens. SJ officers, the dominant type in police departments, believe strongly in rules, and they obey their superiors. SJs feel that they must be prepared for every situation. SP officers, on the other hand, may be just the opposite. They are very restless and do not like routine. They are not particularly disciplined, yet they work best in emergencies because emergencies open up new possibilities. NF officers are so people-oriented that they see good in everyone and want to bring out the best in each person. They are inclined to let their hearts rule their minds.

Of the law-enforcement personnel tested, 67 percent preferred SJ behavior, 17 percent preferred NT, 11 percent preferred SP, and 5 percent preferred NF. When we tested other people in government, we found that about 50 percent were SJs, and slightly more SPs were found among non-law-enforcement government employees than among law-enforcement personnel.

The question then arose whether law-enforcement work itself tends to change one's preferences from the time of entry into the organization until the time of promotion. To explore this issue, we examined a single agency. Officers with five or fewer years of service were asked to complete the MBTI. Forty-four agreed. That testing showed roughly the same kinds of preferences as our earlier tests—that is, a preference for introverted behavior and for sensing, thinking, and judging over intuition, feeling, and perceiving. Exactly half of the sample were either of only two temperament types—14 percent were ESTJs and 36 percent were ISTJs.

These data suggest some possible implications for the future. It appears that law enforcement as a profession may continue to recruit the same kind of people it now attracts and may lack members of other temperament types. Apparently the field attracts people who believe strongly in tradition, in accepting and fulfilling obligations, in being well prepared for tasks; moreover, these people are willing to live in a hierarchical structure and are strong advocates of fundamentals. The kind of person who has these characteristics will accept amounts of responsibility that sometimes are beyond his or her individual ability and energy to fulfill. These people will reward others who act decisively and will try to preserve the morals and ethics of the organization and the community. They may, however, attempt to decide issues too quickly. Today's activities need to be planned and implemented in timely order if the goals of the future, five or ten years ahead, are to be reached. The kind of person who is attracted to law enforcement may have difficulty in dealing with other types—for example, those who rely more heavily on feelings than on logic or are creative or intuitive in their approach to problems instead of drawing exclusively from the past and present.

But in this study, managers in law enforcement or those promoted to key managerial positions differ from line officers in that they more often have an NT temperament. It is possible that a department with NTs as commanders and SJs at other posts throughout the organization will benefit from the strengths of each. This will be true if the department is able to call on one group for preservation of the past and on the other for direction to the future. NT managers may have a tendency to be critical of subordinates, especially when viewed by SJs from their more relaxed point of view. NTs may make too many assumptions about their fellow officers, some of which may be accurate and others not. With NTs in managerial positions, law enforcement may find that the profession will be able both to conceptualize the future and to perform adequately in the present.

NFs apparently are not attracted to law enforcement, and that may be the profession's loss. The special quality of NFs is that they seek to help all other people reach their potential. Where NTs emphasize how to reach goals, NFs think about the possibilities in people. Therefore NTs may help an organization achieve the maximum and NFs may help the individual people reach their goals. Without the NF's natural participation in task forces, group meetings are a little more difficult for the other three temperaments. Whereas NFs have a willingness to listen and are almost automatically empathetic and sincere in their relationships, many people within law enforcement today must try hard to develop these qualities.

## HOW TO USE THE MBTI

The MBTI may be used in a variety of ways to improve working relationships. For example, the police department may use the test simply to learn more about itself. As part of an in-service training program over a thirty-day period, all officers and supervisors might take the test. By participating in the inventory, members of the department can improve their understanding of themselves, each other, the department's managers, and the citizens they serve. Police managers can share the results of their tests with the supervisors and officers, giving their subordinates a better understanding of the managers' point of view.

Another example of the MBTI's usefulness may come from the chief and subordinates seeking to improve their ability to communicate. Officers want a forum where their views can be expressed and heard more readily. After taking the MBTI, officers can discuss the results in relation to how their department operates. They may find that the chief is a sensory-feeling (SF) person while the commanders below are predominantly sensory-thinking (ST) types. Therefore most of the commanders' proposals may not address the issues of employee morale that the chief considers important. On the other hand, the commanders may become frustrated when their logical, precise proposals are consistently ignored.

A lack of feelers (F's) in law enforcement may lead some officers to complain that they are not receiving enough praise or recognition for their work. Although the chief is an F, he may know little about these problems because the commanders (T's) who report to him give little information about employee grievances. In addition, many of the commanders are also J's, who want to make quick decisions on the basis of given facts. Officers below them can become alienated because they are not allowed to participate in these decisions.

The S's may disregard the intuitive N's during the decision-making sessions. They may dominate the discussions without really listening to the creative views of the N's, who are thinking through the implications of the decisions and suggesting possible changes. After the MBTI is discussed, the S's realize the importance of including the N's viewpoints in proposals.

In some police agencies communication issues may involve the preferences of the top commanders and the chief for extroversion (E) or introversion (I). Commanders who are introverts often assess situations in terms of their own reactions, often failing to pick up cues from others in the department. They may not seek contacts with their subordinates to determine sources of difficulty and therefore have little understanding of their subordinates' discontent. Inevitably, since it is the commanders who report to the chief, the chief also knows little about the complaints.

The three practical examples given above show five important uses for the analysis of personality differences through the MBTI:

1. As a team-building tool. Those who take the inventory are able to recognize and accept the differences among them; improved communication can help them work together as a team rather than as a group of individuals.
2. As an aid in looking at issues from different perspectives. People with diverse styles can make different and valuable contributions to a decision-making process. Groups often ignore ideas because the person who presents them has a preference type uncommon to the group—for example, when an intuitor presents ideas for change to a large group of sensory-thinking people (STs).
3. As a data base. To help develop strategies for improving communication and coordination between people with different personalities.
4. As a tool to help police managers understand the ways in which program proposals come across to officers who have different preferences in regard to decision making.
5. As an aid to officers in understanding why they may feel uncomfortable in certain job situations (for example, an ST would not feel comfortable in a job calling for creativity).

Another example of how the MBTI can serve a police department involves the new chief who wants to build decision-making teams. The test can be used as a device to foster better understanding among team members, facilitate the decision-making process, and keep conflicts at a minimum.

Along with other instruments, the MBTI has helped provide a composite of candidates vying for top management positions. City managers have used the inventory in choosing a police chief, but the results are not interpreted on a pass-fail scale. Instead, they help identify the kinds of interpersonal issues that can arise in a given environment. Then, once an applicant is accepted, any differences in style can be explained or ironed out. As an example, if the new chief is a heavy J (judger) and the manager is a P (perceiver), the two (1) can realize that they do not operate in the same time frame, (2) can accept that fact, and (3) can thereby work more cooperatively.

Overall, when interpreted properly, the MBTI is a valuable means of describing people—keeping in mind that it merely identifies preferences and does not label these as being either "good" or "bad." Everyone has different gifts, and it is management's responsibility to appreciate the possible contributions of all these traits. Once people understand that individuals do vary, they can begin to understand that these variations are natural and that coop-eration—rather than competition—can serve to maximize their potential usefulness.

## NOTES

1. *Myers-Briggs Type Indicator* (Palo Alto, Calif.: Consulting Psychologists Press, Inc., 1966).
2. C. G. Jung, *Psychological Types* (New York: Harcourt, Brace, 1923).
3. Mary H. McCaulley, "Introduction to the MBTI for Researchers," *Application of the Myers-Briggs Type Indicator to Medicine and Other Health Professions* (Gainesville, Fla.: Center for Applications of Psychological Type, Inc., 1977), p. 2. Many phrases that appear throughout this article are taken, without quotation marks, from this source. The author is indebted to Ms. McCaulley.
4. Marilyn Bates and David Kiersey, *Please Understand Me* (Del Mar, Calif.: Prometheus Nemesis, 1978), p. 12.
5. Ibid., p. 13.
6. Ibid.
7. Ibid., p. 15.
8. Ibid., p. 54.
9. Isabel Briggs Meyers, *Gifts Differing* (Palo Alto, Calif.: Consulting Psychologists Press, Inc., 1980), pp. 85–86.
10. Ibid., pp. 105–106.
11. Bates and Kiersey, *Please Understand Me*, p. 189.
12. Ibid.

# PART TWO

# Functional Aspects of Police Management

Once police managers understand the importance of the behavioral aspects of dealing with people within their agencies, they then must develop specific methods by which they can make effective decisions.

This section attempts to give them the tools they need to make the rational judgments necessary to maintain a stable organization.

This section opens with a discussion of the techniques of planning behavior. The police manager, in planning and implementing changes within a department, has the responsibility of balancing the concern for risk and the concern for the system. This section discusses his alternatives and their positive and negative features.

The next chapter (Chapter 8) describes a method of decision making that, if employed in the proposed step-by-step process, provides an effective tool for the police manager. This decision-making process is designed so that it can be implemented regardless of the police manager's style of management or communication process. The rational tool will help bring about effective staff work and give a clear-cut direction for all major decisions.

The management by objectives system discussed in Chapter 9 is a process by which a police manager can most effectively use the available resources. The process, which was designed for simplicity, has been tested and proven to be effective in both industry and government.

Chapter 10 deals with the issues of fiscal management, fiscal control, and the budgeting process for a police department. This chapter is designed to help destroy the myths that many police managers may believe about budgeting and the destructive role such misconceptions play in the development, execution, and implementation of a department budget. It is hoped that with this knowledge, police managers will face future budgetary processes with an open mind and a positive attitude as opposed to feeling defeated before even starting.

One of the major obstacles to effective police management seems to be the lack of sufficient time for the average police manager to perform all the required tasks. This section attempts to offer rational tools to help police managers control their time better. By the use of a structured decision-making process, a specific management by objectives system, and a wise utilization of time, the police manager can become more effective on a day-to-day basis.

# CHAPTER 7

# Management Planning

Planning is the foundation upon which much of police management is based. The effective police manager, if he intends to reach specific goals and objectives, begins to develop managerial planning strategies in order to eventually produce effective action. Planning involves the aspects of problem solving, problem identification, problem prevention, and, most importantly, decision making. It is the police manager's responsibility to seek out and weigh alternative solutions and to anticipate their consequences.

Planning should occur both formally and informally on all levels of every police department. These plans should be both short- and long-range. They should be systematically developed by either individuals or work teams. The quality of the final product depends in part upon the ability of the individuals responsible for the planning and also upon the influence that each has in solving problems and making decisions. The role of the police manager as a leader in developing planning strategies is important. Planning is strongly affected by the available facts and information and by the manner in which this information is used in identifying, evaluating, and solving problems.

There are many ways in which the planning process can be approached, but we will discuss only the basic assumptions that can guide the police manager's thinking as he attempts to evaluate information, identify objectives, and use his resources effectively.

## EFFECTIVE PLANNING AND USE OF DATA[1]

The quality and nature of police management planning revolves around two basic sets of concerns:

1. The concern for system, which includes purpose, stability, and entirety
2. The concern for risk, which includes innovation and opportunity

### Concern for System

The three key ingredients within the area of concern for system are purpose, stability, and entirety.

*Purpose.* The first ingredient depends on how aware the police manager is of the importance of individual occurrences in terms of the overall purposes and goals of the police department. In the department, as goals or targets are established, there should be some attempt to establish a system of priorities in the order of their importance to the department's future.

*Stability.* The second ingredient within the concern for system is stability. The police manager should try to reduce randomness and chance in the operation of the department. It is a good policy to try to be in a position to anticipate and prepare for future problems. Standards, policies, rules, and regulations determine how the department should operate. The need for stability is reflected in the police manager's desire to establish some kind of order, sequence, and predictability in the police department as a whole and in the affairs of the individual officers.

*Entirety.* The third major factor that the police manager should be concerned with is the functioning of the police department as a whole. The department can be thought of as a complex system comprising subsystems and units within the subsystems. In planning activities, it becomes the police manager's responsibility to link the information received from the uniform operations with that from departmental records, communications, and training. In addition to the technical aspects, the police manager should be aware of the human and social systems within the agency.

The three ingredients—purpose, stability, and entirety—require careful coordination, for together they make up the concern for system, which the police manager should consider. The more aware the police manager is of the entire system, the better able she is to plan and work toward the department's stability and goals. On the other side of the coin, if she does not have an appreciation for the overall goals and purposes of the department, it becomes difficult for her to carry out her responsibilities effectively and to make worthwhile contributions to the department as a whole.

The degree of the police manager's concern for the system can fall anywhere on a continuum, ranging from a high or positive concern to a low or negative concern.

The police manager should recognize, regardless of what level she has reached on the continuum, that a concern for the total system is necessary in order to maintain the direction and purpose that provides stability within the department. She may be at one end of the continuum, concerned only with the specific facts or elements within the total system and unaware of their interrelationship. Or she may be concerned with events or a combination of elements without perceiving that they are part of a system or subsystem that eventually affects the total operation of the department.

The effective police manager, in creating plans within any system or subsystem, should be aware of the effects that her decisions and planning activities will have on the entire department.

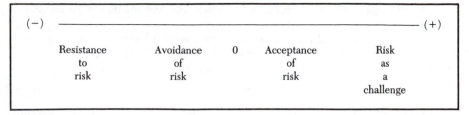

**Figure 7.1** Risk Continuum
SOURCE: *Management Models—The Planning Process*, copyright © 1968 by Educational Systems & Designs, Inc., Westport, Connecticut. Reprinted with ESD's specific permission.

## Concern for Risk

The manager's concern for risk is demonstrated by her attitude toward innovation and opportunity. She should recognize that these factors are closely interrelated.

Almost every decision that the police manager makes involves some level of risk, opportunity, and innovation. The manager may take personal risks or those that affect the department. If the police manager attempts to be innovative by introducing something new into the department, she takes the risk of being rejected, laughed at, or, if the project fails, of receiving a reputation of incompetence. As far as the department is concerned, the risks of innovation include negative public reaction, higher costs, and a decrease in confidence among the personnel.

The decision pertaining to the degree of risk to be taken should be based upon available information, logical decision making, an assessment of the amount of risk involved, and an estimate of the possibility of success. An effective police manager is characterized by her willingness to take the risks appropriate to her level of authority and by her comprehension of the manner in which opportunity, innovation, and risk are interrelated.

The willingness to take risks is represented along the continuum shown in Figure 7.1.

At the positive end of the scale, risk is viewed by the police manager as a challenge and an opportunity to utilize a given set of facts in the best interest of the entire police department. The negative end of the continuum represents resistance to risk. Thus, at one extreme, the police manager views risk as an opportunity rather than a threat, while the manager at the other end believes that the thrust of management practices should always be to avoid risk. From the middle, or the zero point, to the negative side there are various degrees of avoiding and resisting risk and on the positive side of accepting and welcoming it.

## MANAGEMENT PLANNING MODEL[2]

### Explanation

An understanding of the police manager's alternatives in planning behavior is assisted by a model based on his concerns for system and risk.

The management model reflects the following key management issues:

1. To what extent the police manager should be concerned with system
2. To what extent the police manager should be concerned with risk
3. How the police manager should interrelate these concerns in his everyday
   activities

The model (Figure 7.2) is designed to show the four possible relationships between risk and system. The manager may exhibit a high concern for system, purpose, stability, and entirety as well as for accepting risk as a challenge and an opportunity. The manager may be more negative and resistant to risk but still maintain a concern for system. The manager may have a negative concern for system and a resistance to risk taking. He may accept risk as a challenge but may have a negative inclination toward system, purpose, stability, and entirety in his planning activities.

The police manager should be aware that he may have to move from one approach to another, depending upon the issues he faces. In addition, there are varying degrees of system and risk within each approach. For example, although two managers may be concerned with system and accept risk as a challenge, one may view the challenge of risk more positively than the other.

The four segments of the model represent the different approaches of police management to planning:

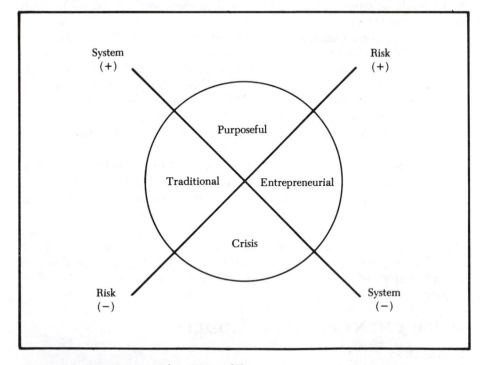

**Figure 7.2**   Management Planning Model
SOURCE: *Management Models—The Planning Process*, copyright © 1968 by Educational Systems & Designs, Inc., Westport, Connecticut. Reprinted with ESD's specific permission.

Purposeful approach
Traditional approach
Crisis approach
Entrepreneurial approach

*Purposeful Approach.* In this approach, the police manager is concerned with system, is willing to take risks, and wants to take advantage of opportunities. Under this approach, the police manager integrates purpose, direction, innovation, and creativity within the system to contribute to the growth of the department. The police manager who uses this approach does not view systems or stability within the department as ends in themselves or as means for minimizing risk but as ingredients important in maintaining a sense of direction and purpose. This manager will weigh the risk against the opportunity, taking into consideration the effect of the outcome on the entire police department.

*Traditional Approach.* The police manager who exercises this approach shows a high concern for system and stability and a desire to avoid risk, innovation, and creativity. This police manager wants to maintain the department in its present form, to support its traditions and precedents, and to minimize the risk situations. Tradition, precedent, and stability are highly regarded. The philosophy of this approach is best described by the statement, "We plan to stay on the same path, avoid rocking the boat, and eliminate any risk to our system."

*Crisis Approach.* This type of police manager demonstrates a minimal concern for system and a desire to avoid risk. He considers every problem that he is faced with, regardless of its importance to the functioning of the department, as a pressing issue that must be solved immediately. Each issue and incident is regarded as requiring quick and firm handling and is normally dealt with on the element or event level with little or no regard to the subsystem or system. Police managers using this planning approach attempt to minimize risk by maintaining a constant surveillance of subordinates and their activities, even if such surveillance stymies the department in its attempts to reach its goals.

*Entrepreneurial Approach.* This approach exhibits a low or negative concern for system and stability coupled with a strong willingness to accept risk and to take advantage of opportunities.

The members of police departments emphasizing this managerial approach are overly concerned with exploration and speculation. In many instances, they take inappropriate risks and may overtax themselves or the department with projects unrelated to specific purposes or goals. Police agencies involved in federal-funding projects that distract them from their long-term direction and goals exhibit the entrepreneurial approach to management planning.

## Responses Within Each Management Approach

The differences between four approaches to police management planning can be further clarified by comparing the attitudes and actions of police managers supporting the different philosophies. The manner in which each management approach relates to the following activities will be described. The activities are:

1. Planning in general
2. Long-range planning
3. The establishment of priorities
4. Structuring of the organization
5. The use of information
6. The achievement of control over activities

### *Purposeful Approach.*

1. Within this approach, the planning activity is designed to bring about sound direction and to help provide stability to the police department. If the opportunity for risk can contribute to the department's overall achievements and purposes, such opportunities are welcomed.
2. Long-range planning is both systematic and flexible in order to encourage innovation and creativity as new facts and opportunities come forth.
3. Priority is placed upon building for the future while maintaining sound direction.
4. The department is organized so as to promote the flow of information among its members. Furthermore, the department's organization helps to handle short- and long-range problems and helps to balance risk taking with the concern for system.
5. The basis for future planning is contained in the information collected by the department. This information is used to provide control and direction for the department as it grows.
6. The department's goals are first examined, and then plans are implemented with systematic controls consistent with the overall purposes. These controls are sufficiently flexible to allow the individual members of the department to exercise initiative in making decisions that will further the department's goals.

### *Traditional Approach.*

1. Planning is designed to produce stable and sound direction. This requires specific procedures and steps as well as checks and balances so that the command level of the department can be assured that the action taken by subordinates is in strict conformity with the established plan.
2. Long-range planning is extremely systematic and is based on present practices and tradition. Whether or not these practices are beneficial to the department is not taken into consideration.
3. The highest priority of this approach is to create a stable organization by developing rules and regulations to minimize risks.
4. The department is organized so that there is a clear-cut chain of command with a distinct delineation between staff and line operations. The staff functions are responsible for the creation and maintenance of the department's stability. The line

operations are permitted to act only on those opportunities approved by the command staff.

5. Much detailed information is collected on a systematic basis in order to reduce the risk of any chance occurrence within the department.

6. The established practices, procedures, and systems are designed so as to allow minimal deviation, thereby guaranteeing the close control of the staff over the entire department.

### *Crisis Approach.*

1. In this approach there really is no need to plan. Most situations that arise are emergencies, and they are dealt with on a day-to-day basis.

2. There is no long-range planning because in law enforcement, the future is totally unpredictable.

3. Priority is placed solely on current needs, problems, and issues.

4. The department is organized so that command-level people will be alerted when a problem arises in order to handle any emergency situation.

5. The information collected usually relates to only the problem at hand. It is designed to identify the cause of the problem, to provide solutions for it, and to prevent it from recurring.

6. Personal inspection by the manager is used as a control mechanism to guarantee that whatever mistakes do occur do not have any effect upon the police operation.

### *Entrepreneurial Approach.*

1. In this approach, action is the key to the department's success and plans restrict its freedom. Activities of the department are basically random and unconnected; therefore planning is impractical.

2. If the department is comprised of sensitive and creative personnel who see opportunities and take appropriate actions, there is no need for long-range planning.

3. Priority is placed on discovering opportunities for improvement and growth.

4. Formal structures such as organizational charts and job descriptions are avoided because they tend to restrict the freedom and flexibility of the police personnel in responding to emergency situations.

5. Risk-taking is promoted and trust is placed in the judgment of the department personnel. Therefore, only a limited amount of information is needed to assist them in solving problems and exploring opportunities.

6. Loose control is sufficient if the personnel possess the imagination and initiative to deal effectively with problems.

## SELECTING A MANAGEMENT PLANNING APPROACH

Before selecting his management planning approach, the police manager should evaluate its positive and negative features and its influence on the future of the department. The amount of energy expended in planning and problem solving should be in reasonable proportion to the potential gain to the department. If the energy expended is excessive, then a quick solution to the problem may well be advisable. The manager should evaluate the potential gains in making a quality decision as well as the amount of effort necessary to obtain additional information. He should also be aware that the delays resulting from a long study sometimes slow up the achievement of the overall goals of the department.

The potential gain or loss that the department may experience as a result of management planning is affected by specific criteria that the manager must weigh prior to selecting the most appropriate management planning approach. These criteria are time, severity, frequency, and "ripple effects."

*Time* is an important factor. Some problems that the police manager faces require an immediate solution. For example, a civil disturbance or a serious criminal investigation must be dealt with as quickly as possible. In addition, long-range management planning is necessary in every police department to help identify the causes of problems, to develop plans and strategies for resolving future incidents, and if possible to prevent their occurrence.

The time demands in solving a specific problem often cause the police manager to consider different approaches to management planning. He may need one approach for short-term needs, another for those in the middle, and still another for long-term needs.

*Severity* is the second criterion affecting the decision about the best approach to use. Usually, when the issue is pressing, such as an immediate threat, then the management approach accomplishing the quickest results is the most effective. With a less severe problem, however, the manager may be willing to extend the amount of time in which to reach a decision, thus permitting the accumulation of additional information and an examination of alternatives.

*Frequency* is a third factor. If the issue is resolved only once, it often will affect only a few people. In this case, almost any of the approaches may be used. However, with greater frequency of the decision-making process, the purposeful approach would be more effective not only in the short run but also in the long run.

*Ripple effects*, that is, both positive and negative side effects, should be taken into consideration. The police manager should be aware of the possible results of using a specific approach to reach his decision. For example, if the department elects to implement a new field reporting system, then the manager should be sensitive to the effect of the system on the other members of the department as well as the operational personnel. In this case, the purposeful approach is the best management planning approach to use because it promotes the flow of information among the employees.

The police manager should realize that the selection of an approach should be based on whether it will promote or hinder the achievement of goals within the department. To select the proper management planning approach, he must take into account the factors of time, severity, frequency, and ripple effects.

## SUMMARY

For many years, police management has defined planning as the writing of a set of procedures and practices. The implication is that there is only one good way to plan. This discussion has focused on the variety of approaches to management planning that are available to the police manager. The approach he selects is determined by his attitudes, assumptions, and concerns. The management planning model built around the two basic sets of concerns shows the particular responses elicited by each approach.

Although this discussion emphasizes that the purposeful approach is generally the most effective, the police manager should realize that only through an analysis of the situation and careful consideration of the criteria can he accurately decide which approach is best for his department.

---

## NOTES

1. From *Management Models—The Planning Process,* copyright © 1968 by Educational Systems & Designs, Inc., Westport, Connecticut. Reprinted with ESD's specific permission.
2. Ibid.

# CHAPTER 8

# *Problem Identification and Decision Making*

Problem analysis and decision making are probably the most important issues that the police manager faces. On a day-to-day basis, he is continually thrust into situations that require logical, sound, and realistic decisions which, if successfully implemented, may lead to the resolution of problems and the achievement of specific objectives. Often, however, police managers are never quite prepared to handle adequately the rational aspects of problem analysis and decision making.

## PROBLEM ANALYSIS

A great many police officers and police managers are not fully aware that there is a difference between the management activities of problem analysis and decision making. They progress through their management careers using these terms interchangeably, and they attempt to apply identical approaches in dealing with both. Problem analysis is nothing more than a careful examination of the facts in order to determine the true cause of the problem so that positive action can be taken. The problem is defined as the difference between what should be happening and what actually is happening.

There are four basic steps to problem analysis:

1. Recognize problems
2. Separate and set priorities
3. Specify the priority problem to be analyzed
4. Test for true cause

### Step 1: Recognize Problems

In the real world, things are all too often not the way we hope they will be. This is especially true in the day-to-day operations of the average police department. The behavior of police officers, supervisors, and civilian personnel often vary over a given time period, as does equipment and the systems for effective use of equipment and personnel. Many times these variations are small and not even noticed. In fact, we generally expect small variations in our daily activities and they do not arouse a strong concern for problem analysis or decision making. Sometimes, however, small deviations, such as damage of a police vehicle or the excessive use of emergency equipment, may be a warning of a trend of deterioration. Such deviations then become significant factors, and their causes should be sought through systematic analysis. The key point in the first major step of problem analysis is to be aware of relevant problems.

To help identify the problem more clearly, the manager should ask the following questions:

1. Who is the cause or what is the identity of the problem we are trying to analyze?
2. Where is the problem located?
3. When does the problem occur?
4. How large is the problem?

## Step 2: Separate and Set Priorities

Among the many problems that the police manager notices, only some demand immediate attention and action. For example, although Part I crimes may be rising at a slow rate, robbery may be rising at a rate twice as fast as any other crime. The consequences, if the police department gives the same attention to the robbery problem as it does to the less demanding Part I crimes, could be disastrous. Problems with urgent and critical demands for attention should be given the highest priority. Other problems can be ranked by their relative importance. The criteria to use are different in each situation, and each police manager should establish his own priorities. Some criteria that can be used are (1) the growth rate of the problem, (2) the financial cost of the problem, (3) the effect the problem has upon reaching stated objectives, and (4) the effects the problem has on such issues as condition of personnel, turnover rate, or morale. A small problem, when ignored, may grow rapidly to serious proportions.

## Step 3: Specify the Priority Problem to Be Analyzed

Once a problem has been selected for analysis, the next step is to describe it accurately. Every problem has four basic dimensions: identity, location, timing, and magnitude. Any thorough description of a deviation should include detailed information regarding these four dimensions. As the heart of problem analysis is the systematic search for deviations, it is essential that the basis for that search be carefully prepared. An accurate description of the four dimensions of the problem provides this basis.

The following six questions, when properly answered, can help analyze the problem and identify its priority:

Identification:
1. What or whom does the problem concern?
2. What is the nature of the problem?

Location:                               3. Where, geographically, does the
                                           problem occur?
Timing:                                 4. When does the problem occur?
Magnitude:                              5. What is the extent of the problem?
                                        6. What is the trend—is the problem
                                           growing, stabilizing, or diminishing?

The matrix shown in Figure 8.1 is a tool the police manager can use in analyzing these six important questions.

## Step 4: Test for True Cause

The true cause of a problem can be determined from careful examination of all the possible causes. Each cause must be tested for a logical relationship with the facts. This is done by tentatively assuming a cause to be true, then testing it against the problem specification (six questions) and its four dimensions. If any of the facts of the specification discredit the cause being tested, that cause should be thrown out as untrue. This logical test is applied to each cause until one cause, or a combination of causes, is found to fit with the facts of the problem specifications.

To find the most probable cause, the police manager must ask, "If this possible cause is the most probable cause, how does it explain both the variations and the stable factors?"

The final test for true cause is demonstrating that the cause actually triggered the problem in question. In the world of tangible objects, this testing or verifying is done through some sort of physical proof such as chemical analysis, measuring, or examining control areas. Less tangible problems centering around human behavior are often more difficult to verify. Reasons for problems in the department's morale must be found through more indirect means, such as in-depth interviews by a skilled counselor.

In verifying the true cause, the police manager should answer the following question: "What tangible, factual, scientific steps or research can I undertake to prove that this most probable cause is the true cause?"

# DECISION MAKING

## General Principles

Three generally broad principles can be applied to the philosophy of decision making. The first rule is *make the decision*. It is extremely important that decisions be made; an effective manager will soon be graded on his ability to *make* a decision rather than by the number of *correct* decisions that may be made. The second general principle is that once the decision has been made, *do not constantly worry about it*. Go ahead and implement it. The only times the manager should go back and change the original decision is if it has been proven dead wrong or if a completely new and more effective approach has

Problem _____

| | Is | Is Not | (a) Differences | (b) Changes (Date & Time) | (c) Possible Causes | (d) Most Probable Cause |
|---|---|---|---|---|---|---|
| **Identity** 1. What or whom does the problem concern? 2. What is the nature of the problem? | | | | | | |
| **Location** 3. Where, geographically, does the problem occur? | | | | | | |
| **Timing** 4. When does the problem occur? | | | | | | |
| **Magnitude** 5. What is the extent of the problem? 6. What is the trend—is the problem growing, stabilizing, or diminishing? | | | | | | |

(a) What is unique or distinct about the "is" of the problem as opposed to the "is not" of the problem?

(b) What circumstances were new, improved, modified, added to, or changed in order to bring about these differences?

(c) What was there in, around, or about these changes that could have triggered or created the problem?

(d) If this possible cause is the most probable, how does it explain both the "is" and "is not"?

**Figure 8.1   Problem Analysis Matrix**

been established. The third rule deals with the question of consideration; the manager *should not try to satisfy everyone's judgment*. Managers are required to satisfy the judgment of those people to whom they are responsible. If the manager attempts to satisfy everyone, it will be impossible to make a sound decision and and perhaps to make any decision at all.

## Types of Decisions

Decisions of effective police managers are few in number but concentrate on solving important systemwide problems and deal with a high level of conceptual understanding. The police manager is not normally put in the position of making decisions quickly but instead, is required to evaluate and manipulate a great many variables in order to arrive at an important decision which, when implemented, will strongly affect the day-to-day operations of the agency. The professional police manager wants to make sound rather than clever decisions.

Before analyzing "how to make a decision," a conceptual framework must be established. In essence, before the police manager even begins to make a serious decision, she must first place that decision in its proper perspective.

The first type of management decision is classified as routine. Routine decision making is an important and daily activity of any police manager. Only through routine decision making can the police department continue to function while allowing the manager the time she needs to solve major problems and make new innovations. Indeed, one criterion of an effective police manager is her ability to keep developing ways in which the routine and unimportant details of daily police activities can be handled. The police manager who is able to delegate as many decisions as possible to her subordinates is the one who will not be spending a majority of her time in routine decision making.

The second type of decision directs itself to resolving specific issues. These issues result from actions taken by members of the police agency or from internal problems identified by external sources. An illustration might be the city manager who feels that the police department is not adequately and effectively using its present resources and who advises the chief to reduce crime as quickly as possible and to provide him with a copy of a new patrol allocation plan.

What happens under this type of decision making is that the total police system is examined and isolated portions of the system are brought out for revising and revamping. An example of this occurs when the police chief recognizes that he does not have sufficient information with which to plan and make sound decisions. After careful examination of the total system, he realizes that the record-keeping function is outdated and neither collects nor analyzes the type of data that is needed to make decisions on a day-to-day basis. Pressure is then placed upon the whole system; this pressure rebounds and directs itself to the records center. The result is the discovery of a serious problem in the records center, and finally some action is taken to develop a new system of record keeping so the necessary information can be collected, analyzed, and properly used.

The third type of decision is designed to generate new ideas and innovative techniques. Innovative decision making in law enforcement is more difficult than routine decision making or problem solving. Many times the police manager lacks hard-core experiments to help him reach adequate decisions. This type of decision making requires the manager to take some risk, because all such innovations or new techniques and ideas will not be completely successful. This type of decision making brings about progress in the profession and is extremely important for vibrant, growing police organizations.

## Means–Ends Analysis

One of the key factors in decision making is the development of a clear picture that shows the relationship between the objectives we are trying to reach and the various alternatives we have to implement.

To build a chain that links together the objectives or ends we have set with the various methods we have available to us, we use a management tool called "means–ends analysis." For example, assuming the problem is with the poor production of records clerks and the records function in general, a specific objective—to increase production of records clerks—is first set. The first question asked is "why?" The answer is to help increase overall departmental efficiency, to cut costs, to avoid conflict that may exist between line and staff activities, and to provide quality information for line operation. Through answering the question, specific broader goals or objectives have been identified at the level above the original objective.

Once the broader goals have been identified, we can proceed to the question of how they and the original objective can be achieved. The answer generated may be better or more supervision, an increase in the number of clerks, or a retraining of the present clerks.

The final means–ends analysis to meet the initial stated objective of increasing the production of records clerks is shown in Figure 8.2.

As shown in this illustration, the mechanics involved in developing a means-ends chain are not complicated. The first question involves the objective to be achieved. A move up the chain answers the question "why?" and a move down the chain answers "how?"

There is some value to the development of a means–ends chain before entering into decision making. First, the means–ends analysis helps show the relationship of an objective at one level to the goal at a higher level, so that meaningful objectives can be set. Second, the means–ends analysis helps stimulate the development of a series of possible alternative solutions to a single problem. Third, it helps develop and translate rather broad objectives, such as increased efficiency, to some very sound actions at the bottom of the chain which can be specifically delegated to individuals; for example, the establishment of a forty-hour course for record clerks.

In addition, the means–ends chain helps depict the numerous relation-

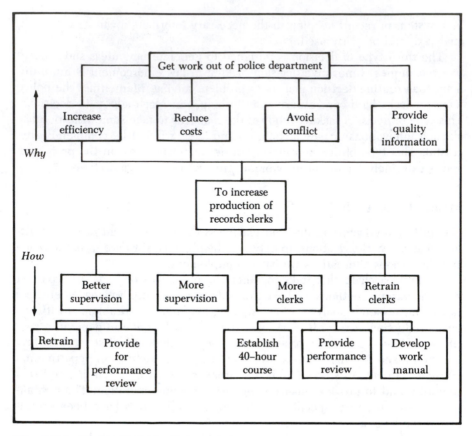

**Figure 8.2** Means–Ends Analysis

ships and dependencies that the police manager must consider in the overall decision. Fifth, it helps to narrow the field of information and data that must be collected in order to make the decision final and to make the one that can be most effective for the police department. Finally, it helps highlight discrepancies between the objectives that have been set and the work that can be done at the bottom level of the working force. Consider the overall goal or objective of trying to reduce costs for the department and the action of increasing the number of clerks at the bottom. These two are inconsistent and would require either restating or eliminating the objective or eliminating the alternative solution of employing more record clerks.

The manager should realize that the means–ends analysis does not help select alternatives, nor will it dictate all the alternatives available. Means–ends analysis is nothing more than an organized method of brainstorming to help bring out objectives that should be achieved along with the methods that can be used to achieve them.

Once the means–ends analysis is completed, the following seven-step decision-making process can begin. This process can apply regardless of the type of decision to be reached. The importance of the decision, the time, and information available for making the decision all affect the way the process is used. The seven steps are:

1. Set the objective.
2. Identify obstacles in the way of the objective.
3. Collect and analyze data.
4. Develop alternative solutions.
5. Select alternatives to be implemented.
6. Develop and implement a plan.
7. Evaluate the results of implementation.

*Step 1: Set the Objective.* Many management decisions become ineffectual because the process starts with a "problem" that, when ultimately solved, does not contribute to the achievement of any objective. In this part of the overall process, the police manager determines the purpose and direction that the total decision-making process is to take by setting objectives.

Too many times, police departments devote the majority of their day-to-day activities to trying to solve "problems." When the whole operation is carefully examined, an immediate question is raised: "Why are you spending so much time solving so many little problems that constantly send you in numerous directions?" The police command level should establish specific directions before becoming involved in the issue of decision making. Consider the police department that revamps its records system without first establishing the purpose and necessity of the records. The money for sophisticated hardware equipment is spent, numerous consultants are hired, new personnel are employed and trained, physical space is revamped, problems generated by the change itself are solved, the new record system is implemented. After a short time, the police manager recognizes that the information received from the new record system is really not that much different from the data generated prior to the expenditure of large sums of money, time, and effort. The efficiency of the records has been improved, but the new system has not contributed to any overall purpose of the police department itself and in many instances may even be distracting it from reaching major goals.

The objective is a statement of reason or purpose indicating that the police manager wants to solve problems and make decisions. These objectives should be tested for consistency against the department's overall goals.

*Step 2: Identify Obstacles.* The second step of the decision-making process is the definition and identification of conditions that obstruct and prohibit the meeting of the objectives. There are two parts to the obstacle identification. The first is the ability to recognize deviations within the obstacles and the second is to separate and set priorities to handle these deviations.

Sometimes it is appropriate at this point for the police manager to go back to the steps outlined for problem analysis. In many instances, however, the obstacles or stumbling blocks are fairly definitive and can easily be identified.

*Step 3: Collect and Analyze Data.* When the objectives have been stated and the obstacles identified, the police manager should begin to determine the data relevant to the issue or the data necessary to make an effective decision. Facts and information should be obtained and organized in some fashion. The police manager should determine what resources of time, money, and personnel are available and then determine the type and amount of information to be collected. It is possible to achieve an endless supply of information, but once its limits have been defined, it can be used effectively.

The police manager should determine how the information necessary for making a decision is going to be obtained. How many times are police managers faced with the situation of examining reams of computer printouts when really only 2 or 3 percent of the data involved is necessary for making some valid decisions? The police manager must determine in advance what criteria are eventually to be used in making a final selection of alternatives. The data that will be useful in examining each of these criteria should be collected.

*Step 4: Develop Alternatives.* In this step, various alternatives for reaching the objectives are determined and identified. If a thorough means–ends analysis is initially prepared, alternative solutions will be delineated in the original means–end chart. The manager should be careful at this point not to restrict the number of alternatives or give consideration to whether or not they can be implemented. The major purpose of this step is to determine as many alternatives as possible, creating a clear picture of the total environment. The police manager can then choose and select the most effective alternatives for resolving the issue.

Another way of stating Step 4 is that the police manager is now in the process of searching for all possible solutions—*not* determining which is the best or most appropriate solution. The question being asked is: "What are the various solutions that can be considered?"

Most police managers recognize that if a solution is not included in the array of possible alternatives, then that solution cannot be chosen. Too often in practice, however, insufficient time is given in the development of a comprehensive list of possible alternatives or solutions. As a result, the effectiveness of the total decision-making process is hampered because only a few hastily identified alternatives are examined. Other alternative solutions that may be even more appropriate for that specific police department are never examined.

Consider the police department that has stated a clear-cut objective of reducing the number of armed robberies by a specific percentage and carefully identified some of the obstacles that are in the way of achieving that objective. The next step might be to collect and analyze only information concerning successful projects or programs in other areas and not information available from the department itself. Too many times the decision-making process then comes to an abrupt end. The police department decides that some program that may have been somewhat successful in another city will be highly successful in its city. In essence, the number of alternative solutions has been greatly reduced by the narrow approach taken by the police manager.

*Step 5: Select Alternatives.*   When various alternatives have been identified, the advantages and disadvantages of each one should be carefully examined and weighed before selecting which one or series of alternatives is to be implemented.

The key factor in this step is establishing criteria for selecting the best alternative or alternatives.

A decision-making criteria chart, shown in Figure 8.3, is available to the police manager. This chart can be an asset to the manager in the analysis of alternative solutions. Four major criteria normally considered in most decisions are included in the chart. First, does the alternative really contribute to the objectives? Second, how much will be spent if the alternative is implemented? Third, is it feasible, are the people available, does the manager have the authority, and is this alternative within the control of the manager? And last, how does the alternative affect the total system, considering the positive and negative side effects?

In completing the decision criteria chart, the police manager assigns weights to each of the alternatives as they are compared with each of the criteria. The weights can either be in a simple evaluation of high, medium, or low or can even be given a numerical value of 1 to 10.

*Step 6: Develop and Implement a Plan.*   This step requires the programming of the decision. Before beginning the implementation of the decision, the resources of the department, especially the personnel, should be taken into consideration. A plan for the orderly process of implementing the selected alternatives should be established. This plan should provide for standards and controls, along with some feedback system. The controls, measurements, standards, specific objectives, time limits, and feedback system are necessary to allow the decisions to be carefully evaluated.

The plan should contain the data to be collected and analyzed in order to evaluate the total process. Ideas become great through their implementation. The police manager should continually strive to implement his carefully analyzed decision. This implementation process is the heart of the decision-making process. It is at this point that the decision or ideas generated earlier become realities in the day-to-day operations of the police department.

*Step 7: Evaluate the Result.*   The decision-making process and its divisions should be evaluated in terms of predetermined objectives and criteria. Evaluation begins the recycling process at the end of any of the steps developed earlier. For example, the collection of data as defined in Step 3 may result in the need to establish new objectives (Step 1). There is no straight line from the stated objective to the evaluation of the implementation in the decision-making process. A constant examination or evaluation must occur with each step.

Statement of Objectives: _____

| Alternative | Contributing to Objectives (Output) | Cost (Input) | Feasibility | Side Effects | |
|---|---|---|---|---|---|
| | | | | Positive | Negative |
| | | | | | |

**Figure 8.3** Decision Criteria Chart

The evaluation process includes specifying measurable objectives, formulating a practical evaluation design, specifying data-collection procedures, and specifying the data analysis methods.

## Pitfalls of the Decision-Making Process

There are pitfalls that police managers will encounter if they are not careful in the overall decision-making process. It is possible to establish objectives that do not provide some framework within which decision making can take place. Objectives using superlative terminology such as "best" do not create a clear picture of what the department is attempting to seek; as a result, no real guidelines are developed.

There could be an inappropriate statement or no statement at all of what can be expected in the way of obstacles to be overcome. The police manager could define the obstacle in such a way as to limit the possibility of alternative solutions. Consider the police manager who decides that the only obstacle to reducing robberies is the judge who hears such cases. In essence, this manager has listed but one or two possible alternative solutions, none of which may be under his control. The result will probably be no action at all.

Another pitfall common to the decision-making process is the failure on the part of the police manager to reexamine the prior steps as each succeeding step is developed. As data are organized, gathered, and analyzed, new obstacles may be identified and even a new objective established. There may be times that the data the police manager collects in the decision-making process are irrelevant. Consider the police manager who constantly examines pages of computer printouts so she can design a project to reduce robberies when a careful examination of but a few of the elements—time of day, location, day of week—may be sufficient to bring about programs that can be effectively implemented to reduce robberies.

There is also a tendency to begin to select alternatives before all the possibilities have been presented, thus limiting the solutions. As personnel work around and near such managers, it becomes obvious very quickly that the alternatives that they both develop and select are those alternatives that the *manager* wants to implement.

The police manager should be aware of the need to establish specific criteria on which to base the numerous alternatives from which those to be implemented will finally be selected. If, for example, cost, time, and side effects are disregarded in the decision-making process, the resulting program will be doomed to failure long before its implementation even begins.

Another and final pitfall that should be avoided is failing to follow up on decisions to guarantee that they were implemented. This means developing checkpoints within the implementation process to guarantee that projects are implemented, carefully evaluated, and readjusted when necessary.

# CHAPTER 9

# Management by Objectives

Management by objectives is a functional process discussed by many authors in many ways. Each author has provided similar but not identical definitions.

A complete volume on this subject, called *Policing by Objective*, has been prepared by Social Development Corporation, Hartford, Connecticut, under the direction of Val Lubans. It now appears as a prescriptive package distributed by the National Institute of Law Enforcement and Criminal Justice of the Law Enforcement Assistance Administration.

The system described in this chapter has been effectively implemented in certain police departments. It is by no means the only system and can and should be adjusted to meet the needs of the individual police agency.

Management by objectives or MBO, as it is more commonly known, may be viewed as a management tool to aid in the decision-making process. The numerous principles developed under decision making also apply to MBO. MBO is designed as a method whereby police managers and their subordinates can identify areas of growth, set standards to be reached, and measure the results against the standards that have been set. MBO relates directly to what is expected of the department and is usually expressed in terms of objectives. It relates to the development of teamwork within all levels of the department by establishing common goals and projects.

The concept of management by objectives is based on a number of behavioral science assumptions. The police manager who emphasizes MBO assumes that all officers want to know what is expected of them and whether they are performing satisfactorily. The manager further assumes that the officers want to participate in and influence decisions that affect the overall purpose and goals of the police department.

MBO may also be viewed as a method of changing the present system of making decisions. It is an important tool in the decision-making process and provides a control component for monitoring success toward the specific goals of the department. MBO can also be used as a training and development tool. It is a method of maximizing the utilization of all personnel within the police department. MBO has been used as a method of enhancing the communication process within police departments.

When examining a police department, it is important to remember the three broad areas of analysis. The first, the input process, consists of the necessary elements before the department can begin to achieve any goals or objectives. The inputs include personnel, money, time, and equipment. The second consists of the activities of the people within the department. If something can be described as "do-able," then it must be included as an activity. Examples include typing, driving, developing plans, patrol, and investigation. The third area involves output, which is the result achieved by the input.

MBO addresses itself to all three areas. It starts with the result, or output, area. The MBO process requires police managers to define carefully what results they are attempting to achieve in a specific time period, usually of three to five years. This careful analysis of goal and objective setting before the agreement on projects is an effective way of increasing the efficiency of the activities within the agency.

Under the MBO process, not every activity of the department should be included. The MBO process is designed to help bring about the changes necessary to upgrade departmental performance. MBO may be viewed as a change-agent tool and should be directed toward approximately 20 percent of the activities within a police department.

MBO can be best implemented in line operational functions as opposed to staff or administrative functions. This is because it is easier to set objectives to define the results. This does not mean, however, to imply that MBO cannot be used in staff functions, but it is generally better implemented first in line operations with the assistance of staff personnel. The disadvantage of this implementation process is that it generally has a tendency toward forcing line personnel to possibly downgrade the role that staff plays in the overall operation of the police department.

Some police managers attempt to implement MBO as a "system of management," claiming that it fulfills all the broad managerial purposes of planning, organizing, controlling, communicating, and staffing. This is not necessarily true. In fact, when MBO is viewed as a system of management, it tends to downgrade the routine activities of the police department.

In viewing MBO, the police manager must constantly keep in mind its role as a rational tool to aid and assist him in making the broad managerial functions of planning, organizing, staffing, and implementation easier. It does *not,* however, take the place of these broad functions. Furthermore, by ceasing to place emphasis upon other activities of the police department and by spending too much time in attempting to implement MBO, the manager may fail to achieve the real purposes of the department. This has been one of the major downfalls of MBO in some government agencies where police chiefs have attempted to implement MBO as a strong control tool instead of using it as a rational tool to assist them in long-range, short-term, and everyday planning.

There is a distinct difference between MBO and program budgeting. A description of what constitutes a program budget will help to clarify the MBO philosophy and system.

Plan-program budgeting is essentially a method of controlling budgetary expenses, with an emphasis on programs such as suppression of crime or investigation of criminal activities. The program budget attaches a dollar cost to every activity within the police department. Under this budget, activities are grouped together in broad categories such as investigation, patrol, management services, and technical services.

The major differences between MBO and program budgeting are as follows: (1) program budgeting does not have specific objectives attached to the programs and (2) program budgeting refers to all departmental expenditures, whereas the MBO portion may amount to only 20 percent of activities within the department.

The cost of implementing an MBO project does not necessarily correspond to the total amount given to the department. For example, if a police department that is operating under a program budget is given $500,000 for control and reduction of crime, that amount must cover the cost of prevention, suppression, investigation, apprehension, prosecution, and recovery of property. In this same department, an MBO program would direct this broad budgeting toward specific objectives, such as a 10 percent reduction of robberies. An evaluation of this reveals that the objective under the MBO program would cost the department only a small portion of the total amount allowed under program budgeting for control and reduction of crime. The manager is able to evaluate the total cost of the broad activity as well as the smaller cost of reaching a specific objective.

MBO is a tool to be used for bringing about the desired growth of the organization; it is not a control mechanism for expenditures.

The police manager who accepts MBO must also respect the personnel in the department and have faith in them. His philosophy must be consistent with the means structure as defined by Maslow and with the assumptions of Theory Y as defined by Douglas McGregor. He should be able to recognize the potential for contribution by the people in his command.

## THE MBO SYSTEM

MBO can best be described as a seven-part process. These parts (shown in Figure 9.1) are:

1. Recognition of community values and departmental beliefs
2. Statement of departmental mission
3. Establishment of long-term goals
4. Establishment of short-term objectives
5. Development of projects
6. Development and implementation of action plans
7. Evaluation of the system

## VALUES AND BELIEFS

Values are defined as the social principles that have been accepted by the community. These include attitudes about honesty, community ethics, level of service, crime, vice conditions, and traffic problems. The values of the

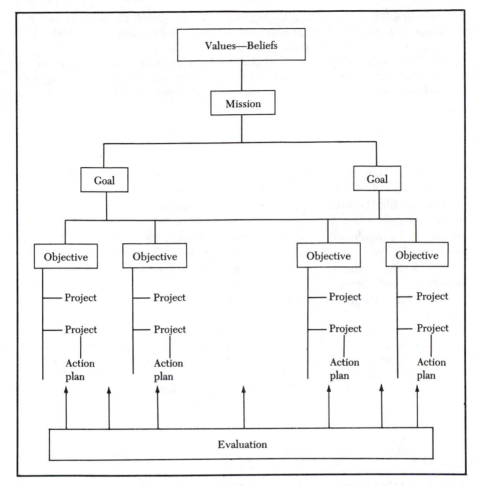

**Figure 9.1** Management by Objectives System

community are usually exhibited through the policy statements issued by the city council. The police chief should help to establish and interpret these policies as they apply directly to the police department. These policy statements are often issued in the form of departmental beliefs.

Examples of belief statements dealing with the issue of crime might read as follows:

> Criminality resulting from poverty, unemployment, and slum conditions is a community problem, not a problem for the police alone. The police have a responsibility to prevent and suppress crime and to solve crimes once they have occurred, but the police cannot prevent or solve every crime that occurs. The police must have the active cooperation, assistance, and moral support of the community that they serve.
>
> For a crime to occur, two factors must be present: opportunity and desire. It is the function of the police department to minimize the opportunities for crime

by such means as open, conspicuous, and aggressive patrol. Desire, however, is a factor controlled by potential offenders and those who influence their thinking. It is a factor over which the police exert little control.

Each police officer is chief of police within the area to which he or she is assigned. Officers are accountable for the crime and vice that exist on their beats and they have a responsibility to prevent crimes whenever possible.

## MISSION

The mission statement is the broadest, most comprehensive statement that can be made about the overall purpose of the police department. Another way of viewing the mission statement is that it spells out the primary responsibility of the police department, which justifies its continuing support by society and provides initial direction for the management of the police organization. The main purpose of a mission statement is to provide a focus for the resources of the police department and for the development of goals, objectives, and projects.

A simple mission statement for a police agency might be the following:

> Our mission is to ensure the safety and protection of both the property and person of all of the inhabitants of our community and to regulate and control the flow of traffic in order to facilitate the movement of persons and goods within our city and to reduce the impact of crime on the inhabitants of our city through investigation, apprehension, and adjudication of persons involved in criminal offenses.

## GOALS

Under an MBO system, goals may be viewed in two different ways. The first is that goals should be idealistic—impossible to achieve. An example of this view would be a goal to eliminate crime. The second and more popular view is that goals should be measurable and within reach, even though they may require a long period of time for implementation.

Goals, although broad in nature, may be specific in terms of the major accomplishments desired by management over two years' time. Examples of such goals might be: "the reduction of Part I offenses by 10 percent within the next two years," or "the reduction of the average monthly traffic accident rate by 5 percent within the next three years."

## OBJECTIVES

Objectives are considered short-term achievements. They must be attainable within a given time period. The maximum time period for accomplishment of objectives within the MBO system is one year. The objectives themselves must be tied to specific measurements. An example of an objective is: "to reduce the number of robberies in the eastern sector of the city by 5 percent within the next six months."

In establishing objectives, it is mandatory that the manager stay away from superlative phrases such as "finest" or "best." Within the MBO system, there should be a minimum of one and a maximum of six objectives for each established goal. Objectives should be used as guides in the planning and implementation of specific projects. They should be seen as tools for measuring the progress that is being made toward the achievement of goals. Objectives should define the results that are to be achieved, not activities that are to be performed.

In addition to being measurable, objectives must satisfy two other conditions—they should be both feasible and cost-effective. The levels of accomplishment within each project must be practical in the sense that they are attainable. The goals and the objectives must also be cost-effective; that is, the expected contribution to the individual project objectives, as well as the overall objectives of the MBO system, must justify the cost of the individual projects.

The following guidelines for setting objectives will help the police manager achieve the most from the MBO system.

1. *Define results to be achieved, not activities.* In stating objectives, the end result should be described, not the activity necessary to meet this stated result. For example, an objective of "putting the stakeout squad in high crime areas," is really an activity that should be designed to meet some stated objective, such as "reduce robberies by 10 percent within the next six months."
2. *The stated objective should relate to goals at the next higher level.* As objectives are established, it is important that the police manager focus on the overall good to be achieved and that she balance the stated goals with the major purpose of the police department, which is the protection of life and property. There is a natural tendency for police managers to set objectives that they feel will be interesting, and they ignore objectives that may be necessary. The police manager, especially if she is at the middle level of the department, should view her role as it fits into the total MBO system and then assist in establishing objectives that can best contribute to the stated overall goals of the department. She must be careful to avoid establishing objectives that are based upon what she herself can or would like to obtain.
3. *Set objectives at a reasonable level.* The objective should be challenging and should call upon the police manager to do better in the future than she did in the past. There is sometimes a tendency for police managers to establish objectives at such a high level that they may be impossible to achieve. In writing objectives, the manager should be careful to balance the need to challenge with the need to achieve. The police manager should not set impossible objectives for herself or her subordinates.
4. *Use language that everyone will understand.* Objectives should be written clearly and simply in language that both subordinates and supervisors can understand.
5. *Emphasize realism.* Objectives are valuable as guides for action only when they are prepared in a realistic manner. The police manager at the middle level should not be trying to impress superiors by establishing objectives that are unrealistic.

## PROJECTS

Once objectives have been determined, it is time to begin to put into action the projects that have been designed to meet these objectives. Projects involve the establishment of the step-by-step process that will be used to reach each of the objectives. It is important to understand that a single project may have an effect upon more than one objective. For example, if the objectives to reduce robbery by 5 percent and burglary by 10 percent have been established, a project using a tactical unit in certain areas of the city may have an effect upon both objectives.

Every project that is implemented under an MBO system must be specifically designed to attain one of the already established objectives. Within the individual projects themselves, objectives can be set that define the time period needed for implementation of the project and the results that are to be achieved by that project. For example, how long will it take to assign personnel to the tactical unit, to have the unit analyze present crime trends, and then to begin to take positive action toward reaching the objectives of reducing robbery and burglary?

Projects should also be designed for the short term. If the objective is to reduce robbery by 10 percent within a twelve-month period, then there may be three or four projects during this twelve-month period in an attempt to reach that stated objective. Each project may require only two or three months. They may be overlapping, or some may begin immediately and continue on through the entire twelve-month period.

Even though a long-range goal and a series of specific objectives have already been determined, it is important that individual accomplishments also be included within each project. These steps for accomplishment are the objectives within the individual projects. It is really these project objectives that are carefully evaluated at the beginning of the process and later analyzed to determine the success or failure of the objectives of the overall MBO system.

## ACTION PLANS

Action plans are the detailed steps of activities necessary for the completion of the individual projects. They dictate the responsibility that has been assigned to particular people, define the mutually acceptable target date, and determine how the task itself will be verified once it has been completed. All action plans relate directly to the projects to which they are assigned.

A simplified form can be used for the development of action plans. Such a form is shown in Figure 9.2.

## EVALUATION[1]

Evaluation in the MBO system is considered one of the most important steps. Evaluation is the process of determining the amount of success in achieving

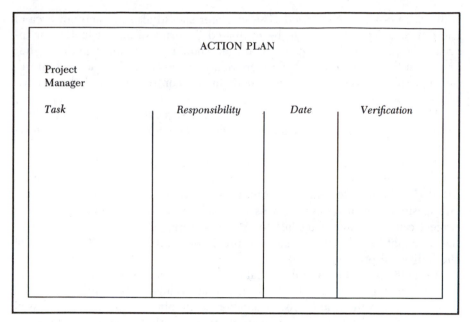

**Figure 9.2**   Example of an Action Plan Form

the predetermined objectives. Evaluation may be interim, to determine the amount of progress that has been made, or final, to determine the ultimate level of accomplishment.

Evaluation information is required for three different types of measurement: (1) external measures that determine the amount of success or failure in achieving the predetermined objectives and goals; (2) internal measures that determine (a) the efficiency and effectiveness of the individual and (b) the difficulties or stumbling blocks that were encountered and describe how they were overcome or why they could not be overcome; and (3) research measures that yield insight into cause-effect and other relationships that are useful as an empirical and theoretical base for future program planning.

The police manager should realize that the best evaluators of the projects that are implemented by police personnel are the individuals who conduct the implementation and manage the organization itself. As individual projects are developed, evaluation criteria can be established for each. Consider the attempt to evaluate a special stakeout unit designed to reduce armed robberies. The criteria for determining the success or failure of this project would be how many robberies actually occurred; how much time, money, and effort was placed into the project; and how long it took to reach the success level that was finally attained.

The police managers can help evaluate this project. First, the area of the city in which the special stakeout unit is to be employed should be examined for its present robbery rate. Then, at the end of the project, the number of robberies must be determined. The manager should also use another area of the city as a "control" area to be evaluated in terms of any reduction or increase in robberies. The police manager should determine whether other crimes in the stakeout area have increased or decreased. The rates of apprehension should also be examined, both in the control area and the experimental area.

Many criteria can be used to determine the success or failure of a project, but the most effective approach is to decide on only a small number of criteria as a measure.

The police manager can establish an evaluation criteria chart similar to that for the decision criteria discussed earlier. The numerous projects can be listed down one side, and the criteria—such as implementation time, cost, and feasibility—can be listed across the other. Information gained from each project can be evaluated against the stated criteria. The police manager then has a simplified evaluation system to use in determining the effectiveness of the individual program.

In addition to the careful evaluation of individual projects at the project level of the MBO system, it is important that evaluation be conducted at the objective and at the goal levels. Evaluation at the objective level can be based upon analyzing the effect of complementary and duplicating projects designed for achieving the same objectives. Whenever possible, the police manager should establish both evaluation and control groups in order to isolate the effectiveness of the individual project from any external effects. In addition, projects that are directed toward the same objective should be separated, either in time or space, so as to avoid a subjective decision concerning which project had the greater effect upon reaching the stated objectives.

Evaluation of groups of projects is also necessary to determine which strategies proved to be most effective in achieving the objectives and goals. In larger cities, projects can be grouped by geographic areas, concentration of target population, or type of area, such as residential or commercial.

Evaluation includes a series of activities:[2]

1. Specify measurable objectives.
2. Formulate a practical evaluation design.
3. Specify data collection procedures.
4. Specify data analysis methods.

This overall process is shown in Figure 9.3.

This four-step process applies whether the evaluation is being conducted at the goal, objective, or individual program level.

## Step 1: Specify Measurable Objectives

In order to have proper output from this first step in the evaluation process, the objectives should be "measurable." Therefore, the output should clearly identify the individual data elements that must be used to determine the amount of success.

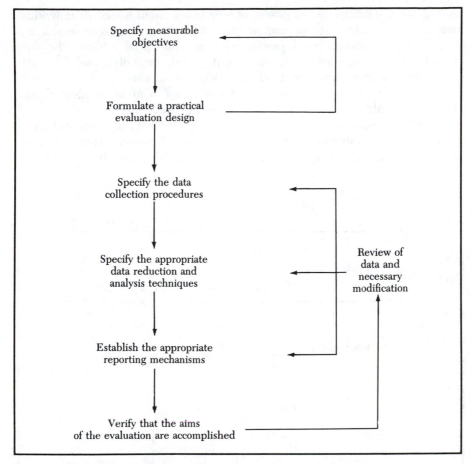

**Figure 9.3** A Schematic Flow Model of the Evaluation Process
SOURCE: Developed for the Atlanta Impact Program (LEAA) by Norman Baker, Edward Unger, Terry Sprott, Thomas Buskirk, and Gordon Miller.

In Step 1, the objectives must be converted to numerical terms. For example, if the objective was the reduction of robbery by 10 percent within a six-month period, then the 10 percent must be translated into numerical figures—from 60 robberies per month to 54 robberies per month.

In addition to translation to numerical figures, there should be an identification of the performance measures that will be examined in the individual projects being directed toward the objective. Using the 10 percent robbery reduction as an example, the basic performance measures would include such broad factors as location, time, and whether the robbery is classified as commercial, residential, or open-space. Once these performance measures have been identified, data elements can be collected and analyzed for each of the performance measures. Data elements for location may be the specific address, reporting area, census tract, patrol beat, or any combination of these. The data elements for time may include the month, day of the week, and hour of the day designated in groups of four hours, eight hours, or individual hours. The data elements for commercial robbery might include banks, gas stations, food markets, and liquor stores. For residential robbery the data elements might include house, apartment, hotel, or motel; and for open space, they could include street, alley, parking lot, or park.

It is important to emphasize that if evaluation is to be conducted, the objectives should be measurable, feasible, and cost-effective.

Step 1 is described in Figure 9.4. As this figure indicates, the output of Step 1 is a measurable objective that is feasible and cost-effective and internally consistent with criteria, performance measures, and basic data elements.

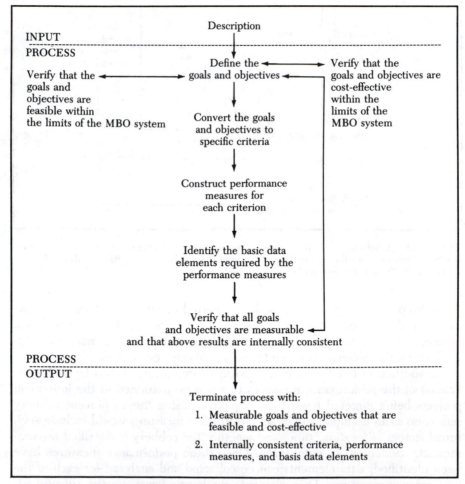

**Figure 9.4**  A Schematic Flow Model of Step 1: Specify Measurable Objectives
SOURCE: Developed for the Atlanta Impact Program (LEAA) by Norman Baker, Edward Unger, Terry Sprott, Thomas Buskirk, and Gordon Miller.

## Step 2: Formulate a Practical Evaluation Design

The important words in this step are "practical" and "design." The purpose of the evaluation design is to assure the police manager that it is possible to distinguish between changes caused by the projects and other changes that may have occurred within the department. Therefore, the evaluation design must separate the impact of other projects from the effectiveness of the projects being evaluated.

The manager has two types of designs from which to choose in evaluating individual projects. The first is referred to as "before-after" design and the second as the "control group" design.

Use of the before-after design is the more common method of evaluating projects in terms of success or failure. This approach involves only one step—comparing the level of activity prior to the implementation of the projects to the level of activity after the projects have been implemented. A simple example is the comparison of robbery rates in a certain area of the city during the first six months of Year I (prior to the implementation of the MBO system) and the robbery rates of the same area of the city during the first six months of Year II (after the projects have been implemented). The difference in the robbery rates during these two time periods is an indication of the success or failure of the MBO system.

The control-group design is based on the assumption that it is possible to identify two environments, two geographical population areas, that have similar characteristics. One area is designated as the experimental group, and the other as the control group. The basic data elements are collected for both groups, with the further assumptions that the factors influencing one group (except for the projects being implemented in the experimental group) also influence the other. The assumption is that the only difference between these two groups during the period of program implementation is the project activity. Therefore, it is safe to assume that the difference between the performance measures found in the experimental group and those in the control group can be attributed directly to the projects that are being implemented in the experimental group.

At least one of the approaches should be used in order to guarantee some valid evaluation; however, in many instances it is impossible to use both the control group and before-after approaches.

The evaluation design must also be practical. It should be possible for the police manager to collect and manage the required data elements so that careful evaluation can be made. In this instance, the manager should consider such questions as: (1) Are the data we need currently being collected for some other reason? (2) If the answer is no, then can these data be collected only by implementing minor modifications of the present data collection system? (3) Would it be necessary to develop a completely new data collection system?

The manager must also examine the cost of obtaining this information, and he should know whether or not this information will be reliable and valid.

Step 2 is shown in graphic form in Figure 9.5. The results of this step are (a) a practical evaluation design, (b) the identification of required basic data

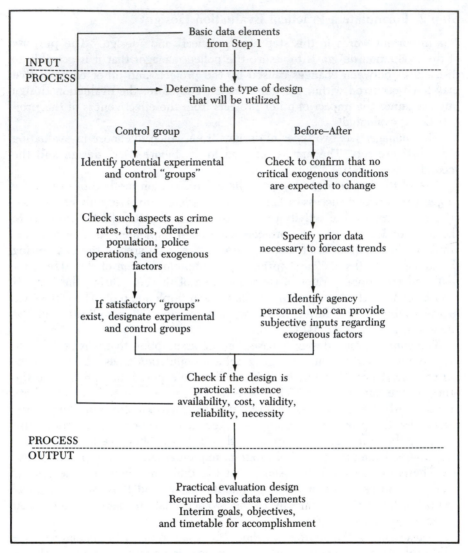

**Figure 9.5** A Schematic Model of Step 2: Formulate a Practical Evaluation Design
SOURCE: Developed for the Atlanta Impact Program (LEAA) by Norman Baker, Edward Unger, Terry Sprott, Thomas Buskirk, and Gordon Miller.

elements, (c) the specification of interim goals and objectives, and (d) the timetable for the accomplishment of these interim measurements.

## Step 3: Specify Data Collection Procedures

Within this step, the police manager should perform the following activities:

1. Determine how the data will be collected.
2. Specify by whom the information will be collected.

3. Decide upon the frequency with which the information will be collected.
4. Design forms that will be used to collect the information.

These activities should be formulated for all of the required data elements that will be collected and analyzed.

The information system presently in use should be examined in considerable detail, and it should be used as much as possible. In some instances, the police manager may determine that the information necessary for evaluation *is* being collected but is not being used for output purposes. Therefore, minor adjustments should be made that will produce this information in the output process. For example, if the manager wants to know whether robberies have been directed toward gas stations, liquor stores, or banks, he may find this information in the field reports. The manager would then only have to take this information from the field reports and have it analyzed on a monthly basis. If, however, the information is not currently available, then the manager must take the necessary steps to guarantee that the information will be collected and analyzed.

The process of Step 3 is shown in Figure 9.6, with the output being the specification of the information collection procedures.

## Step 4: Specify Data Reduction and Analysis Methods

This step is necessary to enable the police manager to measure the success of projects in reaching the goals and objectives. This step also helps to describe relationships between projects, and it provides knowledge that may be useful in future planning and project activities.

It is important to measure the success of each project so that the police manager may have a way of monitoring, controlling, and directing the activities within each project from its inception to its conclusion. By assessing the program's failure or success and that success's contribution to the overall objectives and goals of the MBO system, the police manager can make recommendations as to whether the individual project should be continued, modified, or eliminated. In addition, the description and explanation of the data produced from the projects can be used to analyze the reasons for the degree of success or failure of the total MBO system. The manager can use this analysis to improve management practices and upgrade the operation of the entire department.

With regard to the measures of success, the police manager should attempt to determine the degree to which the projects have achieved their individual goals and objectives as well as the objectives of the MBO system. This data analysis can also help to formulate a value judgment as to whether the projects should be continued or expanded to other units within the department.

The data reduction and analysis methods include such activities as weekly reports, monthly reports, comparisons of the before and after, comparisons of the control group to the experimental group, and the use of maps, charts, and graphs. In the larger police agencies, this data reduction and analysis

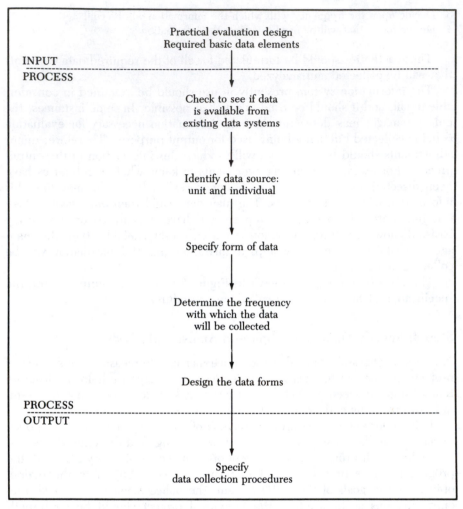

**Figure 9.6** A Schematic Model of Step 3: Specify Data Collection Procedures
SOURCE: Developed for the Atlanta Impact Program (LEAA) by Norman Baker, Edward Unger,
Terry Sprott, Thomas Buskirk, and Gordon Miller.

would include the use of computerized information systems and highly technical procedures for summary evaluation of the information.

In addition to specifying the data reduction analysis methods to be used, the police manager should identify the individual who is responsible for the evaluation analysis. In many instances this can be personnel who have already been assigned to activities such as operations analysis, research and development, or crime prevention. The manager should also determine when interim evaluations will be conducted. The number of interim evaluation points depends on the length of the project, its cost, and its complexity. Within this step, the police manager should also specify how the evaluation results will be used, especially with regard to the overall management practices and procedures of the department.

Step 4 is described in Figure 9.7, with the output being the full specifications of the evaluation process.

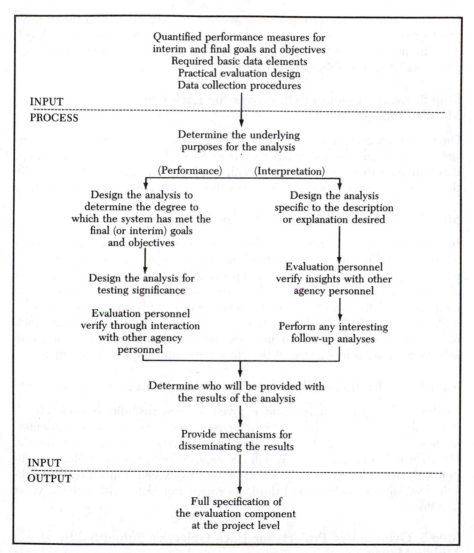

**Figure 9.7** A Schematic Model of Step 4: Specify Data Reduction and Analysis Methods
SOURCE: Developed for the Atlanta Impact Program (LEAA) by Norman Baker, Edward Unger, Terry Sprott, Thomas Buskirk, and Gordon Miller.

# IMPLEMENTATION

Once the manager has some understanding of the MBO system, he must develop such a system and begin to implement it within his department. The MBO system is most effectively put into practice through the use of 9, 9 team management. It must also be based on the assumptions of Theory Y.

## Step 1: Establishment of Goals by Top Managers

It is the responsibility of top-level managers to determine long-range goals and to give direction and set parameters for the managers at the middle level. It is the middle managers who are responsible for the development and implementation of the objectives and projects.

## Step 2: Establishment of Objectives for Each Goal by Middle Managers

Once top management has determined the goals for the agency, middle management must submit a series of objectives for each stated goal. In this step, it is important that the managers at both levels have an opportunity to clarify the stated goals and proposed objectives through effective communication.

## Step 3: Selection of Objectives by Top Managers

In this step, top management reviews the objectives with middle management. Depending upon the ability of middle management to implement the management by objectives system, top management selects from one to six objectives for each stated goal. The selection of objectives by top management should follow as closely as possible the priority listing of objectives by middle management. It is top management's role to carefully evaluate each of the objectives submitted for inconsistencies and to adjust the measure of achievement in each objective if they feel it is either too low or too high.

## Step 4: Finalization of Objectives by Middle Managers

In this step, middle management is given the responsibility of finalizing all stated objectives, even though top management can place certain guidelines on how each objective is to be stated. For example, they may require the objective to state, first, what it will accomplish (reduction of robbery by 10 percent); next, the cost of the objective (not to exceed limits already established within the budget); and third, its completion date (within the next six months).

## Step 5: Overview of Projects for Each Objective Submitted by Middle Managers

In this step, middle management is required to submit for approval by top management a list of projects to be implemented in order to reach each objective. This step requires close coordination between top and middle management as well as horizontal coordination between the middle managers. The projects should be carefully screened to avoid duplication and to evaluate all possible consequences and side effects. Consider a project to implement a special tactical unit in one control area and a special stakeout squad in another high-crime area. If both projects are implemented at the same time, even though both have merits and will have some effect upon the overall objective of robbery reduction, the effect of transferring personnel within the patrol force to handle both projects may seriously hamper the overall operation of the uniformed forces. The negative side effects may cause more harm and prevent the department from reaching its overall goal of reducing robbery.

## Step 6: Development of Detailed Projects by Middle Management

After the projects have been approved by top management, the middle managers must develop specific formats for the implementation of each project. The middle manager should refer to the seven-step process developed under decision making and use it to develop the individual projects. Each project has its own objectives, it defines the obstacles to completion of the project, and it determines the data that is to be collected and analyzed. In this case, it would not be necessary to develop alternative solutions because the project has already been selected. But the manner in which the project is to be implemented can be developed according to how it will be evaluated.

A simple one-page information sheet can be developed to give all necessary data concerning each project. This information sheet should include such items as (1) who will be responsible for the project; (2) the stated objectives of the project; (3) which overall objectives the project might affect, as well as its effect on the objectives of the MBO system; (4) what results are expected; (5) what steps are to be taken and who is responsible for each step; and (6) the beginning date, the interim evaluation dates, and ending date.

This form should include such items as (a) *staffing*—the personnel who will be involved with the project in each of its steps; (b) *coordination* of the individuals from within the department, as well as those outside the department whose services will be necessary for the successful completion of the project; (c) *training*—what additional training of individuals is necessary; and (d) *evaluation*—the determination of the overall success or failure of the project.

## Step 7: Evaluation

Steps within each project should be carefully evaluated on review dates for success as well as failure and for determination of any changes that may be required. This evaluation should be flexible enough to allow project directors to initiate changes they deem necessary or to recommend that the project be cancelled because of its lack of success.

This step-by-step implementation process forces the police agency and the manager to plan systematically.

# ADDITIONAL USE OF THE MBO SYSTEM

As a police department evaluates its direction, it views numerous issues to help define where it is, and it examines its values, beliefs, major problems, environmental factors, and the elements contained in the evaluation process. In order to define direction, it establishes a mission statement, goals, and objectives. In order to analyze and describe how it is going to achieve the mission, goals and objectives, projects, and action plans are developed.

*Environmental factors* may also affect the MBO system. Environmental factors are defined as those over which the police department has no direct control. Typical examples might be the appointment of a new city manager who emphasizes values and beliefs different than those already established by the police department or a new governing board that places priorities in a different order—or it could be a new law passed that requires a different course of action or which changes present procedures in the police department. Such environmental factors can easily be integrated into the MBO system.

*Specific problems* that require immediate action might also arise during the implementation of the MBO program. These can easily be integrated into the total MBO system. The police manager must recognize that if serious problems do arise—for example, (a) a high turnover rate, (b) a reduction or freeze in spending, or (c) a type of crime that drastically increases, such as robbery—he will be able to use the MBO system at any level in order to take positive action to overcome the specific problem.

Let us assume that armed robberies are suddenly increasing at an alarming rate. Within the MBO system, there might be an objective dealing with armed robberies. However, the objective might either be too low-priority or the projects themselves might not really deal with the areas of the community in which the problem exists. With new information developed through the evaluation process, a new objective can be established, an old objective can be changed, new projects can be implemented, or old projects can be upgraded in order to help meet the newly established objective that is designed to overcome the problem.

When MBO is viewed as an ongoing system of assisting in day-to-day operations, it takes on a new meaning and an added dimension. The total picture of how the MBO system operates is shown in Figure 9.8.

# PITFALLS OF MANAGEMENT BY OBJECTIVES

*Management by objectives is by no means a panacea for all management ills.* The police manager must constantly realize that she is responsible not only for the implementation of projects designed to meet specific objectives and goals but also for day-to-day implementation of the many functions and activities necessary to bring about a successful police operation. The police manager cannot seriously deplete organizational units such as the patrol force in order to emphasize the implementation or meeting of a specific objective.

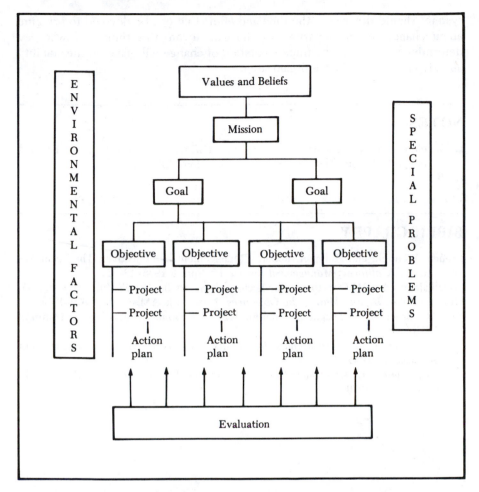

**Figure 9.8**  Management by Objectives System

*The manager cannot allow MBO to override the responsibilities or caring for day-to-day activities.* The police manager's job is to decide which objectives are to be sought, at what point in the organization they are to be implemented, by whom, and to what degree the total effort of the organization should be devoted to reaching some stated objectives.

*Another pitfall in the implementation of MBO is the attempt to involve every member of the agency in some way in attempting to obtain the objectives.* This may upset the stability that has already been created and may do more harm than good. Consider the police department that has an adequate record and information system. To force them to revamp their present practices and procedures for the sole purpose of doing a "better job," may be highly expensive, frustrating, and in the long run, bring about more negative than positive side effects.

In summary, then, the police manager, in the implementation of an MBO system, should determine the time and effort that can be devoted to bringing about change in the department, who can devote this time, and who can determine what effect the implementation of change will have on the stability already created within the organization.

## NOTES

1. Developed for the Atlanta Impact Program (LEAA) by Norman Baker, Edward Unger, Terry Sprott, Thomas Buskirk, and Gordon Miller.
2. Ibid.

## BIBLIOGRAPHY

French, Wendell, and Hollman, Robert. "Management by Objectives: The Team Approach," *California Management Review* 17 (Spring 1975):13–22.
Gazell, James A. "MBO in the Public Sector," *Business Review* 27 (July 1974): 29–35.
Humble, John. *How to Manage by Objectives*. New York: AMACOM, 1972–1973.
Kirchoff, Bruce A. "A Diagnostic Tool for MBO," *Personnel Psychology* 23 (Autumn 1975).
McConkey, D. D. *How to Manage by Results*. New York: American Management Association, 1965.
Morrisey, George L. *Management by Objectives and Results*. Reading, Mass.: Addison-Wesley, 1970.

# CHAPTER 10

# *Fiscal Management*

The police department's budget is one of the most important policy statements made on an annual basis. It reflects the values that are predominant and the thinking of the managers of the police department, the city or county administrator, and the political leaders of the community.

## DEFINITION

The most common definition states that a budget is a plan expressed in dollar terms by which a set of programs is authorized for a future period of time, usually one year. This definition is many times questioned. One of the first issues raised is whether the budget is really a plan, or if it is just an agreement or a contract between the governing board and the department heads on how much money they may spend in the upcoming year. Although the budget is expressed in dollar terms, it is seldom viewed strictly as a fiscal device. In some instances, it is a device used to indicate priorities and to indicate the role that department heads may play in conjunction with other department heads, the city manager, and the governing board. Under a strict economic definition, a budget is an allocation of scarce resources among competing demands from different departments, including the police department.

A more acceptable definition is that a budget is a comprehensive plan, expressed in financial terms, by which an operating program is effective for a given period of time. It includes estimates of services, activities, and projects comprised by the program; the resultant expenditure requirements; and the resources usable for their support.

## PURPOSES OF BUDGETING

The budget is significant from several standpoints. First, it encompasses comprehensive reviews of police department activities, usually on an annual basis. Second, it specifies limits as to what the police department can do; in this sense, it serves as a legal document. Third, it is used to accomplish managerial ends such as designating who is responsible for what, setting a pattern for centralization or delegation of authority within the police department, and mandating economies that must be brought forth in the future. It sets out what the police department will or attempt to accomplish. In this sense, it is a workload plan. It is used to enact new programs or significantly change existing ones within the police agency. It helps bring information to the proper level necessary for decisions and, when implemented correctly, provides upward and downward information, so that these decisions may be properly carried out at all levels within the police department.

There are two overall approaches to the establishment of a budget as far as the chief of police is concerned. There is what is known as *incremental budgeting* and at the other spectrum what is known as *zero-base budgeting*.

Under incremental budgeting, there is an assumption that activities that have occurred within the past fiscal year are presently effective and will become the foundation for the future. This budget focuses upon revenue growth. A typical example might be the police chief who is obligated to submit the budget in a format whereby he discloses how much he spent last year on a certain item (such as new vehicles), how much he intends to spend this year, and the difference between these two figures. For example, if he requires an additional $3,000, then a justification is needed for the additional expense. The assumption is that the amount of money spent for purchasing during the last year was spent in an efficient and effective manner.

Zero-base budgeting, on the other hand, implies a review of the entire budgeting process. It requires the setting up of priorities; communication to the police department of the relationship between these priorities and their costs; and the establishment of goals, somewhere in the department, not only for the upcoming year but also for at least three to five years into the future. In essence, the police department must know where it is headed and how it will get there; it will then be able to measure its effectiveness. This budget explains, on an annual basis, why the police department exists.

In reality, there really is no budgeting system that is 100 percent "incremental" or "zero-base." Usually, budgets are built on some aspects of each system.

## STAGES IN THE BUDGETING PROCESS

There are four broad stages in the budget process. The first is the *preparation stage*, which is the responsibility of the executive branch of the government, including the police department. The budget calendar is established by the city manager, who works backward from the legal date required for the enactment of a budget. For example, if a budget must be enacted by July 1, then the city manager may demand that the police department's budget be submitted to her at least forty-five days in advance. It then becomes the police department's responsibility, under the direction of the police chief, to establish its requests. The police chief must first know the date required for his submission of the initial budget requests to the city or county manager, the budget director, or whoever may be responsible for first reviewing the police department's budget. Depending on the size of the police department and the amount of involvement required by members within the department, the commanders of the police agency can establish a budget schedule designed to meet the required date for initial budget requests.

The second stage in the budget process is *adoption*. This is a legislative function that requires some legal action, such as a special ordinance passed each year or a resolution by the governing board. Each police chief should carefully review the state's statutes governing the budgetary adoption process for his individual community so that he will be aware of the legal requirements and the formal process that must be followed.

The third stage is that of *execution*. This is an executive function and is a fairly detailed process of the establishment of some kind of fiscal control system, usually at the direction of the city or county manager. The police chief, therefore, need not be concerned with the development of an execution process. His primary concerns should be to have a clear understanding of how the budget forms are to be used, what forms are to be submitted for what types of requests, how the summary information presented to him can best be used for the upgrading of the police department, and how well the department is proceeding in implementing the programs and expenditures of its approved fundings.

The execution process includes the development of purchase orders, some kind of preordering, receipts to be received for merchandise purchased, and the disbursement of funds. Each of these procedures is generally citywide or countywide in nature; the individual police department is usually not responsible for developing special procedures for the police agency.

The fourth major stage in the budget process is the *postaudit stage*, which is a legislative function whereby, on an annual basis at the close of each budget year, an audit is taken so that the city and the police department are protected from any accusations of misappropriation of funds. This stage clearly shows that the funds have been properly expended, that the police chief has not overexpended his budget, and that the budgeting has proceeded in a clearly legal manner.

These four stages and their relationship are shown in Figure 10.1.


## TYPES OF BUDGETS

There are three basic types of budgets. The first is the *line-item* or *object budget,* the second is the *performance budget,* and the third is the *program budget*.

The *line-item* or *object budget* groups expenditures by classes or objects. It concentrates primarily on efficiency, focusing the dollar amounts on inputs (what the police department intends to purchase), not on outputs (what the department intends to achieve). Normally, only the increase in any specific amount is questioned by the budget director, city or county manager, or governing board. This type of budget forces the police chief to concentrate on the incremental philosophy of budgeting. The line-item or object-type budget was created to resolve problems of corruption that existed at local levels many years ago. Today it is used as a strong control tool by fiscal man-

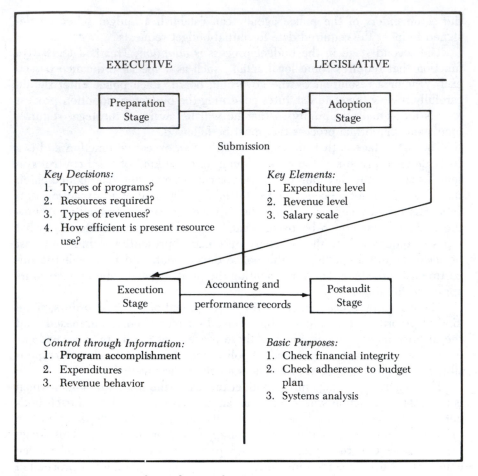

EXECUTIVE                                    LEGISLATIVE

Preparation                                    Adoption
Stage                                          Stage

Submission

*Key Decisions:*                               *Key Elements:*
1. Types of programs?                          1. Expenditure level
2. Resources required?                         2. Revenue level
3. Types of revenues?                          3. Salary scale
4. How efficient is present resource
   use?

Execution        Accounting and               Postaudit
Stage        performance records              Stage

*Control through Information:*                 *Basic Purposes:*
1. Program accomplishment                      1. Check financial integrity
2. Expenditures                                2. Check adherence to budget
3. Revenue behavior                               plan
                                               3. Systems analysis

**Figure 10.1**   Stages in the Budget Cycle

agers; it really does not assist in the development of departmental programs or explain the purpose for the individual police department.

The police manager must recognize that a line-item or object-type budget will always be present someplace within the budgetary process. It may be the sole budgetary style, or it could be part of a different type of budget, such as the performance or program type. It may be used as a planning tool or as a means of auditing expenditures. A line-item or object-type budget, therefore, is important for all police managers to understand. Although this type of budget may be on the whole more negative than positive in nature, it is surely one of the more common types of budgets in law enforcement today. In addition, a clear understanding of its value can assist the police chief in the overall fiscal management of the police department.

Line-item budgets are usually divided into the following four major categories: (1) *personal services,* which includes salaries, fringe benefits, and other costs relating directly to costs allocated for people; (2) *operating and maintenance,* which includes supplies such as gas, oil, forms, pencils, and even paper clips; (3) *charges and services,* which covers special contracts, rentals, travel funds, and training, and (4) *capital outlay,* which is the money expended for the purchase of equipment such as cars, desks, or weapons.

An example of the format of a line-item or object budget is shown in Figure 10.2.

A *performance budget* specifies activities of the police department, the performance data being the information by which the police chief determines the necessity for incremental increases or decreases. The format is much like that of the line-item or object-type budget. It normally measures activities such as number of tickets written, crimes solved, property recovered, and calls for service handled. It is divided into these types of services by organizational unity. For example, it compares the number of calls for services handled by the Uniform Operation Division to those handled by the Criminal

| *Item* | *Amount* |
|---|---|
| Personal services | $25,000 |
| Contractual services | 5,000 |
| Supplies/materials | 5,000 |
| Miscellaneous items | 500 |
| Capital outlay | 10,000 |
| *Total* | $45,000 |

Sample—Object Budget with Divisional Breakdown

| *Item* | *Amount* | *Total* |
|---|---|---|
| I.  Personal services | | |
| A.  Salaries | | |
| Headquarters | $5,000 | |
| Patrol | 5,000 | |
| Detective | 5,000 | |
| Services | 5,000 | |
| | | $20,000 |
| | | |
| B.  Fringe | | |
| Headquarters | $1,250 | |
| Patrol | 1,250 | |
| Detective | 1,250 | |
| Services | 1,250 | |
| | | $ 5,000 |
| | *Total personal services* | $25,000 |

Note: Contractual services, supplies/materials, miscellaneous items, and capital outlay categories would all have similar breakdowns.

**Figure 10.2** Line-Item—Object Budget

Investigation Division. An example of the performance-type budget format is shown in Figure 10.3.

*Program budgeting,* developed by the Rand Corporation for the U.S. Department of Defense, demands an analysis between cost-benefits and cost-effectiveness. This first requires the statement of the goals of the police department, such as what effects they will have upon crime and calls for service. It then focuses on what programs and activities will be used to achieve these goals. Finally, it emphasizes output measures. Budgeting then becomes a planning tool in helping in the everyday operation of the police department. It demands a justification for expenditures for new programs or for deleting old programs that have not met their objectives and are no longer effective because of changing conditions within the police department. Program budgeting requires that the decisions for implementation be left with the police department and not be controlled by some outside agency.

The program budget is also a means of planning future costs on the basis of past experience and forecasted events and conditions.

There are numerous broad programs in which law enforcement can become involved. Some of these include prevention of crimes, investigation of crimes, apprehension of violators, presentation of criminals for judicature, services to the public, and career development of personnel. An example of a program-type budget format is presented in Figure 10.4.

The police department shares the broad responsibilities of its overall program with such other agencies as public works, traffic engineering, and fire departments. Each agency contributes to the program objectives, and they need to show those expenditures in their respective budgets.

| | | |
|---|---|---|
| *Accident investigation* | | *Amount* |
| Personal services | | $85,000 |
| Contractual services | | 5,000 |
| Supplies/materials | | 1,250 |
| | *Total* | $91,250 |
| | | |
| *Performance statistics* | | |
| Investigate (initial) | | |
| Property damage | | $ 2,000 |
| Personal injury | | 500 |
| Fatal | | 10 |
| | | |
| Arrest and follow-up | | $ 2,400 |
| | | |
| Cost per accident | | |
| Property | | $    25 |
| Personal injury | | 75 |
| Fatality | | 375 |
| | | |
| Issue summonses | | |
| Hazardous violations | | $20,000 |
| Nonhazardous violations | | 15,000 |

**Figure 10.3**  Performance Budget

*Program—Community Safety*

| | | | |
|---|---|---|---:|
| *Subprogram—Crime Prevention and Suppression* | | | $100,000 |
| Program Elements | (a) | High school education | 10,000 |
| | (b) | Preventive patrol | 50,000 |
| | (c) | Crime prevention, security-oriented | 25,000 |
| | (d) | Crime prevention, treatment-oriented | 15,000 |
| | | | |
| *Subprogram—Investigation and Apprehension* | | | $ 25,000 |
| Program Elements | (a) | Crimes against persons | 7,000 |
| | (b) | Crimes against property | 15,000 |
| | (c) | Community security | 3,000 |
| | | | |
| *Subprogram—Movement and Control of Traffic* | | | $ 30,000 |
| Program Elements | (a) | Traffic patrol | 15,000 |
| | (b) | Accident investigation | 7,000 |
| | (c) | Traffic regulation | 3,000 |
| | (d) | Traffic safety education | 5,000 |
| | | | |
| *Subprogram—Maintenance of Public Order* | | | $ 10,000 |
| Program Elements | (a) | Civil disturbance prevention | 3,000 |
| | (b) | Noncriminal investigation | 7,000 |
| | | *Total* | $165,000 |

*Program—General Management and Support*

| | | | |
|---|---|---|---:|
| *Subprogram—Staff Support* | | | $ 80,000 |
| Program Elements | (a) | Information services | 20,000 |
| | (b) | Technical services | 10,000 |
| | (c) | Discretion and supervision | 40,000 |
| | (d) | Planning and evaluation | 10,000 |
| | | | |
| *Subprogram—Employee Development* | | | $ 20,000 |
| Program Elements | (a) | Employee training and education | 12,000 |
| | (b) | Employee recruitment | 8,000 |
| | | *Total* | $100,000 |
| | | | |
| | | *Grand Total* | $265,000 |

Note: Each program element contains the "objective" and cost summary by object—
personal services, operating and maintenance supplies, charges and services,
capital outlay.

**Figure 10.4**  Program Budget

Regardless of whether the budget is designed as a performance or a program budget, a line-item budget must be prepared to support the theories behind the overall budget process. The line-item document may be developed and kept at the police department level, or it may be a separate document helping to support the performance or program budget request.

## ROLES OF MAJOR PEOPLE IN THE BUDGETING PROCESS

The budgetary process is by no means entirely under the control of the police department. Numerous parties become involved in it, each playing a separate role and each affecting the decisions of the others.

The first key person in the budgetary process is the chief of police. Working with other members of the police department, his budget reflects the professional or expert approach to resolving the problems that face the police department. The police chief is oriented primarily toward successful completion of his mission and in some instances tends to be too expansive in his budgetary requests. His responsibility is to initiate most of the policies that are eventually accepted into the budget.

The second key person is the budget or finance officer. She is usually an administrative generalist and is oriented to financial and managerial norms. The budget or finance officer tends to be more restrictive in her budgetary recommendations and carefully considers the progress of the police department, the goals it has established and whether or not they are being met, and how well guidelines established within the present budget have been met.

## SUMMARY

This chapter was not designed to make budgetary experts out of police managers but to give the manager an overview of the budget process, the types of budgets available, and the roles that different people play in the budget process. All this has a strong effect on how the police department obtains its funds and how much flexibility is given for day-to-day operations.

Police managers should not be overwhelmed by the budgetary process. It can and should be carefully studied, analyzed, and understood by all commanders in the department so that they will be able to assist the chief of police in preparing the police department's budget, negotiating its approval, and executing its mandates.

# CHAPTER 11

# Management of Time

Police managers must recognize that the delegation of tasks is one of their most important functions. By distributing work, they are able to use their time effectively.

The police manager should realize that time is one commodity available to all people. Time cannot be stockpiled, nor can it be recycled. And unlike money, material, and ideas, it does not increase with added responsibility.

There are two types of time that the police manager faces. The first is defined as *management time:* that time spent in planning, organizing, leading, and controlling. The second, *vocational time,* is that time spent performing activities that only the police manager can perform. Examples include attending special staff meetings, meeting with the city manager or members of the city council, and honoring specific invitations to attend meetings of civic organizations and professional associations.

What often happens is that as police managers are promoted within the organization, they maintain the same amount—if not more—of vocational time that they previously had. As a result, the necessary management time is never totally available. The manager may attempt to find this extra management time by staying extra hours, starting with an eight-hour day and constantly adding to it until he or she is spending twelve to fourteen hours a day performing the police management role. If it is impossible to continue to find this time at the police building, the manager may take the work home. The end result is that both the professional activities of the department and the manager's personal life begin to suffer.

The solution is to delegate tasks as much as possible, redefining activities and functions, and passing these responsibilities on to subordinates. The police manager can make more effective use of management time by having some system for using the rational tools of management.

## DEMANDS ON THE MANAGER'S TIME

The first demand on the manager's time is made by associates. If the police manager is an assistant chief, then time must be allocated for conferences with the chief of police. The chief of police must spend time with the city manager, the mayor, or the city council. Usually there is an immediate priority on this part of the manager's time. In this situation police managers are playing the role of employees and are acting in compliance with the requests of superiors. They are performing work, and the rewards and the risks are usually extremely low. It is important that the police manager and his or her superiors, the city manager and mayor for example, agree to meet at definite times during each work week. The professional manager will do all that is possible to help assistant managers use their time more effectively. It is the police manager's responsibility, however, to bring this issue before the relevant superiors and arrive at some consensus as to how they can best work together to conserve the time that is needed for each to perform adequately.

The second demand on the police manager's time is created by the system or organizational structure itself. The demand of the system is the time the police manager must spend inspecting, evaluating, and attempting to bring about conformity within the department. Depending upon the nature of the required activity, the manager could be supervising or possibly even doing the work of subordinates. It is important that the police manager carefully evaluate each task and be certain that he or she is not doing something that should be done by subordinates.

Consider the police captain who constantly establishes daily work schedules and daily assignments because six months earlier a new subordinate asked him to perform the task once. The captain continues to perform the activity. The result is that the subordinate finally accepts as fact that the captain intends to devote his management time to performing the activity which is really the responsibility of the subordinate. The police captain, as a police manager, should redelegate that task to the subordinate, where it rightfully belongs, thereby giving the captain more time to operate as a manager rather than performing as a first-line supervisor.

The third major demand on the manager's time is categorized as self-time. Here the police manager is thinking, planning, and evaluating information to assist in future decisions. It is important for the police manager to set aside a time each week when he can be creative, innovative, and carefully think out and plan for the future. If used well, the time spent in this category can bring about change and progress.

The effective police manager, recognizing that there are three demands on her time, could establish her work week in half-day blocks as shown in Figure 11.1. She could then assign specific and designated time periods within each day as to how she will allocate her time during the normal work week. For example, she may allot only two blocks of activities that require her time away from running the police department. At least one or two blocks may be set aside for developing ideas, for planning, and for making best use of her ability to help the department grow. Each police manager should carefully evaluate the amount of time she spends with her organization and the amount necessary to be spent with her city manager or superiors. She should assess the present ability of her subordinates to handle the delegated authority and the amount of time she must spend in helping them develop the

|  | *AM* | *PM* |
|---|---|---|
| Monday | Review and inspection | Self-development |
| Tuesday | Inspection | Public contacts |
| Wednesday | Personnel conferences | Self-development |
|  | Department staff |  |
| Thursday |  | Division staff |
| Friday | Public contacts | Weekly evaluation |

**Figure 11.1**   Manager's Work Week

ability to accept added responsibilities. The pressures placed upon her by the community, the law enforcement profession itself, and any other priorities must be taken into consideration. The final judgment, of course, belongs to each individual police manager.

Only through a careful evaluation of how she spends her time on a day-to-day basis and a recognition of the necessary high-priority activities can she learn to use time periods during the work week most effectively.

## THE ART OF DELEGATION

Delegation is the art of gradually giving increased responsibility to one's subordinates. This means, first, defining the functions and responsibilities for which the subordinate is responsible. When these functions and responsibilities have been defined, then the level of authority to accomplish each of these tasks is established between the police manager and the subordinate.

There are three levels of authority. At the initial level, the subordinate is obligated to report first and is allowed to act upon approval. The subordinate must first come to the police manager to explain his decision and how he intends to implement that decision; he then receives permission from the police manager. Needless to say, it is a time-consuming method or level of authority and requires close contact between the police manager and the subordinate. The next level is defined as authority to act first and then report. Within this category, the subordinate has the right to implement his decision but is responsible for constantly advising the police manager of his activities and their results. The third level is defined as complete authority. It assumes that trust has been developed between the police manager and the subordinate and that the police manager is confident that the task will be accomplished effectively.

Consider, for example, the simple task of establishing a monthly work schedule. The police manager can initially request that his new subordinate complete the schedule, bring it to the police manager, and—upon approval of the police manager—the subordinate can begin to implement the decision. After two or three such schedules have been developed by the subordinate, the manager begins to gain confidence in the subordinate's ability. He can then raise the level of authority by advising the subordinate that there will be no further need to bring the schedule to the manager before implementation but that the subordinate is to advise the manager of the schedule. The reporting can actually occur after the schedule has been implemented. Once a high degree of trust has been established between the manager and the subordinate, the manager can advise the subordinate that he is fully, totally, and completely responsible for the development and implementation of the schedule. The manager will only inspect periodically to determine that the quality of scheduling still meets the level agreed upon prior to the granting of the complete authority.

When the function and responsibilities as well as the level of authority have been defined, the results can be established for each task. In this way the subordinate can be evaluated and held accountable for the success or failure of the task. For example, in the issue of scheduling of police officers, once the manager has agreed upon the minimum number of police officers to be available for specific days and time periods, the subordinate knows what results are expected and is responsible for achieving them.

Delegation is the transferring of responsibilities and involves a four-step process. First, the police manager must transfer his responsibility to his subordinate. Second, the subordinate must accept this responsibility. Third, a mutual trust must develop between the police manager and his subordinate, and fourth, there must be some system of follow-up of the responsibility that has been transferred and accepted.

What can delegation accomplish for the police manager? For the manager himself, it will help ease his job pressure; it will therefore provide more time for planning, organizing, leading, and all other management functions and activities that bring about growth of a police organization. It will also give the police manager the opportunity to improve the quality and quantity of his own personal operation. And last but by no means least, it may actually leave time for the manager when he can be absent from the department while still feeling confident that the agency will continue to function in the most effective manner possible.

Delegation, by the same token, has effects on the subordinate who accepts the responsibility. First, it tends to make the police activities and responsibilities of the subordinate more satisfying because she is making a large number of the decisions at her level not only in implementation but also in evaluation. Second, it encourages and helps the subordinate grow and develop within the department. Third, it brings about increased motivation on the part of the subordinate and those who work for her. In essence, it begins a chain reaction from the top of the department all the way to the bottom. For the person accepting the responsibility, the receiver of the delegation, it fosters initiative and competence to the point where someday she too can effectively perform the art of delegation.

## EFFECTIVE RULES OF DELEGATION

In order to make delegation an effective tool, the manager should follow certain general principles. First, the police manager must be willing to delegate part of his clarified responsibilities and authority so that he is sharing his overall responsibility with his subordinates. Next, the police manager must carefully describe the responsibility delegated to the subordinate so that there is a clear understanding of exactly what is being delegated. Third, the manager should exercise patience and allow subordinates the opportunity to assess possible difficulties that may arise in accepting added responsibility. Fourth, there has to be some agreed-upon follow-up so the manager is guaranteed that the authority is used in the manner intended. This is best accomplished through agreed-upon, stated objectives. Fifth, and probably most important, the manager must have faith and trust in the subordinate. If such trust does not exist, the delegation process is doomed to failure from the beginning.

There are certain cardinal don'ts that the manager must remember. First, the police manager should not wait until she is "snowed under" before exercising the art of delegation. Next, she should not expect subordinates with this new authority and responsibility to perform perfectly right away. In every organization, there has to be both the freedom to succeed and the freedom to make mistakes. Third, the manager must not become a "back-seat driver." She should allow her subordinates to experiment with their new responsibility until they become as confident as the manager. Finally, the manager should not wait for things to explode before stepping in and offering help. Through a fairly controlled system that may be considered tight in the beginning, the manager can prevent the project from becoming bogged down before she can help overcome obstacles and move the project toward its stated objectives.

Once the subordinate has accepted more and more responsibility, the police manager will find it easier to delegate more projects, activities, and responsibilities. As the manager helps subordinates develop, she is gaining more time for her own management activities.

## RULES OF MONKEYS

Consider the average police chief when he is first assigned to his new position. In a few weeks he has moved from sitting at an empty desk, going home at a reasonable hour, and having spare time to do some planning to the life of a harried individual, always being late for supper, taking home at least a briefcase and three extra piles of paper, and constantly spending fifteen to twenty hours a day performing tasks that could and should be performed by subordinates. How does the average police chief find himself in this situation?

In the beginning, the police chief will usually be extremely cautious in delegating authority and responsibility. After a quick examination of his subordinates, he realizes that it is their activities that have caused him to be in this predicament.

An examination of the situation may reveal that his first key assistant is an average individual named Charlie, who is assigned to research functions and activities of the department. Charlie considers it his job to submit to the chief of police numerous memoranda that call for decisions. He submits one memorandum, request, or decision at a time, and the chief has to consider each of these separately, as it hits his desk.

Joe is responsible for the service functions of the department. He normally sends the chief, for his approval, weekly status reports that include a statement of problems and recommended solutions. The police manager doesn't even have time to eat, much less act upon these reports. Joe is the type of individual who would act only after the chief has sent him a memorandum approving specific recommendations.

Next comes Sam, who holds a staff position responsible for administrative activities such as budgeting and purchasing. Sam is uncertain of his responsibilities and authority. He daily brings every single question that is asked of him to the chief and refuses to make a single decision on his own. In fact, if forced into making any kind of a decision, he always prefaces it with "the chief wants."

The fourth individual is Louise, the chief's administrative assistant. An energetic extrovert, she is responsible for public relations, establishing the chief's schedule, and writing speeches for him when needed.

The police chief suddenly finds himself working from seven o'clock in the morning until six o'clock in the evening at the office, taking large quantities of work home, and spending at least one or two more hours away from his family each night in attempting to solve numerous problems which he feels only he, as the chief, is capable of resolving.

The work week eventually expands to include at least a half a day each Saturday. One Saturday, while en route to the office, the chief sees Charlie, Joe, Sam, and Louise getting ready to tee off at the local golf course. Upon his arrival at the police department, the chief carefully analyzes the piles of paper on his desk and reexamines his conversations during the past week with his four key subordinates. He quickly realizes that they constantly say to him: "How's it going?" It becomes obvious that the four subordinates do not report to him but that the chief is literally working for the four subordinates. In fact, the chief has been afraid to visit with them, to have a cup of coffee with them, or even to go to lunch with them—afraid that he could not answer their favorite question: "How's it going?"

How does the average chief of police get out of this situation? The answer is by implementing the following five "rules of monkeys." A "monkey" is defined as a task or an assignment of work, some function or activity that must be performed. The five rules of monkeys that bring about effective delegation are the following:

1. *Feed it or shoot it, but never let it starve to death.* Either the manager must be willing to stipulate that the monkey, or task, is not to be performed at this time

within the department for whatever reason there may be or, if he feels that the task is one that must be performed, he must be able to "feed it." Feeding of monkeys means that the manager takes the time and the effort, after delegating the task to a subordinate, to converse with the subordinate at designated times so as to keep track of progress. This can be accomplished by the use of a tickler file system.

2. *Only have those monkeys out that you can afford to feed.* The manager must not delegate so many tasks or activities that he loses control of the operation under his command. It becomes necessary for the manager to delegate only the activities or monkeys he has time to follow up and only those monkeys that subordinates are qualified to work. The number of monkeys the manager can have running about the agency depends on his time commitments, the ability of personnel to accept the responsibility of working the monkeys, and examination of activities within the agency.

3. *Never conclude a feeding without scheduling the next feeding session.* The manager should never accept statements from subordinates such as "as soon as possible." Every time a discussion is completed concerning where the monkey is then, a new time must be scheduled and specific results agreed upon before the next monkey feeding date.

4. *Subordinates will find the time to work the monkeys if you have time to feed them.* What this means is that if the manager takes the time to delegate responsibilities, to give the monkeys to the subordinates instead of working the monkeys himself, he will have time to act as a manager and play the role of advisor, inspector, and monkey feeder.

5. *Keep the monkey off your back.* This rule means literally what it states. It is not the manager's role to become involved in constantly making sound decisions, but it *is* his role to see that the sound decisions are reached. The best way this can be accomplished is by consistently delegating to subordinates the authority and responsibility to feed and handle the monkeys, thereby allowing the manager to be a monkey supervisor and not a monkey keeper.

In the previous example, how does our chief go about implementing these five rules and bringing about successful delegation? For illustration purposes only, the necessary action is dramatized in two steps.

*Step 1.* In this step, the police chief comes to work at 9:15 A.M. on Monday morning instead of the usual 7:30 or 8:00 A.M. He then interviews Charlie. Prior to this interview, all of Charlie's memoranda are placed in a neat pile. As Charlie enters, these memos are returned to him with the following instructions: "Charlie, I want you to divide these memos into three separate stacks by Wednesday at 10:00 A.M. The first stack should contain those recommendations that you feel qualified to handle; the second pile will deal with matters on which you feel you need more information but that you believe you can eventually handle; and the third pile will deal with matters that only I can resolve."

Next, the chief asks Joe to examine the status reports carefully and to do the following: redline all the problems already solved, greenline all the problems that need immediate attention, and blueline the problems that need more study. Joe is then told to return by Wednesday at 11:00 A.M.

Sam is then interviewed. He is asked to carefully write out his job activities in the following format: "I do such-and-such for so-and-so in order for this to be accomplished." Sam is asked to return by Wednesday afternoon at 2:00 P.M.

Next, the chief asks Louise to examine the weekly calendar carefully and underline those commitments that only the police manager can handle, setting aside all other commitments and reviewing the information at each of those meetings so that she, Louise, can represent the police manager.

*Step 2.* The first action the police manager should take is to begin to relax and unwind. Then, as Charlie reenters on Wednesday, at his designated time, the manager can examine the piles of memorandums that Charlie brings with him. Charlie can be congratulated for handling those tasks that he has felt able to perform. At this time, the manager can restate his confidence in Charlie and redefine Charlie's authority. Upon completion of this, Charlie is asked to review those memorandums that he feels the manager must act on. Charlie is then asked to return at a specific date and time.

As Joe enters for his second visit, he also is congratulated for having accepted responsibility and having already solved the redlined problems. As for those that have been underlined in green, Joe's new authority is established by the manager. Based on this new definition, Joe can accept as many of the greenlined problems as possible. In addition, Joe is requested to reexamine the bluelined problems (those that allegedly only the manager can handle or that need more study), and Joe is asked to redefine these problems. Prior to Joe's leaving, another monkey-feeding date is established.

As for Sam, his authority is carefully delegated to him. It should be noted that the authority delegated to each of the key subordinates need not be equal. In fact, the amount of authority and responsibility that each subordinate receives depends on the task to performed, the amount of time that the manager intends to spend with the subordinate, and the subordinate's individual ability. As for Sam, the amount of authority delegated to him may be less than that given to Joe or Charlie. Sam is asked at this time to redefine the tasks that he can delegate to someone else, to redefine tasks that other units in the agency should really be handling, and to outline the steps whereby he intends to accomplish the remaining tasks. Again, another monkey-feeding date is set.

As for Louise, she is congratulated on the amount of information she has gathered and on her ability to comprehend the total organizational problem. Then she is given the responsibility of making as many appearances during the week as possible to free the manager to handle the more important functions and activities. A monkey-feeding date is set, possibly at the end of the week, in which the manager reviews the results and establishes new tasks and activities for Louise.

The results of implementing the monkey-feeding system as shown in steps 1 and 2 are to force the subordinate into the position of making decisions. The specific time frames that have been established allow the police manager to plan his work schedule and actually have productive management time allotted during each week. As for the individuals themselves, Charlie will be spending more time doing the job for which he is being paid; Joe will quickly realize that he has been writing memorandums to himself and will begin to take action on problems as they arise. Sam will be defining his own authority and job ability; and Louise will begin to become involved in the whole scope of department activities and will serve her true purpose, alleviating the responsibility of administrative tasks from the police manager.

Furthermore, decisions are now being forced down the ladder and will eventually be made at the lowest possible levels. Controls have been established through the use of the monkey-feeding system, and tasks are being returned to the subordinates.

Probably the major result that has come about is that now the police manager travels to all his divisions, meets with his subordinates, and asks the question: "How's it going?"

## STAFF MEETINGS

There are three types of staff meetings:

1. General staff meetings
2. Problem-identification meetings
3. Brainstorming meetings

The first type, the general staff meeting, can be used to pass information from the top to the bottom of the organizational structure. In such instances, it is usually a good idea to use an agenda to organize the meeting. These meetings are designed to advise agency personnel of decisions that have already been reached. Information concerning the stages of implementation for certain projects is usually passed back and forth. Staff meetings do not usually resolve problems, nor do they develop creativity or resolve conflicts that may exist.

The second type of staff meeting is designed specifically for problem identification. This is actually a series of meetings, the first having been designed to establish or name problems that are serious obstacles to the achievement of departmental objectives. Once all of the problems have been listed in some manner, a second staff meeting is conducted about a week later with the primary purpose of listing problems, in priority, as they are to be dealt with. Three to five major problems are chosen: the remainder are usually given a secondary status by the command level of the agency.

In this role, the police manager is really focusing on the major problems or obstacles in the department. After the priority list has been established, a third meeting is held to set specific objectives and develop a time schedule for resolution of these major issues.

The third type of staff meeting is for brainstorming. To initiate the process of brainstorming to assist in problem solving and problem identification, simply gather the members of the decision-making team, state the problem, and invite each participant to call out ideas that he or she might have concerning the issue involved. There are some guidelines that should be followed. First, no criticism or evaluation should be allowed during brainstorming. Comments such as "That's not a good idea" will only tend to cut off the communicative process and will lead some team members to defend rather than generate ideas. Second, team members should be encouraged to come up with as many ideas as possible. It is much easier to reduce the number of ideas at some later time than it is to bring up new ideas. Third, at this point, the emphasis should be placed upon quantity, not quality. The more ideas and possible solutions are developed, the more likely it is that good ideas or good solutions will eventually to turn up. And fourth, the team members should be encouraged to build upon each other's ideas. In a police department, a brainstorming session is usually most productive after the police manager has developed a high degree of trust with the other members of the decision-making team.

# Modern Police Management: Major Issues

Once police managers understand the psychological and functional aspects of their role as chiefs of police or commanders, they are ready to begin making changes. This section attempts to show police managers how such changes may be instituted. It further deals with the major issues of law enforcement today.

In Chapter 12 the manager is made aware of the issue of power—"power" being defined as the ability to influence others so that the goals of the police department may be met. In this chapter, the police manager is given information concerning the types of power, techniques for using power, and the reasons for seeking power or influence.

A major issue facing police managers today is civil liability. Chapter 13 attempts to assist police chiefs in a broad manner so that they will be able to deal with their roles as managers within the framework of law. This chapter is not meant to be a complete text on legal responsibilities but only an overview giving police managers some understanding of the issues that must be dealt with in the broad context of civil liability.

Chapter 14 discusses the issue of labor management. Again, it is not an in-depth study of the problem but presents, in outline form, the steps that police managers can take to deal with unions and possibly prevent their development while also preserving the police managers' right to develop new programs within their police departments.

One of the most thorny issues and one that can have serious repercussions is that of promotion. Chapter 15 deals with the latest techniques for designing an effective promotion process. It discusses the role of assessments centers and how they can help police managers to run their departments more effectively.

Chapter 16 deals with conflict and change. This chapter shows police managers how to deal with people in fixed positions when there is potential conflict; it also describes how the police manager's personal negotiating style can help to resolve conflict. This chapter also focuses on the principles of change and the reasons for resistance to change.

Chapter 17 discusses the organizational development process. Included are such issues as foundations for organizational development, strategies that may be employed, management of team building, and how to understand the organizational culture of the police department.

Part III ends with Chapter 18, a discussion of the future.

# CHAPTER 12

# *Use of Power*

Police organizations use the terms "authority" and "power" interchangeably. "Authority" is defined as the formal power that goes with a given position in the department. For example, the chief has more authority than the captain. The fact that such authority exists does not mean that the chief will be more influential than the captain in the running of the police department.

"Power" is defined as the ability to influence others toward stated goals and purposes. In this chapter, we will attempt to deal with three major issues with regard to power: (1) types of power, formal or informal; (2) approaches to the use of power; and (3) reasons for seeking power.

## TYPES OF POWER

### Formal Power

There are two basic types of power—formal and informal. Formal power is that which is granted to the police managers by the nature of their position in the organization. Formal power has certain distinguishing characteristics.

Formal power comes in an instant. Police managers can point to the date, time, and place when they received this power as dictated and the position that goes with it. However, they are generally aware that this power can also be lost in an instant—when they are demoted, dismissed from the police department, or retire. Such people no longer have the formal power associated with their positions in the department. Police managers recognize that formal power comes from outside. It is therefore entirely controlled by the manager's actions or behavior.

Police managers who rely heavily on formal power may be caught in the ultimate trap of believing that they are more important than they really are. The result is that subordinates tend to play organizational games, making the formal power of the police manager less effective.

### Informal Power

The second type of power, informal power, is power that one earns over a long period of time. Where formal power can be granted in a moment, informal power can only be earned through long-term relationships and the kind of reputation necessary to demonstrate to the world that one is capable of dealing with the issue of power.

Informal power is internal in nature and is long-term both in terms of development and of use. It does not relate directly to one's position within the police department.

Police managers who may hold the rank of lieutenant or captain and who teach in the police academy may have greater degrees of informal power than others of higher rank within the same agency. It often happens that people with informal power are able to help reduce conflicts and bring about changes in a police department even though they are not directly related or involved in the conflict or change. The police captain in training who is able, through informal power, to influence the actions of other captains and commanders by bringing them together to resolve a conflict may have a greater effect on the outcome of patrol operations than will individuals who are directly involved in the Patrol Division or Section.

Effective informal power gets things done through other people. It does not depend on wealth or status and it cannot be bought—it must be earned. Informal power might require sitting at a large desk in a large office, but it is not directly related to the size of the desk, the number of phones, or even to the office's position in the building or the number of people being managed. Instead, people with strong informal power have the ability to use such power for good purposes. Police leaders with informal power clearly show that they know what they are doing, how they are doing it, why they are doing it, and what other people are doing about it.

Informal power helps bring out creativity within the individual and his or her co-workers. It also tends to foster a high degree of self-confidence.

When police managers are able to mix both formal and informal power in day-to-day operations, their level of influence in relation to both subordinates and superiors seems boundless.

Police managers who receive formal power should feel confident in accepting such power, but they should not take the acceptance or maintenance of formal power alone as a great and serious matter. If, instead, they see it in terms of something they could easily put aside, they will never become slaves to it. The growth of formal power is fostered by adherence to sound values and the use of this power to help others grow.

In order to keep developing informal power, the police managers must first learn to establish priorities and be willing to learn about the various approaches to this end. There are three major steps in developing informal power:

1. *Being visible.* That is, making themselves available so that subordinates can get to know them as human beings. In short, being visible means being available.

   When something must be done, the leader with informal power is available and usually knows how to do it.

2. *Maintaining integrity*. Integrity is the willingness to be open and maintain one's values and principles.

   Leaders who strive to develop informal power have a clear idea of their strengths, limitations, and goals. They also have a clearly defined system of values. They do not appear lazy or dependent on others. When they value a principle, they have chosen it carefully, cherish it, and pursue it on a day-to-day basis. Police leaders with informal power know how to trust themselves as well as others.
3. *Maintaining performance*. Performance is the ability to listen, to be open and honest, and to live up to one's word. This, the production side of management, is especially important in the development of informal power.

Police leaders with power are capable of doing a job and doing it well. They are dependable and willing to take on a variety of tasks within their police departments. For example, the effective police leader who attempts to build an informal power base is not reluctant to take assignments in almost any unit within a department.

A technique common to many informal police leaders is to carry in their pockets a small notebook or set of blank cards. When discussing issues in the hallway or in someone else's office, they make note of dates and commitments so that they can follow up on this information later on, making sure that they keep their word and perform. Police managers who have a high degree of integrity and can be counted on to perform develop an informal power base that is almost impossible to destroy.

With regard to relationships within a police department, the formal power of police leaders is not of primary importance. Power or influence is the capacity to get things done, and police leaders clearly recognize that such power is unevenly distributed among their personnel.

Police managers who take over new sections or departments have to consider the methods that were in use before their arrival. For example, if someone takes over as chief of police and finds that the agency has previously responded to the formal power structure, then the new chief will have relatively more formal power and may be able to initiate rapid changes. In instances where departments have been more responsive to informal power, the new police chief does best to work closely with the most influential (informally powerful) people so that they will help to initiate needed change. Normally, a new police chief can transfer and possibly even dismiss or force into retirement people who have depended on formal power in the past. But to try to use the same techniques on those with informal power tends to undermine the implementation of change, creating conflicts between the new police chief and informal leaders.

## APPROACHES TO THE USE OF POWER

There are four basic approaches to the use of power: (1) control, (2) manipulation, (3) threat, and (4) coordination.

## Control

Control is formal use of power. It emphasizes rank and organizational position and bases the use of authority on controlling other people's behavior.

At first glance this approach may seem negative; however, it, like all approaches, has advantages and disadvantages.

The advantages to the use of control include the ability to control a situation quickly, to coordinate activities, and to coordinate activities with those of another department. It also allows the police manager, when necessary, to conceal the motives for the use of such power. This approach brings about conformity and can affect many people simultaneously. It is effective in short-term projects or emergency situations.

When a police department is mandated, for example, through court decisions to perform in a certain way, then the use of formal authority as an approach to power is an effective method.

There are negative features as well. Sometimes accuracy is lost in relying upon control. It tends to create moral issues, especially when the decisions reached under this approach affect the lives of individuals and groups within the department. It sometimes brings about frustration and, when relied upon exclusively, tends to generate organizational game playing. Also, once this approach is uncompromisingly and rigidly implemented, it becomes difficult to reverse or to modify.

## Manipulation

The second approach is manipulation—which depends largely on more or less indirect methods of ensuring cooperation and getting things done. Manipulation may be either positive or negative, depending on how it is viewed by those who are being manipulated. It has five main aspects.

1. The withholding of full information as to the reasons behind certain actions. For example, an officer may be asked to undertake advanced training without being told that this step is connected with plans for his future promotion.
2. Dependence on long-term personal relationships. For example, a police lieutenant may be able to persuade a police sergeant to observe departmental principles or rules on the basis of their earlier effective implementation in which they both cooperated.
3. Reliance on hierarchy. For example, it is difficult for a lieutenant to manipulate a captain or major; downward manipulation is generally easier.
4. Ability to exploit others' needs for approval or participation. For example, a police commander may announce that meetings will begin at a certain hour and that people who are late will be excluded. By closing the door once, the commander will have threatened the latecomers' sense of participation. This tactic can be very effective in preventing subsequent tardiness.
5. Dependence on cumulative effects. The use of power through manipulation is built upon one example after another. It is difficult to manipulate people to a great degree during the first few days of a relationship, as when a freshly promoted officer is new to a department. But as the newcomer becomes accustomed to the new milieu, then this approach may become more useful.

Manipulation can be negative when it is used in a predominantly self-serving way, to aggrandize the manipulator rather than to get things done while also considering the needs of others.

## Threat

This is the third approach. It is unlike manipulation in that here the police manager is going outside the rules. The police managers use threat when they try to influence the behavior of subordinates by suggesting that the failure to comply can bring personally damaging consequences. For example, a captain may try to coerce a police sergeant to perform an unethical although not illegal act by threatening to have the sergeant transferred to a less favorable post should she fail to cooperate.

People who are tempted to submit to threats must recognize they are the final controllers of their own behavior and that they must decide they should submit to the coercion of anyone else. It is the author's personal belief and experience that the more people submit to coercion, the more they are likely to be coerced, and that people who try to use this approach to implement their power are usually recognized fairly quickly and generally disciplined by way of disgrace, demotion, or dismissal and a consequent loss of power.

## Coordination

Coordination is the fourth method, which involves the sharing of power. It includes the involvement of other people and is the most effective use of both formal and informal power, although it is also the most time-consuming. This approach is best used in attempting to bring about changes and in resolving conflicts.

Some people see their power as limited, believing that if they delegate some part of it, they will be left with less. The truth is that power is more closely related to an issue such as love. The parent who has one child and is then blessed with a second does not have less love for the first child as a result; instead, the circle of love simply grows. The same is true of power. The police manager who is willing to share power with subordinates as well as superiors (and in some instances, depending on the issue involved, with other city or county departments) usually becomes far more powerful and influential within the entire community, both directly and indirectly, than one who is basically unwilling to share power and authority with others.

# REASONS FOR THE USE OF POWER

There are three basic reasons for using power: (1) personal, (2) social, and (3) survival.

Although these three may seem mutually exclusive, police managers in day-to-day operations generally balance them and do not normally use their power for any one of these reasons alone. They usually follow a set of priorities and will use one of these mainly, another secondarily, and the third only as a last resort.

## Personal

The manager who uses power for personal reasons is generally trying to enhance his own status; therefore personal power is essentially self-serving. Although this may seem like a negative thing, it can sometimes be justifiable. For example, if the police manager recognizes that he may have to stand on his own reputation in some conflict situation, as with a community group or another department head, personal power may help him to carry out not only his personal goals but also those of the police department. Another example would be that of the police official who has developed an influential base in the community and therefore can effectively defend the police department against arbitrary and unjustified attacks from the media.

## Social

Social power is exercised when a police manager uses his or her influence over others to achieve some common good. Here power is used mainly to influence people within the agency, on other levels of government, within the criminal justice system, or in the community. An example would be that of the police manager who is able to use his unique background to educate the community on the subject of crime and its prevention.

## Survival

The third reason for the use of power is for survival. For example, a chief might be willing to use his power in order to implement the plans of the city manager even though he, the chief, does not especially favor these plans. In other words, he "goes along" in order to "stay alive" in his position as chief. Another example might be that of a police executive who agrees to implement performance evaluations within his or her department, even though such evaluations seem unnecessary and unconstructive, simply because he or she considers it politically risky to oppose them.

In studies throughout law-enforcement agencies, it appears that most police managers do tend to place a higher priority on social power than on the other two. Personalized power usually ranks second, with survival being lowest. The only time survival power seems to come higher in the order of priority is when the chief of police feels the need to survive for a short period of time—for example, for two or three years prior to retirement.

Data[1] indicate that people with a strong need for personalized power seem to exhibit certain common characteristics. These include (1) dominance, the desire to be in charge of the situation; (2) aggression, willingness to criticize others rather than defend their own principles; and (3) exhibitionism, or the need for personal attention. Police managers who strive for power for personal reasons usually have low needs for (1) nurturing, or caring for others; (2) perception, or understanding the reasons why others behave as they do; and (3) deference, the willingness to defer to others solely because of the others' position.

Police managers who demonstrated a strong need for socialized power usually scored high in (1) perception; (2) achievement, or the desire to excel; and (3) dominance. They scored low in (1) abasement, the need to accept guilt for themselves or others' behavior, and (2) aggression.

Police managers who sought power for survival reasons usually had high scores in (1) guilt, (2) nurturing, (3) deference, with low scores in (1) dominance and (2) achievement.

## CONCLUSION

Any police manager must be skilled in the use of power. As police managers, we are dependent upon the activities of other people—our peers, our colleagues, our subordinates, and our superiors—as well as those who attempt to influence the operation of the department from the outside.

Power is established in a personal relationship through the ability to lead people, especially during a crisis situation. Therefore, police managers are evaluated on their professional reputations and track records and through the ideas they implement within their departments.

In conclusion, in using power at any time, either formally or informally, successful police managers are sensitive to what others might consider to be legal, ethical, and moral considerations. Police managers need a good intuitive understanding of power and influence and how their power affects other people. Successful police managers develop different types of power and are good at using the appropriate methods in dealing with various situations. They are able to take advantage of their resources and do not feel that power should be used to avoid risks. Instead, they look for opportunities that will help them to enlarge their base of influence in a prudent way. Finally, effective police managers recognize and accept the fact that they, by the role they play, clearly influence other people's behavior.

---

## NOTE

1. Tests conducted from 1980 through 1984 by the Institute of Government at the University of North Carolina.

# CHAPTER 13

# Civil Liability

The role of the police manager has been in a state of flux for some time, and—while some challenges have been completely met and subdued—new ones constantly surface to complicate the job of the law-enforcement manager.

There was a time, not long ago, when police managers could count on exercising some degree of control over the crime rate and keeping their agencies scandal-free; this sufficed to give them a sense of security. Today, however, they have additional and more pressing problems while still having to contend with the old ones. Many of these problems have already been addressed in this text. But recently, more and more police managers are feeling troubled by the presence—very real and expensive—of liability for the actions of their personnel and of judgments against their agencies that in some cases run to seven figures. But before addressing the more specific ways of confronting the liability issue, we should think in terms of what is called the "police manager's bulletproof vest"—the multilayered protection that will allow police chiefs to walk their beats—the protection offered by policy, support, training, discipline, supervision, and evaluation. Each item will add more protection; any item alone will not offer enough protection. It is only by depending on the interaction of all these factors that the police manager can feel fairly secure.

Another approach is to make sure that the manager selects, appoints, trains, supervises, entrusts, retains, and directs personnel so that an officer's misconduct on the street at 2 A.M. can be shown to have occurred despite the manager's best efforts. The trail of evidence that might indicate culpability should not lead to the police manager's door. Then it would appear that the officer acted independently and that there is no vicarious element to the responsibility. Liability has increased for a number of reasons: the greater the number of lawsuits in our society, the greater the scrutiny given to the actions of police officers and the greater the accountability demanded by the public and recognized by the courts.

Years ago police officers were rarely sued, but today, suits are filed almost automatically where there is any possibility that the actions of the officers fell below the standards required by the courts. Possibly these lawsuits for "police malpractice" are a sign of the profession's coming of age.

Police managers must be familiar with current terms, concepts, and trends in the civil courts; they must keep track of the recent decisions and their awards so as to understand what is expected of them and their person-nel. By monitoring the decisions of various courts across the land, the man-ager can learn valuable lessons and perhaps avoid potential lawsuits.

The following story concerns a question given to candidates for a ser-geant's promotional examination in England:

> Q. You are on duty in the High Street when there is a large explosion, which causes a large crater in the middle of the road, a main trunk road in fact. The explosion blows a van onto its side and upon investigation you discover in it a man and a woman, the woman being the wife of your sergeant, who is currently away on a course. Both are injured. At this point two dogs, neither of which is wearing a collar, begin to fight in the middle of the road, and they are encouraged by drinkers from a nearby public house who are quite obviously inebriated and dis-orderly. In the confusion a car and a coach collide and you discover that the car is being driven by your chief constable and that the bus driver has taken a shotgun from his cab with obvious intentions of using it. A man runs from a house shouting for a midwife and a woman informs you that there is a fire in the large garage around the corner. You then hear someone shouting for help from the nearby canal where he has been thrown by the original explosion. Bearing in mind the provisions of the Justices of the Peace Act, the various Mental Health Acts and particularly, section 49, Police Act, 1964, what should your course of action be?
>
> A. Immediately—immediately remove your helmet and mingle with the crowd.

But this is no option for us. We cannot slough off our responsibility, for it is the "deep pocket" that the plaintiff's attorneys will go after. Says a UCLA law school professor: "Robbers and muggers do not have liability insurance, and they do not have assets. The job of the lawyer is not simply to find the negligent party but the negligent solvent party."[1]

The "deep pocket" theory makes it advantageous for the plaintiff's attor-neys to name as many defendants as possible, from the officer who committed the alleged act, to the supervisor, to the chief. Therefore, it is important that the chief, as the agency head, be able to sever himself from the suit by prov-ing that he or she did everything that could be expected to supervise and train the highest-quality officer.

We readily agree that the number of lawsuits in the past few years has increased almost geometrically, and a partial cause could be publications that give a comprehensive treatment of the liability issue, complete with sample forms. They lay out for any attorney the obvious points of attack and infer that police are asked to perform an impossible task. In addition to such jour-nals, there are now quarterly newsletters that raise additional points and highlight cases and awards. *Police Misconduct: Law and Litigation,* for ex-ample, is a valuable tool for the police manager because it indicates the course of action, the points of attack, and the simplicity with which suits can be filed.

So, given the magnitude of the problem, it is necessary that police man-agers achieve a greater familiarity with the concepts, terms, and principles guiding the courts as well as with the rules for lawsuits; that they have a

comprehensive overview of news from the "liability front" and from juris-
dictions around the country; that they glimpse a projection of future trends
and issues; and that they understand the major areas of liability: civil rights
violations and negligence. Finally and most importantly, managers must know
how to develop liability protection programs for both themselves and their
agencies. All this to minimize the risk of "self-inflicted wounds" such as those
from which the profession is suffering now.

Lawsuits resulting from police misconduct fall into two major categories:
civil rights violations and negligent employment and supervision. Police managers must become familiar with the various ways in which causes of action
under these categories can be filed and the resulting decisions of the courts.
While not always consistent from jurisdiction to jurisdiction, these decisions
should be tracked to monitor trends. The emphasis in this chapter is on the
management of liability; the technical and legal aspects of civil rights and
negligence will be treated only in outline form.

## CIVIL RIGHTS VIOLATIONS

Civil rights violations, based upon the deprivation of a person's rights under
the Constitution when an officer is purporting to act "under color of law," are
the grounds of the most frequent complaints filed against law-enforcement
officers. The Civil Rights Act of 1871 gives rise to these causes of action under
42 Section 1983. Liability under this law does not necessarily have to be
based on the intent to violate a person's constitutional rights, for liability is
based upon the doctrine that the officer's conduct had a natural and obvious
consequence and that, without intention, the officer's conduct resulted in a
denial or deprivation of the person's rights.

The Civil Rights Act of 1871 provides that:

> Every person who, under color of any statute, ordinance, regulation, custom,
> usage, of any state or territory, subjects or causes to be subjected, any citizen of
> the United States or any other person within the jurisdiction thereof to the de-
> privation of any rights, privileges, or immunities secured by the Constitution and
> laws, shall be liable to the party injured in an action at law, suit in equity, or
> other proper proceeding for redress.

The specific causes of action under this law are as follows:

- False arrest and detention
- Excessive force and physical brutality
- Illegal search and seizure
- Denial of counsel and illegal interrogation
- Denial of First Amendment rights
- Denial of medical attention
- Discriminatory or retaliatory prosecution
- Use of perjured evidence
- Verbal abuse and/or harassment

- Failure to provide police protection
- Misconduct resulting in death through use of deadly force

The vital points are that (1) *intention* to deprive is not a necessary prerequisite to legal action and (2) an action can be brought for failure to prevent a violation (that is, when an officer does not take positive and affirmative action although he or she knows that a violation or deprivation is taking place).

## NEGLIGENCE

To understand the basics of a liability or "tort," it is necessary to consider its four requirements:

- A duty owed
- According to a standard of care
- A failure to perform that duty according to that standard
- A loss or injury resulting from that failure

The major areas in which actions can arise are as follows:

*Negligent Appointment.* The plaintiff can show that the officer who injured her was unfit for appointment and that the appointing authority knew or should have known about this unfitness.

*Negligent Detention.* The plaintiff can show that the officer who injured him was unfit to be retained as a police officer and the retaining police manager knew or should have known of this unfitness.

*Negligent Assignment.* It can be shown that the police manager has assigned an officer he is attempting to terminate to a sensitive post or that he has acted similarly with regard to an errant officer who has been reinstated by the civil service authority despite the chief's wish to terminate.

*Negligent Supervision.* Plaintiff can show that the administrator was under an affirmative duty to supervise her subordinates and that, in failing to do so, caused the plaintiff to sustain injuries or loss.

*Negligent Training.* It can be shown that the police manager has not trained his officers—especially in highly critical areas such as firearms, driving, defensive tactics, and first aid—and that the plaintiff was injured as a result.

*Negligent Direction.* It can be shown that the police manager has failed to anticipate problems arising in the field, to minimize police discretion at the operational levels, and to promulgate comprehensive written directives guiding police actions and behavior. Failure to do this is equivalent to not assuming the duty to direct personnel, and the manager is responsible.

## SYSTEMATIC APPROACH TO SELECTION AND TRAINING

One of the surest ways of reducing the potential for lawsuits is to do everything possible to staff the police department with the best possible people. A systematic approach to selection and training starts with the assumption that, for the most part, the selection and training process goes on at each one of the six steps or phases in this approach, which are:

1. Recruitment
2. Initial selection
3. Psychological evaluation
4. Academy training
5. Field training
6. Probation

*Recruitment.* The manager selects by *where* he recruits, by *whom* he is recruiting, and by *who* does the recruiting. The chief actually filters people out by the very way he goes about the recruitment process. In other words, the quality of the recruits may depend in large part on the design of the recruitment program.

*Selection.* At this point the chief applies certain selection criteria, utilizing background checks, polygraph recordings, and whatever else he may want to use within legal and ethical guidelines.

*Psychological Evaluation.* The courts have recognized and accepted psychological testing for police officer candidates. It is recommended that tests be administered to candidates, then scored and interpreted by a psychologist who will also interview each candidate and make recommendations to the police chief. The psychologist should be familiar with the police profession and able to defend her decisions in court, present findings logically and professionally, and be willing to recommend the rejection of unqualified candidates. A final caution: psychological evaluation only gives an assessment at a particular point in a person's life. The chief cannot use the test to guarantee predictions of how a person is going to handle the job three years down the road or when unforeseen events (a broken marriage, financial problems, friction with a difficult supervisor) cause stress.

*Academy Training.* For too long, methods of training have not received much scrutiny, but they will in the immediate future. There is an old saying: "If you think training is expensive, try ignorance!" A proper training program for recruits is based on a job task analysis and the subsequent validation of a curriculum that includes performance objectives for each block, a plan of instruction, and a training guide. Evaluation of both courses and instructors, along with simulation exercises and role playing, should be considered essential.

*Field Training.* This innovation has, over the past ten years, been one of the most beneficial ways of providing officers with both training and job-related evaluations. It does much to counterbalance the "street nullification" so common in the past, and it is exactly the best preparation for solo assignments.

One problem is with the development of supervisors. Supervisors are often trained by the supervisors they served under, who may, in many cases, be inadequate. And so it goes. The department may thus only perpetuate inadequacies and may not take the steps needed to improve the system. Supervisors are usually not trained prior to their promotion, and few are really trained afterward. Field training programs for supervisors and managers can reap a great harvest for the future. Such programs can also reduce the effects of negligence.

*Probation.* This is a legal right that has seldom been employed properly, but it can challenge recruits to maintain their drive and prevent them from just sliding through this period. It is during this time that the manager can make the most knowledgeable and intelligent choice of who has the most potential to be the best officer in the organization. In most instances the decision to allow officers to enter career status and achieve tenure is made when they graduate the academy; at that time, much of the incisive information and evaluative material that is almost strictly job-related has not yet been gathered. During this period, supervisors must be conscious of their responsibility to continue the training of the recruit officers in certain one-on-one situations by critiquing their performance and offering advice.

The components in this systematic approach are not new, but taken in combination, where each part complements the others, they can help to put better-prepared officers into the system and into individual police departments.

## THE PROTECTION CIRCLE

The alarm has been sounded often enough to warn police managers about the imminent dangers of lawsuits and adverse judgments. What is now needed is the description of a comprehensive liability protection program. Regardless of the level at which the manager is operating, given the vulnerable areas that have to be improved and protected and the burden of responsibility lying on the manager's shoulders, these suggested steps will provide a framework on which a liability protection program can be built. Simply put, the protection circle as it applies to liability consists of three equal parts or phases— direction, maintenance, and assessment—operating in three consecutive time frames as follows (see Figure 13.1):

1. Protective: policy and support from the executive
2. Active: training and supervision
3. Reactive: discipline and evaluation

There is no way that policy can be effective without training and discipline. Each function must flow from and be consistent with the one that precedes it, for the protection circle is a combination of policies, training, and discipline so integrated that each follows, supports, and then improves the next while indicating changes necessary to improve the overall process.

To expand on the protection circle, and to lay out a series of steps that

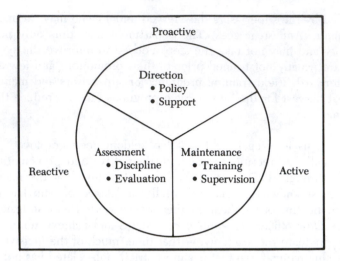

**Figure 13.1** The Protection Circle

will, if followed, make it possible for concerned police managers to assess their danger and react accordingly, it is necessary to start with the chief, the top-level manager. The chief needs to:

1. Be knowledgeable, stay informed, keep abreast of trends and precedents, read the literature. Identify a number of agencies that are trend setters and regularly ask for their policies, find out what they are changing, and start a running dialogue with their chiefs of police.
2. Identify the areas of greatest concern for liability, preferably after completing a job task analysis of personnel. List the areas that are producing the most lawsuits, both for the agency and for others in the area, and track the general trends from around the country. These areas might be firearms training, supervision, medical assistance, defensive tactics, arrest procedures, and pursuit driving.
3. Make an annual review of policies, practices, and procedures with respect to these areas of liability. Simple changes in policy language may be enough to head off a lawsuit—or at least eliminate the chief from it—if they are coupled with some training and appropriate discipline. Match the areas of greatest concern—the critical tasks—with policies, practices, and procedures and ask whether all of these elements are articulated adequately (i.e., what personnel must do, whether the practices are described in the manner desired, and whether the procedures are the best that the state of the art can offer). If the chief is not completely satisfied, then she can proceed to make changes where necessary.
4. Identify the standards of care with regard to these critical tasks. It is against these standards that actions will be judged by comparing them with recognized, accepted performance levels in both emergency and routine circumstances. Check state statutes to see what they require, then the policies of other departments, then the literature, and then court cases and reliable experts on these various topics.

5. At this point, have available the services of dependable legal counsel—one who is not just an attorney but is also familiar with this topic—who can offer expert legal advice and will be able to look after the department's interests. It profits little to have just any attorney work on policies. Your attorney must work on *your* policies and must be familiar with the demands of your profession, your personnel, and current legal thinking.

6. Prepare written directives for the police department, using a format that includes definitions and states pertinent policy in the clearest, most direct language, making sure that related policies are reviewed and changed accordingly where they are affected by these revisions.

7. Train personnel accordingly. Simultaneously with the training itself, document the qualifications of instructors. Don't allow someone to train just because they're "available" or "have always been doing it." Be critical of training methods and require written lesson plans, which should follow training guides developed along with the new major policies on such matters as deadly force, high-speed chases, and medical attention for those taken into custody. The manager needs to be careful that the right way of doing something is emphasized and that inappropriate or wrong methods are clearly indicated. They must be particularly careful about documenting everything pertaining to the training, such as reviewing attendance-taking procedures, whether by roll call, sign-up sheets, or having the instructor take the attendance according to a seating chart. It is advisable to give tests (competency-based examinations) of one sort or another to assure that the training is adequate.

8. Keep everything current—instructors' qualifications, lesson plans, and their contents, which can quickly go stale because of new state laws and new policies.

9. Have discipline conform to the policy and training. Make sure that it is consistent and progressive. The manager must be certain that records are kept of all disciplinary actions for violations of any particular policy. Checking on disciplinary records is used to review the effectiveness of the policy and training. An increased number of disciplinary incidents might indicate the need for further revision in the policy or for additional emphasis in the training.

10. Keep in contact with professional groups by maintaining an active membership and demanding that they provide professional assistance. The police manager can also work closely with other police departments and exchange copies of policies and procedures, thereby producing model policies or adopting uniform policies. Regional or statewide policies are easier to defend, since they indicate a more general consensus of professional opinion on what should be required; on the other hand, it is more difficult to have expert witnesses develop standards and have them imposed, as it were, by the courts. The manager must realize that police agencies can no longer afford the luxury of not cooperating. As in other things, there is strength in unity. All this can be done without sacrificing autonomy.

11. Make the next year one of consciousness raising on the subject of civil liability. Lay out a plan of attack, actually a training plan with goals and objectives for the whole department. The plan, for example, can provide for two days of training in liability for everyone, with additional days in high-liability areas. Task forces and study groups can be formed to examine practices and procedures in the department on an ongoing basis. Incidents in the high-liability areas should be reviewed as training examples. Personnel can be debriefed on these incidents and the department can gain much value from them. Special attention can be paid to

the supervisors, and it can be made undeniably clear that they have a direct responsibility for the conduct of their subordinates.

Although these steps will not eliminate lawsuits (anyone can sue anyone at any time), they may help to forge a multilayered "bulletproof vest" for the police manager behind which he can be safer while he does his job.


## TRAINING IN THE FUTURE

Two important developing trends will soon make greater demands on the law-enforcement profession and its training system. Although tremendous progress has been made in the past fifteen years in police officer training, too much emphasis has been placed on the quantitative process and not enough on the qualitative one. We are currently entering a time when, for a number of reasons (lawsuits and adverse judgment among them), much more emphasis will be placed on the qualitative side of training.

It does not seem that attorneys who represent the plaintiffs really understand the inadequacies of our training system when matched against the norms or standards and the newer approaches that have become the state of the art in the profession. Once these attorneys become more sophisticated, they will begin to zero in on negligence in training.

Finally, it appears that the courts themselves are giving the law-enforcement profession credit for a higher quality of training than might really exist. In the immediate future, the courts may—in addition to an award of, say, $500,000—stipulate that the police agency submit a forty-hour training program acceptable to the court. It may further demand that all personnel be exposed to this training within a certain time period.

Better that the police chief understand these developments and take action to improve the local training academies (by active participation on advisory boards, by the elimination of shoddy techniques, by the assignment of the best personnel to the training function, and by elevating the status of training) than to have to live with the consequences of inaction.


## ACCREDITATION

The formation of the Commission on Accreditation for Law Enforcement Agencies has given rise to discussion and generated strong opinions around the country, even though the concept does not apply to every police agency. The police department itself decides whether or not it wishes to seek accreditation. Another movement represents an even stronger potential for the imposition of standards, and with hardly any direct input from the profession. This development has been gaining momentum for the past five to ten years and it is likely to impose standards on law enforcement from outside the profession itself.

There are many examples of expert witnesses testifying that police officers violated certain standards of care in the use of their firearms, in pursuit driving, in arrest procedures, or in the use of less than lethal force. Depending on what the expert witnesses declare is the "standard," on how the jury accepts the testimony of the witness, and on the verdict, a standard is, in effect, formulated as a result, and this becomes a precedent. As more and more cases are decided in great part on the basis of whether or not the officer's actions are up to the standards of care, those cases and the standards they spawn become criteria that the profession has to adopt in order to avoid judgments. This happens in the absence of uniformly agreed-upon standards accepted by the broad segments of the law-enforcement profession.

If the profession were to agree on certain standards and there were uniform policies and practices around the country, "standards" would exist. First of all, expert witnesses would not carry the weight they now do and professional associations and managers of other police agencies could be more supportive of the policies in effect in the police department under suit. The profession would have the chance to stand together and develop its own standards, thus improving image, productivity, and cost-effectiveness.

But the profession, not outsiders, *has* gotten together and developed some standards, hammered out over a couple of years by professional associations that represent almost all of the law-enforcement interests in this country. It is those standards that some agencies want to acknowledge, to accept for their own. Those standards and subsequent accreditation will provide a degree of protection to the agency and its managers.

Accreditation is here to make its standards available to those police agencies that want them. Furthermore, police managers should not confuse uniformity with lack or loss of autonomy. With lack of uniformity and subsequent imposition of standards from without, there is a loss of autonomy. Uniformity to a degree can lighten the burden of police managers, for they can then rest assured that broad segments of the profession will line up with them and stand by them (since one department's policies cannot be pitted against another's). Uniform policies, standards, and accreditation are ideas whose time has come, and they will go a long way toward helping police agencies in the courtroom.

## CONCLUSION

The police manager's ability to manage liability is the direct result of his knowledge of the accepted standards and the initiation of liability protection programs in the police department. Nothing can prevent the manager from being sued, for "anyone can sue anyone at any time." But managers can take steps to protect themselves and their department from serious judgments.

Liability can be seen as public enemy *or* public ally number one. It can be a moving force for great change, which might not have taken place if there were not the danger of liability. It can exert tremendous leverage on the system and, if properly countered, can be a force that helps to initiate needed change and increased professionalization of law enforcement. With the proper resources, it can be managed.

## NOTE

1. *Time* magazine, June 13, 1984.

# CHAPTER 14

# *Labor Management*

Police employee organizations, whether they be called unions, benevolent associations, or anything else, have risen both in number and in power since the mid-1960s. This has created a new issue—collective bargaining—with which police commanders must be able to deal in devising their management systems and implementing their programs.

At the present time, not all states have collective bargaining. It is mandatory, therefore, that the individual police manager first review the laws within his jurisdiction concerning this issue. A typical example is the situation in Dade County, Florida, where collective bargaining had been carried out for several years before the state of Florida enacted enabling legislation (in 1974) requiring all police agencies to become involved in collective bargaining. In such states as Illinois and Maryland, state legislation does not exist; however, individual municipalities engage in collective bargaining with police employee associations or organizations representing the police officers within that municipality. Some states, such as North Carolina, have no collective bargaining law or even ordinances enacted at the local level.

When police officers organize, a fundamental shift occurs in internal relationships. What may have been a "one team" police department embracing both senior and junior police officers can start to divide, and these two distinct adversary groups may become respectively "management" and "employees."

Before the appearance of collective bargaining by police officers, there were few encroachments in the area of management policy. This condition is now starting to change, and police officers are beginning to win an increasing voice in policy formulation. As this transformation continues, changes cannot be ignored; they must be recognized and adapted to by the police manager as soon as possible.[1]

Proactive management is no guarantee against the emergence of a police union. Peer-group pressure, family background, and the examples set by other public and private sector labor organizations are some of the factors that may also make police receptive to unionization.[2]

Hopefully, prior to either the formal or informal recognition of a police officers' group, the police manager will have certain policies established, including a selection and placement program, a promotion program, a classification and pay program, grievance procedures, a fringe benefit package, and personnel policies, to mention but a few of the major areas that must be developed.


## WHY THE GROWTH OF POLICE UNIONS?

Today police agencies in some instances are overmanaged and in many instances overcontrolled. Police officers currently do not appear ready to accept the rigid control that may be imposed upon them; nor are they likely to accept it in the future. They may resort to overt acts of retaliation, sometimes amounting to outright sabotage of the individual police department and its efforts to achieve law and order. Typical examples are where police officers deliberately misuse departmental equipment or resort to the tactic of the "blue flu" in order to emphasize their power and achieve their demands.

Once police officers have experienced the freedom to participate in problem solving and decision making, as they do today in their homes, their schools, and other activities, they begin to demand the same rights as police officers. The granting of higher fringe benefits, such as increased pay, or the provision of special equipment does little to settle the unrest that exists in many police agencies at the bottom level. Police officers today are not always willing to make personal sacrifices for the economic security of belonging to a police agency if this personal sacrifice does nothing to provide some form of self-fulfillment for them as individuals.

This feeling of restlessness, anger, and sometimes even hatred has come from the rules defined for police officers that provide no challenge or variety and from supervisors and managers who are inconsiderate and strongly autocratic in their leadership. The new breed of police officers have doubts about the ideals of efficiency. They are unwilling to exchange the loss of personal pride, the constant monotony in the performance of mundane tasks, and the constant stress of working for poor managers in return for the highest wages that law-enforcement officers have received in the history of our country.

To many police officers today, the idea of success involves some kind of personal self-fulfillment and is not geared specifically to material rewards. If these needs are not satisfied by management, another organizational structure within or parallel to the police department begins to take form. In many instances, this turns out to be a police union.


## PREPARATION FOR COLLECTIVE BARGAINING

The police manager must know about collective bargaining laws, his budget, and the relationship between his department and other agencies within city or county government. The police manager should have a fairly concise and accurate idea of the city's or county's political stability as he enters into bargaining.

The next issue he must face is whether to develop in-house negotiators or to hire outside consultants to do the collective bargaining. The police chief must recognize that collective bargaining is a time-consuming business.

There is divided opinion as to whether the chief of police himself should be a part of the talks conducted at the bargaining table. Most city managers and police chiefs seem to agree that their role is not one of actually conducting the bargaining but rather of being constantly aware of what is proposed and agreed upon. The police chief, therefore, should try to get help from people who have experience in negotiating management contracts, whether that experience be in dealing with police or governmental unions. Such assistance can be an asset to him whether he decides to participate in the negotiations personally or to leave this responsibility to other managers in the department.

Some of the strong reasons why a chief should not be on the bargaining team include the fact that he may have risen through the ranks and may strongly identify with the rank and file, thereby prohibiting the bargaining team from presenting a unified front. Furthermore, it is the responsibility of the chief of police to implement any contract agreed upon. If the actual contract negotiations were strained, the chief's role as the manager of a department could be hampered. There is no question, however, that a commander within the department, a personal representative of the chief, should always be part of the bargaining team.

The police chief should, after making a decision as to whether he will or will not be a negotiator, develop a negotiating team that will represent his points of view. This team could be made up of personnel from within the department, such as top commanders and middle managers. The chief must also decide whether or not an outside consultant should be brought in to assist. If there are experienced and qualified negotiators within the police department, there is no need to bring in an outside consultant. This is especially true if the managers have been carefully trained and clearly understand the legal and political implications of collective bargaining. If a department's management staff has not received such training, outside consultants can provide a tremendous amount of assistance at least for the first negotiating and contract session.

Whether the police chief elects to partake in the bargaining or whether this is delegated to his commanders, the chief must recognize that he has to give the necessary authority to his commanders to participate in the bargaining and to make binding decisions.

There is no magic number as to how many should be on the management team. However, members of the team should be able to understand the demands being made by the police union, the role of the police officer within the community, and the needs and desires of the chief of police as to the amount of control he feels is necessary in operating the department. They should be aware of the budgetary restrictions placed upon the department. The team should know the laws governing the bargaining session, the contract, and the arbitration that may be necessary. In order to ensure these skills, outside consultants may be called upon to assist. Sometimes these consultants are attorneys who bring with them expertise in bargaining as well as knowledge of the law. Other management teams are made up of police department managers and representatives from other city departments, such as finance or personnel.

Once the bargaining team has been formed, it must collect and analyze information in advance of any meetings with the union representatives. It must also develop in close conjunction with the chief of police the management demands that will be made during the bargaining sessions. This is where such issues as the management's "rights clause" and what it means are agreed upon by the management bargaining team.

In its initial meetings, the team should establish certain criteria to be used in reaching decisions about all key issues. Once identified, these issues can then be analyzed and discussed one at a time. A simple planning form such as that in Figure 14.1 can be used. This form lists the topics to be discussed, what management is attempting to secure within each topic, what its initial position will be, its fallback position, its final position taken, and any remarks that may be necessary for the management team to analyze as it begins bargaining with the union representation.

It is generally agreed that members of the governing board should not be part of the bargaining sessions or the management bargaining team.

Whoever is on the bargaining team, the team surely should include at least the following types of people: an attorney, a financial expert, a representative of the chief of police, a representative of personnel, and a chief negotiator who is a labor–management relations expert. If this negotiator comes from within the police department, it would help strengthen the bargaining team. It is important that the chief negotiator be open and honest and create a feeling of trust between both sides as the negotiations continue. Usually when the police department hires a professional negotiator, the police union is inclined to do the same. In situations where the police department does not hire an expert, the police union will not normally do so.

Team Leader—

Team Members—

| Topic | Objective | Initial Position | Fallback Position | Final Position | Comments |
|-------|-----------|------------------|-------------------|----------------|----------|
| Contract length | | | | | |
| Wages | | | | | |

**Figure 14.1**   Planning Form for Collective Bargaining

The following checklist of items that should be researched prior to negotiations comes from the Management Information Service of the International City Management Association.[3]

1. Anticipate union demands and prepare counterproposals.
2. Review contracts and awards that have been negotiated in police agencies within the general area.
3. Review department policies and procedures in this regard.
4. Review any literature that has been prepared by the police union and distributed to their members to determine what promises, if any, have been made.
5. Be thoroughly briefed and familiar with all local and state legislation regarding collective bargaining and management's rights.
6. Keep complete and thorough records of all grievances, because many times these grievances eventually become the demands of the unions.
7. Review any previous contract talks and analyze what notes were made and what issues were dropped, compromised, or held on to in each of the prior meetings.
8. Review the recommendations of first-line supervisors or middle managers as to the feasibility of any proposals that have been developed by the top managers in the police department.
9. Have the information readily available concerning the present work schedules, fringe benefits, and any other data that may be discussed during the bargaining session.
10. Review economic and labor market information for current cost of living and trends that may be developing.
11. Compile information on officers in general, including their average age, length of service, turnover data, absenteeism, overtime, and the actual dollar cost for the present fringe benefits being given to police officers.
12. Insist upon receiving any proposals from the police union in writing.
13. Formulate objectives for each of the union demands.
14. Establish ground rules for determining when negotiations will begin, what information will be released and when, whether the bargaining talks will be open or closed to the public, who should make the press releases, when the negotiations will be held and where, and what shall be on the agenda.

With these kind of agreements reached in advance, there will be few surprises at the bargaining table itself.

## ASSISTANCE AVAILABLE TO POLICE MANAGERS

If police departments, with their many employees represented by various police union organizations, are to function effectively in collective bargaining, police managers must be able to develop the skills of union leaders. They must feel confident that they are on a par with those they face across the bargaining table. In administering and developing a contract between the police union and the police department, the management team must be able to show knowledge and techniques at least equal to those of the union bargainers. In order to achieve this result, the police manager must be aware of the political, social, and legal ramifications that result from the decisions reached. Education and training hold the key to the police manager's successful fulfillment of their additional role.

Educational institutions must be advised by police managers of their needs in this field. Academic courses, special seminars, and workshops can assist the police managers in developing necessary skills. In-house training programs should be conducted to provide information to management teams that would be responsible for representing the police department at the bargaining table.

Through the National Criminal Justice Reference Service of the Law Enforcement Assistance Administration, the police manager can keep abreast of the latest journals and newsletters as well as the special labor relations training programs available at different times and in different parts of the country.

Reference material is available from the International Association of Chiefs of Police through their publications *The Police Labor Review* and *The Public Safety Labor Reporter*. The annotated bibliography *Police Unionization and Bargaining*, published by the Traffic Institute of Northwestern University, could also be an asset to the police manager.


## MANAGEMENT RIGHTS

"Management Rights" is perhaps the only clause that, if properly structured, truly represents the police managers' interests and rights under a collective bargaining agreement. Such a clause provides protection from having an outside arbitrator rewrite the contract because of a lack of specific language, reserves certain operational rights, and has a psychological impact on the police union by demanding such management rights in writing.

A list of the more significant rights to be preserved by the police manager is as follows:

1. The right to hire and fire
2. The right to determine the size and composition of the individual organizational units
3. The right to allocate work assignments
4. The right to determine geographical assignments of officers
5. The right to determine the level of service and the types of service to be offered by the police department
6. The right to discontinue operations or discontinue performance of operations by the police department and police officers assigned to those functions
7. The right to establish and change schedules and assignments of police officers
8. The right to transfer, promote, and demote police officers consistent with personnel regulations
9. The right to discipline police officers for violations of department policies, rules, regulations, this discipline being consistent with the procedures established within the department to handle such matters
10. The right to develop and enforce policies, rules, and regulations

11. The right to schedule and assign overtime based upon needs and situations that face the police department

This listing is not intended to be exhaustive but is offered only as a guide to the police manager for his review of existing agreements and to assist him in the developing of any new agreement with a police union.

The key concern of police managers should be to protect the police agency's ability to offer the required services to the public in the most effective manner. A good management rights clause enhances the police manager's flexibility. Protection of operational authority should be one of the police manager's primary goals during any collective bargaining session and during the term of any agreement between management and the police union.

## AVOIDING THE DEVELOPMENT OF POLICE UNIONS

One way to prevent the formation of a union in a police department is through good management. If police officers are pleased with their present benefits and feel they have a good rapport with management, they are not likely to feel a need to unionize.

Many unions are created because the police officers believe that through the union organization they can relieve their feelings of frustration and boredom and achieve some prestige and recognition. If the police chief using systems management techniques achieves this same result—that is, of decreasing the frustration levels within the department, decreasing the level of boredom or number of mundane tasks assigned to police officers, and giving them a chance to achieve personal satisfaction and recognition—the chance of unions being developed will be very low.

The police manager must strive strongly to develop confident leadership qualities so that officers under her, although they need not feel personally close to her, respect and trust her judgment as their leader. The police manager does this by keeping open communications, by meeting as often as possible with the police officers—whether it be on a social basis, at monthly meetings, or by roll calls, or just by making her presence seen and known by walking through the building and talking on an informal basis with the officers.

Some of the things that the police manager can do to avoid the creation of a union is to see to it that the police officers receive fair treatment from their immediate supervisors. Once they believe that their immediate supervisors and the management team are sensitive to their needs and protect their rights, police officers generally will not seek any outside type of assistance in order to reach these objectives. The police chief should attempt to give as much personal recognition as possible to police officers. She should see to it that the officers do not doubt their job security but have adequate benefits, standard wages, and fair personnel policies and benefits. All the above should be clearly spelled out in some form of written directive and should be known by each member of the department.

Another technique found fairly successful by police managers is for all key managers in the police department to take an active part in the basic or recruit training program and any in-service programs that may be conducted. The police manager, by his presence in the recruit program, allows the issues and doubts raised by the new recruit to be answered directly by management. This is an effective manner of dealing with rumors that the recruits may have heard during their formal training or during any type of "on-the-job" training they receive during this basic training program.

All in all, the police manager who treats her people fairly and equitably, is open and honest with them, and develops the qualities listed earlier in this text will probably not be faced with the necessity of dealing with a union.

The police manager must recognize, however, that even if she is effective as a leader, she might possibly be required to deal with a union because of the ineffectiveness on the part of the managers above her or of the governing board. If this is true, it is the obligation of the police manager to show to these people the effect that they are having on the police department by not recognizing the worth of the individual police officer and by not meeting the professional standards established by the police manager for her agency.

## SUMMARY

Like in any other successful operation, effective collective bargaining—which includes careful planning, rational decision making at the bargaining table, and fairness and honesty—will not only assist police management in achieving its objectives, but also help police officers to build a unified police department. Police managers need not fear police unionization, nor should they take the opposite view—that the police union should fear them. If a police union is voted in, police managers must accept that fact and be willing to work within the framework of careful preparation, bargaining, and implementation.

In each stage of the collective bargaining procedure, different roles are played by various individuals. It is important that these roles be played carefully and well. If they are not, the whole process fails in its objective and strife ensues. Separate roles exist on both sides of the bargaining table, and seldom does the ability to play these roles come naturally. The requisite skills must be learned and practiced if they are to be used effectively. Learning by trial and error is dangerous for the police manager, since errors in the bargaining process may be of such magnitude as to place the police manager at a severe and lasting disadvantage. Any police manager having a role in collective bargaining should familiarize himself with the extensive literature on the subject. He should discuss tactics at length with others in the field of collective bargaining and, if at all possible, observe the collective bargaining process before becoming a direct participant.

This chapter has not been designed to teach the police manager how to go about collective bargaining with officers' associations but is rather intended to give a broad overview of the issue. Much has been written in this field;

each police manager should study this literature, review the legal requirements within his jurisdiction, and work closely with his legal adviser, city or county attorney, and the city or county manager.

## NOTES

1. "Impact of Collective Bargaining on Law Enforcement," Jim Morgan, Public Safety Research Institute, St. Petersburg, 1976.
2. Molley H. Bowers, "Police Administrators and the Labor Relations Process," *Police Chief Magazine,* January 1975.
3. "Police Unions," *Management Information Service Report,* Washington, D.C., International City Management Association, March 1976.

# CHAPTER 15

# Assessment Center Process

## OVERVIEW

Through an assessment center, candidates for promotion can be observed and evaluated over a specific period of time, such as one or two days, during which they undergo a series of exercises designed to test specific characteristics. In some situations, assessment programs can be used to guide career development, the selection of new personnel as well as supervisory and management candidates for the future, and the identification of training needs. The assessment program process allows individual candidates to be evaluated on the basis of their observed capabilities and behaviors. Exercises are geared specifically toward real-life situations within the agency and the dimensions are related to the position being sought.

Assessment centers have proved to be effective for promotions to management positions. However, when numerous candidates seek first-line supervisory positions in medium to large police departments, assessment centers can get caught up in a cumbersome bureaucratic process and this may fail to produce the desired results. They appear to be more effective in testing candidates for management positions. Overall, assessment programs can be useful in filling executive positions, but they become less practical as one moves down the line in the organizational structure.

In running an assessment center, the police manager must be aware of the question of trust between agency personnel and the assessors. That is, it may be necessary to use outside assessors until such trust is developed. Usually, in the first few assessment centers, police managers have a tendency to use a combination of inside and outside assessors. It is advisable to use at least one inside assessor on each exercise in order to deal with special policy questions as well as to clarify the exact meaning of phrases that may be unique to the individual police agency. Prior to the implementation of any assessment center, it is important to train both assessors and candidates and to conduct a job analysis from which criteria can be established.

Many police departments use aspects of the assessment center approach for promotional testing to the positions of first-line supervision and full assessment centers for mid- and top-level management positions. The assessment center concept combines a various array of performance tests, both written and oral, with evaluations by human observers. That is, this center includes the observation of actual behavior and is considered more job-related than many traditional methods.

There are benefits to be derived both by the participants and by those conducting the evaluation. Normally, a promotion made on this basis—as opposed to the more traditional written test and/or oral interview—can be made with greater confidence.

One major issue to be overcome by large police agencies, especially in first-line supervision, is how to select the candidates for an assessment center. This issue is still open for debate, and many agencies are in the process of testing different devices. The most common method involves some form of a written test with a short oral interview by a board made up of personnel from within the department. These exercises are scored in some way and then the top twelve to fifteen, depending upon the number of open positions, are included in the assessment center itself. If this does not produce enough candidates for promotion, follow-up assessment centers are conducted.

In many instances the assessment center approach benefits the assessors as much as or more than the candidates. Many industrial agencies such as General Electric believe strongly that the benefits of assessor training are great; they therefore increase their assessor:participant ratios in order to expose more personnel to the experience. Among the benefits to assessors are improved interviewing skills, broadened observation skills, increased appreciation of group dynamics and leadership styles, new insights into behavior, strengthened management skills through repeated exposure to case problems and situations, a broadened repertoire of responses to problems, the establishment of standards by which to evaluate performance, and the development of a more precise vocabulary with which to help describe behavior and feedback processes on a day-to-day basis.

Assessment centers offer benefits to all officers regardless of whether or not they are promoted. The two major benefits for the police department undertaking an assessment center are (1) the identification of management potential and (2) the development of the candidates' skills. Most assessment programs help the candidates—those who are promoted and those who are not—to recognize their individual strengths and weaknesses. This affords the candidates insight into how their management potential can be enhanced.

If the procedure is to aid the individual candidates significantly, they must behave in a certain way. For example, they need an opportunity to talk with those who evaluated their behavior. This is normally done in the feedback process. There is a need to be honest and candid when isolating weaknesses and strengths, and candidates need to seek ways in which they can improve their conduct or behavior patterns.

In any promotional process, it is extremely rare to find a single individual who greatly excels all other candidates in every facet of an assignment. This is also true of the assessment center. Normally candidates have a tendency to score well in some parts, and poorly in others. Such evaluation of an individual officer's strengths and weaknesses prior to promotion gives the police chief an opportunity to see which areas may require more intensive, personal attention. Thus the chief can be more effective in helping a new commander to become an effective member of the management team.

Sometimes consultants work closely with the individual police department in helping them develop their assessment program. Usually the personnel department sits in on the meetings in which the consultants play the role of facilitators. Questions are raised, examples of how to deal with issues are addressed, and eventually an assessment center is put together. The consultant plays an advisory role for the first assessment center, in many instances participating as an evaluator. Once the first assessment center has been completed, the consultant helps by evaluating the program itself—whether its purposes were met and how future programs might be made more effective. After the first couple of assessments, the police department usually conducts its own programs. Sometimes outside evaluators are called upon to sit as individual assessors, but normally they have little to do with the development of additional centers for the police agencies.

In many instances, police departments will use psychological testing as part of their assessments. These tests are designed to assist the newly promoted candidate and the supervisors or managers to work better in the future. They carry no weight in terms of the assessment itself. The most common tests used include the Myers-Briggs Type Indicator, the Edwards Preference Test, and the Styles of Management Inventory. If these tests are used, the candidates are given either group or individual interpretations of the results.

## ADVANTAGES AND DISADVANTAGES

On the positive side, an assessment center approach is usually seen by police personnel as a "fair" system. Therefore its results are more easily accepted not only by those promoted and those who did not receive promotion but also by other members of the agency. A second positive feature involves the process whereby the officers receive feedback about their strengths and weaknesses. Just as important, top-level managers and the chief receive feedback concerning what might be serious issues that need immediate attention. For example, it may prove that some candidates for assessment resent the performance evaluation system more than the department's top managers had realized. Upon being informed of this, the police chief may be able to check out the process more thoroughly and make immediate changes if such are necessary. Solutions offered during the exercises may produce useful ideas for the police department. In this way, even unpromoted candidates sometimes get to feel that they have a stake in the growth of the police department.

A third reason why assessment centers are popular in government is that they are generally accepted by the courts as being legally fair.[1] This allows police chiefs to implement affirmative action programs and meet other legal requirements.

Like any management tool, the assessment center contains negative features. It is time-consuming. A promotional process that involves only a written examination can be conducted in a half to a full day; however, assessment programs may run anywhere from two to five days. This does not include the time necessary for preparation, training of assessors, or final evaluation and analysis.

A second problem is that of locating good assessors. Experienced assessors are not common because of the newness of this approach. As more assessment centers are implemented, qualified assessors are becoming more and more common.

A third negative consideration is the cost. Assessment centers can be expensive, especially by comparison with more traditional methods. Usually the cost of the first assessment center includes that of the consultants who help to develop it. It may, in some instances, require a job analysis, which is used as a basis for the development of dimensions. In many areas assessors are paid honorariums or at least expenses. As a result, the overall cost can rise. But when agencies in a general area tend to train assessors and share such personnel the costs are reduced.

Experience shows that assessment centers normally provide highly detailed feedback to the police chief. This information is developed and presented in a few days, sometimes short-cutting years of informal feedback.

An assessment center approach may help avoid lawsuits that would require a police department to defend its present practices. In essence, assessment centers are more likely to be realistic in demonstrating that they actually test for the abilities a candidate will need in his or her new position.

Assessment centers are used to help enforce departmental policy. For example, in agencies that believe in encouraging the personal growth of their employees, the assessment center can serve as a tool to test such growth. Individual plans for personal growth can be developed with the help of the assessment program. In one police department, the police chief recognized the strengths and weaknesses of each of the candidates after conducting an assessment center. The chief offered each candidate the opportunity to develop his strengths and overcome each weakness.

Assessment centers tend to identify training needs, especially in the human systems approach to running the police department.

In implementing and developing an assessment center, it is useful to have the personnel department involved. Personnel departments usually help by providing job analyses and developing adequate dimensions that are consistent with personnel practices. Personnel departments may bring about community involvement, either through input prior to the actual assessment center or by providing people from within the community to act as assessors.

Personnel departments can assist in the physical arrangement of an assessment center. They also play a key role in coordinating it, thereby taking care of the numerous details such as housing for assessors and outside candidates, providing meals, and, when necessary, providing role players.

Although an assessment center approach might be expensive, it tends to reduce the chances of promoting people to positions for which they are not qualified. As a result, the cost of the assessment center tends to be far outweighed by the quality of personnel promoted.

## DEVELOPING THE ASSESSMENT CENTER

There are eight steps to be taken from the stage of early discussion to final completion. These include (1) job analysis, (2) development of dimensions, (3) creation of a matrix, (4) developing guidelines, (5) development of exercises, (6) training of assessors and candidates, (7) conducting of the assessment center, and (8) ensuring feedback.

### Job Analysis

In this first step, either a formal task analysis can be performed or personnel from within the agency can be called together to carefully discuss the behavior and traits required by the sought-after position. In general, agencies have a tendency to bring together personnel of the rank of police captain or deputy chief and discuss what these people perceive to be the more important characteristics of their positions. These characteristics then become the job analysis. Available to police agencies are numerous consultants who have experience in the development of a task analysis study for the police department. The expense incurred, however, is sometimes prohibitive, especially for smaller agencies. In many of the larger police agencies, a continual job analysis is being performed by the personnel department, and its findings often serve as a basis for the assessment center.

### Developing Dimensions

In the second step, dimensions are developed. Dimensions are the behavior traits to be examined during the assessment center. These dimensions fall into four broad areas. General dimensions may encompass commitment to handling responsibility and authority as well as command presence. The second area includes technical skills such as work perspective, handling of complaints, and career development. The third general area includes rational skills, including the ability to handle written communications, decision making, management of time, planning, fact finding, and control. In the final area, human skills, the candidate is observed and examined for those characteristics that are necessary for personal development as well as to foster growth in others. Human skills are usually the main category. These include such dimensions as leadership, oral communication, interpersonal sensitivity, stress management, the handling of people, and team development.

An example of a list of dimensions is included in Figure 15.1.

Once dimensions are agreed upon, it is important that they be prioritized. It is impossible for an assessment center to test for all possible dimensions

1. General
   a. Command presence
   b. Commitment to service
   c. Handling of responsibility and authority

2. Technical skills
   a. Work perspective
   b. Technical and professional knowledge
   c. Career development
   d. Handling of complaints
   e. Dealing with rumors

3. Rational skills
   a. Communication (written)
   b. Judgment
   c. Decision-making skills
   d. Management of time
   e. Planning and organizing skills
   f. Fact-finding skills
   g. Control skills
   h. Delegation skills
   i. Problem analysis
   j. Follow through

4. Human skills
   a. Leadership
   b. Emotional maturity
   c. Oral communications
   d. Interpersonal sensitivity
   e. Assertiveness skills
   f. Adaptability
   g. Fairness
   h. Flexibility
   i. Attitude toward development of personnel
   j. Stress management
   k. Attitude
   l. Handling of people
   m. Power
   n. Enthusiasm
   o. Patience
   p. Integrity
   q. Intuition
   r. Team development
   s. Stability
   t. Organizational climate

**Figure 15.1**   Assessment Center Dimensions

the candidate may need in order to perform his or her assigned job. In a world of reality, the dimensions that can be tested in an assessment center number somewhere between twelve and fifteen. Once the dimensions are prioritized and the most important ones are established, it is possible to move on to the third step.

## Developing Matrix and Exercises

In this step a matrix is developed listing the dimensions on one side and the possible exercises across the top. Normally each part of the assessment center will test for six or seven dimensions. It is possible for dimensions to be tested in more than one exercise. The more important dimensions are tested in three out of a possible four exercises. In some assessment centers a dimension may be tested once; for example, command presence in the role-play situation.

Figure 15.2 shows an example of a typical matrix in exercises for an assessment center for a police department.

## Developing Guidelines

Once the matrix and exercises are agreed upon, guidelines are developed for each part of the assessment center. The guidelines include the purpose, a brief definition of the individual dimensions, and examples of behaviors that should be considered as positive and those that should be considered as negative. In the guidelines, specific behavior patterns for the individual police department are given so that assessors can understand which behaviors would be rated high and which might be rated low. For example, in the dimension of written communication, high grades might be given for complete sentences, conciseness, and correct spelling. Low grades may be given for poor spelling, improper arrangement of paragraphs, or incomplete sentences.

## Developing Exercises

In the fifth step, each exercise is developed in great detail. In the oral interview panel, the assessors are selected and questions that are common for all

|  | Project Development and Presentation | In-Basket Exercise | Leaderless Group Exercise | Oral Interview |  |
|---|---|---|---|---|---|
| 1. Work perspective |  | X | X |  | (2) |
| 2. Command presence | X |  |  | X | (2) |
| 3. Oral communication | X |  | X | X | (3) |
| 4. Written communication | X | X |  |  | (2) |
| 5. Interpersonal sensitivity | X |  | X | X | (3) |
| 6. Decision-making skills |  | X | X |  | (2) |
| 7. Stress management |  |  |  | X | (1) |
| 8. Control skills | X | X |  |  | (2) |
| 9. Emotional maturity |  |  |  | X | (1) |
| 10. Delegation |  | X |  |  | (1) |
| 11. Planning and organizing | X | X | X |  | (3) |
| 12. Flexibility |  |  | X | X | (2) |
|  | 6 | 6 | 6 | 6 |  |

**Figure 15.2** Evaluation Matrix Position: Assistant Chief

candidates are developed. In the role-play situation, a role-player is selected. Instructions for the role player as well as the candidate are prepared. It is also decided whether to use audio or video equipment. Video can be used for two purposes. First, it can allow the command personnel of the police agency to identify the behavior patterns of each candidate after the completion of the assessment center. Second and just as important, it is a way to give individual feedback to candidates on how they were graded and how they appeared during their part of the assessment center.

Special instructions for each exercise should contain as much detail for the assessors as possible. For example, in the in-basket exercise, instructions may include even the fact that the name should be placed on envelopes. Instructions should be read carefully, and if extra answer sheets are needed, assessors can provide them. For leaderless groups, the instructions might include the fact that the assessors should provide name tags and solicit questions prior to the actual beginning of the exercise.

Instructions are provided for each exercise. One set of instructions goes to the candidates. In a role-play situation, the instructions may designate the information to be provided for the candidate. They may say that the candidate is to play the position of captain and that he is going to interview a disgruntled employee who has received an attached performance evaluation report. In addition, instructions are provided for the assessors. These are usually one or two paragraphs in length and are concise, so that the assessors understand their role in the process.

Next, the problem is defined for each exercise. The written plan problem may be long in its detail. It may include pages of data from the department's annual and monthly reports. In another instance, it may contain information from other facets of the department, such as memorandums from the chief and policy statements. The last part is the scoring form, which is necessary to help assessors see that they complete the scoring as consistently as possible and in the terms and manner in which the police department deems most effective.

## Training

In the sixth step, assessors and candidates are trained. In assessor training, it is common practice to hold a short meeting with the assessors for each exercise, usually the night before or a few hours prior to the beginning of the assessment center itself. In some areas of the country, a general pool of assessors is trained at a community college; they may then be called upon by individual agencies within a general area. Usually this short-term training program is conducted by giving an overview of the assessment center and then going through the guidelines for the individual parts for the assessors in great detail. Emphasis is placed upon the assessor's understanding of his or her role and of the definitions of each dimension as it applies to that individual agency. In most assessment centers, one assessor is assigned the responsibility of playing the lead role. Usually this is the more experienced assessor, especially for that individual exercise. In this step some agencies have taken the opportunity to prepare individual candidates for an understanding of the assessment center approach. This training usually takes a maximum of five hours and involves explaining the meaning of the dimensions and how candidates will be graded.

## Conducting the Center

In the seventh step, the assessment center is conducted. It takes place in a neutral locale and the coordinator does not take part in the exercises. The coordinator is responsible for seeing that candidates are on time and that assessors' questions are answered. One of the major tasks for the assessors is to get together at the completion of the center and meet with the police chief to give their personal views of each of the candidates. This kind of feedback is not designed to qualify any candidate but only to give to the police chief the personal impressions of the assessors. It is important to stress that this feedback is given after the center has been completed and all scores have been tabulated. In this way, scores or rankings cannot be adjusted and the integrity of the assessment center approach is not compromised.

## Ensuring Feedback

The eighth and final step includes giving feedback to the individual candidates. This is done within two weeks of the completion of the center. It is imperative that each candidate receive as much information as possible, avoiding comparisons but simply helping candidates understand their performance and what steps they might take to improve it in the future.

A common approach of feedback is for a single assessor to receive comments from other assessors, study the individual scoring forms, and then hold a personal interview of about thirty minutes with each candidate. In some police agencies, candidates are required to appear before a departmental assessor from each exercise. In this manner the candidate has four feedback sessions with separate assessors as opposed to one summation. Either method is satisfactory. The important factor is whether the candidate is provided feedback within a reasonable time.

# COMPONENTS OF THE ASSESSMENT CENTER

There are numerous exercises available to police chiefs who wish to implement an assessment center. The most common exercises include oral interviews, leaderless groups, in-basket problems, role-play situations, oral presentations, a written plan, and scheduling.

## Oral Interviews

In the oral interview phase there are three assessors, although many times a fourth is also included. Three is usually the more effective number, and two tend to make the interviews not inclusive enough. Four, on the other hand, can create a situation where the issues are discussed only superficially. Three assessors, however, generally have enough time to let each one ask specific questions. Time frames are extended for top-level management positions. For example, for the position of police chief, the time might range from 1½ hours up to as much as 3 hours. For positions such as first-line supervisors, where there are many candidates, the time frames are shortened to 45 minutes. A minimum of 30 minutes for each interview is normally necessary in order to get the necessary information.

An additional quarter hour should be allowed to give the assessors a chance to score the candidate immediately after the interview. The interviewing process, although very common in police departments, is not necessarily the most effective measure of future behavior patterns. Usually the interviewing panel is made up of one member of the department, another member of city government, and a third member with a special skill, as in psychology or a technical area relevant to the specific position.

It is imperative that each candidate receive the same questions in oral interviews. Sometimes candidates are given as many as ten to fifteen questions, which is too large a number to permit answers of any depth. When the questions are restricted to four or five, they can be open-ended. An example of such a question would be the following: "Assuming the police chief asks you your opinion on a certain issue such as the color of vehicles, would you state your honest opinion?" At this point the questions continue, regardless of what the answer might be, leading the candidate through his or her approach not only to the chief but also to other managers, fellow supervisors, and subordinates. The real issue is at what point the candidate is able to distinguish the priority of two values—loyalty to the police department and honesty toward subordinates and superiors.

In the oral interview, it is advisable to develop specific questions to which the police agency requires answers. For example, if the police department is facing an affirmative action program, questions dealing with how such a program might be implemented would be important. If change or dealing with conflict are other important issues, then questions geared to them should be developed. It is not advisable to have stock questions that have no clear-cut relevance to the examining police department. For example, a question such as "Do you believe in professionalization?" does not really help the assessors to tell how the candidate would behave in the new position.

Sometimes questions asked in the oral interview have no special value to the grading process but are designed to provide feedback for the police chief. Such questions may focus on what the candidate may have done to prepare for the position, what he or she perceives the position to include, and how he or she would rank the individual candidates. This last question provides the police chief with feedback about how the candidates perceive one another and who they think is really the best within their grouping.

## Leaderless Groups

Leaderless groups are designed to test an individual's ability to work in a small group. The minimum number needed to make such an exercise effective is usually five. The maximum number is eight. There are two approaches to the kinds of questions to be asked within a leaderless group. The most common method is for the police department to develop one large issue or a series of small issues that are important to the present environment. For example, policies that are presently under study can be presented for discussion by the leaderless group. Such policies might include off-duty working hours, the use of firearms, or reorganization. In some instances, more than one problem is given. For example, three small issues might be (1) whether the department should accept gifts at Christmas time; (2) whether the agency should issue press releases, and if so, on what incidents; and (3) whether cars should be assigned to personnel on a permanent basis.

Sometimes fixed problems that have nothing to do with the police agency are also used. Examples include group problems such as "Lost in the Desert," "Lost in the Arctic," or "Man on the Moon." In these exercises, some answers are recommended by experts; however, the purpose of this part of the assessment program is not to elicit the "correct answer" but to see how the candidates work together.

A third approach involves asking each member of the leaderless group to play a specific role. Persons seeking the position of assistant chief of police can be asked to role-play other department heads, and the issue can be how to best reduce the citywide budget. This may give each person the opportunity to show some understanding of how other agencies have to deal with problems similar to those within the police department. Some departments restrict the role playing to positions within their own agency. Of the many types of problems available, this last seems to be the least effective as it restricts the individuals involved. It therefore is not necessarily used when a large amount of information is to be analyzed during such a leaderless-group problem.

The leaderless-group problem usually lasts forty-five minutes to an hour. In order to add additional stress, sometimes the assessors will collect the answer, have a short discussion among themselves, and then advise the group that the solution it has produced is not adequate. They then ask the group to continue to work on the exercise for an additional fifteen minutes. Usually this additional fifteen minutes tends to place people under high stress, so that they begin to show behavior patterns that may not have been evident before.

## In-Basket Problems

The in-basket exercise is considered an especially effective one as it explores the candidates' ability to set priorities and their understanding of departmental policies, rules, and standards.

In most police departments, a series of real-life memorandums are gathered approximately sixty to ninety days in advance of the assessment center. Copies are made—changing names and dates—and most of the items in the exercise are then based on them.

The most common approach is to bring all the candidates together in a room and present the in-basket at that time. The answers are written on pieces of paper, and each candidate, upon completing them, places them in an envelope. The envelopes—one for each candidate—are then returned to the assessors. In some instances, names are excluded and candidates are judged only by assigned numbers. In this format, the only knowledge the assessors have is through the written documents provided by the candidates.

Another approach has the candidates complete the in-basket problem in the usual forty-five minutes. They are given the memorandums, asked to prioritize them, and required to describe briefly what they would do in each instance. Upon completion of this task, they present their written answers to three evaluators. The assessors read the answers and then take approximately twenty to thirty minutes to question each candidate concerning any issues they may feel are not totally resolved in the written responses. This allows a wider range of information to be evaluated.

In the in-basket exercise, the departments provide a priority listing and model answers. Priorities are listed as those that should be handled within eight hours and those that could wait twenty-four to forty-eight hours. Model answers are usually one or two sentences at most, and these serve to guide the assessors as to the direction that the correct answers should take.

## Role-Play Situations

Here individuals are asked to play a specific part dealing with an individual role player. The most common example involves the use of a disgruntled officer who is objecting to his or her performance evaluation report. In some instances, women play the role of complainants of sexual harassment or blacks complain about discrimination. Sometimes a combination is used to focus on more than just one issue. For example, a black sergeant might complain to the candidate, who is role-playing a captain. The sergeant complains that the performance evaluation report is not fair—that it is based predominantly on racially discriminatory attitudes on the part of his lieutenant. In such situations, it is imperative that the same role player be used in each instance.

A police department can use a role player from within the agency. This individual may play the part of a captain with candidates seeking the position of assistant chief. The role player may be accused of taking something from the scene of the crime, and it is up to the assistant chief to conduct an interview to determine whether the accusation had any merit. In some instances two role players, both of whom are professional actors, can be used. They role-play the parts of two employees, subordinates to the candidate, who are involved in a conflict concerning the best way to implement a certain project. Each takes an opposite point of view and, during the role-play situation, both indicate severe stress by raising their voices, standing, and pacing about the room.

In another instance, the candidates seeking the position of police captain might be brought into a room and advised they are to give a speech to the chamber of commerce within ten minutes. A specific issue is presented—one on which the candidates already know the department's point of view. They will also already have the data they would need to deal with this issue as police captains. Each candidate is asked, after ten minutes of preparation, to present a ten-minute speech and role-play the situation as if she were speaking to members of the chamber of commerce. The evaluation would include not only the role-play presentation but also the candidates' handwritten notes.

Usually the role-play situation is limited to thirty minutes. Assessors are given an additional fifteen minutes to agree upon their ratings.

## Oral Presentations

In the oral presentation, the candidate is given a specific question and is asked to respond within a short time period, such as five to ten minutes. Oral presentations include such issues as, "Why do you seek this position?" "What do you feel are your personal qualifications?" or "How do you view your strengths and your weaknesses?" The weight given to this part of an assessment program is usually small, as it does not require a tremendous amount of forethought on the part of the candidate. Because of the nature of the questions and the amount of time provided, an in-depth analysis is not required of the assessors.

Some police agencies include an oral presentation in conjunction with a specially developed personal qualifications appraisal task. A series of questions and tasks are given to prospective candidates at least thirty to forty-five days in advance. For example, the candidates may be asked to interview people in their professional and personal life, summarize what they have learned from these people, and supplement such knowledge with their own perceptions of themselves. They may be asked to write a short scenario about where they would like to be in their personal lives in five years. This would include such issues as life-style, vocation, organizational life, family, and free time. They are also asked to write an outline of their expectations for the police department within the next five years. During the oral presentation, they are given fifteen minutes to explain their written document and are granted an additional thirty minutes in which to expand on their plan on the basis of questions provided by the assessors.

## Written Plan

In the written-plan exercise, candidates are given from ninety minutes to three hours to prepare a written document concerning a specific issue within the police department. The problems are varied, depending on the nature of the position sought. For example, in one police department, because the position being sought was in management, the problem involved planning for a rock concert at the civic auditorium. Other written plans have included broad issues such as (1) what promotional system should be implemented within the police department, (2) how the department should go about recruiting additional women and blacks in order to meet the requirements of the city's affirmative action program, and (3) how to develop team management practices.

The police department may give candidates approximately forty-five days in which to develop a five-year budget plan for the police department. The budget documents are submitted at the end of that time. The assessors are then given approximately two weeks to read through these documents. Each candidate is given ten minutes to explain additional information and then an additional thirty minutes during which to answer questions from the assessors. Only after all of this information has been gathered is the written plan evaluated.

It is imperative for the police chief to recognize that a written plan is a good exercise only when the position being sought requires people to write such plans. For example, a police department that has a Research and Development Unit, should not necessarily demand a long written plan from every candidate for a supervisory position. Only for those seeking posts in the Research and Development Unit would such an assignment be appropriate.

## Scheduling

In the scheduling exercise, the candidate is given the personnel roster of a given unit and asked to allocate the time of these people—that is, to develop some kind of scheduling system—in order to achieve the overall goals of the police department. To create stress, the problem may be complicated by introducing additional information halfway through the thirty-minute exercise. For example, individuals may resign, call in sick, or need to be scheduled for training programs. In this way, flexibility and the ability to make decisions under stress can also be analyzed.

# RATING SCALES

## Numerical Scales

There are different ways in which scoring scales can be developed to evaluate the individual candidate during the assessment program. In most cities, a specific numerical value is assigned to each exercise. For example, an oral interview might be worth 40 points; an in-basket exercise, 30 points; a leaderless group, 20 points; and a role-play situation, 10 points. Each candidate, upon completion of the assigned exercise, is rated individually by each assessor. Once the individual ratings are completed, assessors discuss the ratings and come to a consensus as to the final numerical score. After all candidates have completed an exercise, the raters examine final consensus scores given to each and make any adjustments necessary to clearly show differences that may be greater than originally agreed upon. For example, suppose that candidate A received 28 out of 30 points, and candidate B received 26. The assessors may later agree that candidate B was not 2 points but 3 points behind. Thus the second person's score might be changed to a 25.

In using numerical ratings, it becomes difficult to show large differences between the candidates, especially when the maximum score is below 20 on any exercise. It is recommended that when numerical ratings are used, each exercise be graded on a score of at least 30. The total scores of all exercises can be computed to reflect an overall grade of 100 percent. For example, if there are four exercises, the first might contain 30 points, the second 40, the third 50, and the fourth 60, for a total of 180 points. This score can easily be computed to a scale of 100 percent. (Divide the applicant's score, say 120, by the total of 180, for a final grade of 66.6.)

## Strengths and Weaknesses

A second approach is to use a rating form that discusses the strengths and weaknesses of each candidate. Under this form of rating, however, no numerical grade is given, and the police chief receives feedback on the strengths and weaknesses of the individual candidates in each of the dimensions in each of the exercises. The final judgment as to the value of strengths and weaknesses is left up to the person responsible for the final promotion.

## Composite Graphs

The third method is to develop a composite graph. Here points are given to each dimension instead of each exercise. For example, if decision making is examined in three of the four exercises, then the number of points given to decision making is placed on a bar or line graph denoting the score for each exercise. In this way, the person responsible for the promotions has a composite graph from which to analyze individual scores on each dimension and where dimension scores may appear the strongest and the weakest. Again, using decision making as an example, an individual may be an effective decision maker in a one-to-one situation such as role playing during an oral interview process, but he may not have exhibited strong decision-making skills in the leaderless group. Thus the police chief has an understanding of how the candidate will behave in different situations.

## Forced Choice

Another approach is to have assessors rate the candidates on a forced-choice scale. They have to rate candidates first, second, third, and fourth during each part of the assessment center without giving assigned weights. This system has not proved to be effective in giving an overview of the candidate's behavior during the total assessment center.

## Consensus

In the rating process, it is important for individual assessors to rate the candidates prior to any discussions between themselves. Once they have completed their individual ratings, the assessors discuss them and come to an overall consensus. All the scoring is given to the candidate during the feedback process. In this way, the integrity of the assessment center is maintained and more data can be analyzed before the final consensus is reached.

# CONCLUSION

In conclusion, police chiefs must recognize that assessment centers will not solve all promotional problems. They are designed to serve as a tool in police agencies where such tools may be useful. History has shown that the assessment center approach may help to pinpoint quality candidates and, more importantly, lend a sense of fairness to the promotional process. These are both important criteria, especially in government agencies. The assessment center must be recognized as only a tool; therefore the belief that this approach always produces "the best" is not necessarily justified. Police chiefs must recognize that they must personally be strongly committed to anyone who is promoted to a key management position. Assessment centers can help to develop that commitment by identifying the strengths and weaknesses of persons to be promoted. This tends to reduce the amount of time it takes a police manager to learn about key managerial personnel. Conflicts are thus reduced and working relationships develop more quickly and effectively.

Although assessment centers may not be the final answer, they are surely helpful in identifying the assets and liabilities that a candidate may bring to a new position.

---

# NOTE

1. *Kirkland* v. *New York State Correctional Services*, 711 F. 2d 1117 (1983).

# CHAPTER 16

# *Change and Conflict*

## THE NATURE OF CHANGE

The job of effectively bringing about changes in a police department is one of the most complex tasks confronting today's police manager. No other activity is as filled with frustration or resistance as that of upgrading and changing a police organization and its personnel. Often, the police officer views the change process as indicating that she is considered incompetent. Further, because the manager is the one to implement changes, his personnel often assume that he considers himself "better" than anyone else in the organization. It is little wonder, therefore, that police managers have been reluctant to even suggest change, much less to plan for its implementation or to devise strategies to bring about commitment to the change.

Many police managers find themselves in the position of being change agents. A police manager may be transferred to a specific unit that is seriously hampering the overall effectiveness of the police department, or he may be hired as police chief in a new city to initiate change in its present police organization. These police managers must identify, plan, and successfully implement change strategies. Once the police manager has committed himself to the overall objective of bringing about changes in attitudes and behaviors of his subordinates, he is faced with a serious situation, one that may easily dictate his success as a police manager. Once the police manager understands both the change process and the strategy preferences of his personnel, he can develop a specific step-by-step program to implement the changes necessary to upgrade his agency.

Meaningful and enduring change is extremely difficult to effect within the police department because police managers and personnel hold beliefs about change that often have no foundation in fact.

One key assumption concerning change is that if a police officer can be sold on a certain procedure, then her attitude will change, and the change process can then be brought about effectively in the department. This assumption has merit but does not go far enough. There are other factors operating within the change process that must be considered by the police manager.

More important than the change that is to be brought about is the police manager's attitude toward the following three criteria: (1) freedom of choice within the change process, (2) reliance upon new information and experience, and (3) involvement of the people to be affected by the change.

## Change as a Function of Freedom of Choice

By involving the police officer in the change process and allowing him to develop alternatives that he feels will most effectively bring about the desired change, the manager is more likely to effect genuine change in the subordinate's attitude toward the procedure and its consequences. Research has demonstrated that individuals who are subjected to strong pressures to follow a certain course of action yield to the pressure and conform to some extent. But when individuals are given a greater freedom of choice, they actually experience a sustained change in their attitude and behavior. This is because when a person is involved in choosing alternative actions, he searches for attitudinal support for his choice. As the subordinate is allowed to test the alternatives, he will continue to reexamine his current attitudes and, with new information and experience, may very well adopt a new attitude toward a specific practice within the department.

## Change as a Function of New Information and Experience

Another reason why new practices and procedures initiated by a police manager may help bring about change is that the changes themselves may provide the opportunity for departmental personnel to gain new experiences and to learn from the new information. The subordinates soon learn the consequences of the options they are allowed to consider. Many times, this experience and new information have the effect of changing the subordinates' negative perceptions toward the change process, which can then be appraised in a realistic and nonthreatening manner.

## Change as a Function of Involvement

Group decision studies have indicated that when people agree about some proposed change, action, or direction, the barriers to change are removed or are at least lessened, and a new attitude—one supporting the change—begins to play a more prominent role. Many times commitment to the change process satisfies the ego needs of those who have planned the change and are in the process of implementing it. The probability of experiences and information having a positive effect on the subordinates depends on their openness to the new information and to what extent this new information allows them to become involved in planning the change process.

The police manager's attitudes and behavior are extremely important in the change process. His assumptions and beliefs determine the strategy of change that he is likely to select. These strategies, in turn, dictate the extent of subordinates' involvement, freedom of choice, and openness to new experiences. The police manager's assumptions are reflected in the way he uses his power, formal and informal, to effect change and to inspire commitment to change.

In police departments where changes are based upon trial and error, rather than upon any careful planning and understanding of the change processes, changes tend to be short-lived and unpredictable. The police manager must conceptualize his particular change strategy very carefully, and he should be able to predict with some degree of assurance the consequences of his action and the strategy he chooses.

## WHY PEOPLE RESIST CHANGE

Police officers resist change for numerous reasons. Probably the most important is that the subordinate often views the police manager with little trust and does not believe what she says. The police manager's prior actions indicate to her subordinates whether or not she really believes they should become involved in the change process. If, for example, all changes in the police department originate with top management and are implemented by middle management, the people at the bottom of the organization do not see themselves as part of the change process. If the police manager uses outside consultants to determine what direction the department should take and then attempts to sell the change process to members of the department, she will lose their respect and meet resistance to the change.

Consider, for example, the police manager who alone carefully plans what changes should be made in the field reporting system. She may seek outside assistance, but once she reaches the decision, she orders the report forms, which are usually copied from some other agency or from a specific management consulting contract. This change process does not involve the subordinates. They immediately question whether they will be able to receive any of the information as a result of the new reporting system. Many times the new reporting system does nothing to increase the amount of information returned to them. Furthermore, they question why they were not allowed to help design the report forms on the basis of criteria established by management. And, finally, they quickly recognize that their involvement is only passive: they are being told what to do without being involved in reaching the decision as to whether the reporting system is needed, whether the one selected is best for the department, or how the system should be implemented.

Some members of police organizations will resist change if they think that top management has become complacent and somewhat set in its ways. For example, officers at the bottom of the ladder may have a clear indication that the crime rate within the city is going up, but top management may be saying that the department is really doing a good job because the crime rate in their city is not increasing as quickly as the crime rate in others. Eventually, when management attempts to implement some change, officers feel that such change is being forced by outsiders (such as the office of the city manager) and that top management is not committed to any great degree to improving the department.

Coupled with this may be the preconceived notion—on the part of department management, middle management, first-line supervisors, or the officers themselves—that whatever is to be implemented really won't work.

The change is doomed to failure from the start when such a belief exists. If a police department is the kind that refuses to examine new pieces of information, to question its own procedures and practices, and to establish clear-cut objectives for the future, a negative approach to change will continue within the department.

Fear of the unknown also creates resistance to change. This fear is easy for management to overcome; all that is required is close communicative ties with the people who will be affected most by the change. An honest report to them of the process whereby the planning, implementation, and evaluation of change is effected is most important.

Probably one of the greatest causes of resistance to change is the fear some people have that they will lose power and authority as a result of the change. How many times have we heard police managers vehemently justify their present positions and attempt to justify their importance in relation to the department? The police manager should recognize that people do not normally like to give up their power, whether this power is real or imagined. The change process has to consider the possible loss of power on the part of all persons involved. Consider the trend in many cities today to merge the police and fire departments into a new agency: the public safety department. Police managers may agree that their role is to help reduce the overall cost of police operations and to become more effective in their work, but when it comes to reorganizing the department and establishing new rules, these same managers often find reasons for holding on to their authority and responsibilities.

## THE MANAGEMENT OF CONFLICT

Conflict and disagreement are present in almost every department and organization. The police chief differs with his personnel on how specific jobs should be handled. Middle managers disagree with the philosophies and policies of top management. The police officers disagree with the wages, hours, working conditions, and rules and regulations of the department. These kinds of conflicts may vary from minor differences of opinion to intense differences in attitudes that bring about serious disruptions.

The police manager should be realistic and accept the fact that conflict is an ingredient of every police organization. He should also realize that conflict is not only inevitable but also has a positive effect on initiative, creativity, and decision making. Many police managers attempt to find ways to avoid conflict, but the most effective manager learns to recognize and deal with it in a logical and effective manner.

There are two kinds of conflict: emotional and rational. Emotional conflict is unrelated to facts and stems from differences of opinions based on differences in background. Rational conflict comes from differences in values, experiences, and points of view. The police manager must understand that almost all conflicts have rational and emotional elements and he must learn to deal with both.

In some instances, conflict can be resolved only by approaching it rationally, with facts and figures. In other situations, a subjective approach—which takes into account personal feelings, attitudes, and relationships—is most effective. The police manager, then, in order to be effective in resolving conflict, must be aware of both dimensions and should have the ability to distinguish between the rational and emotional elements in each major disagreement.

## The Role of Emotion

If one member of the department disagrees with another and neither is strongly committed to a specific solution, the conflict may be resolved by analyzing the facts. If, however, emotions are the key factor in the situation, the facts themselves will probably fall short of resolving the conflict. Some elements contributing to this resistance are:

1. Defensive attitudes
2. Group loyalty
3. Self-image
4. Saving face
5. Interpersonal relations

*Defensive attitudes* may be defined as attitudes concerning a certain issue that prohibit the individual from viewing it with an open mind. Defensive attitudes are conclusions already drawn by the person in the conflict situation. The police manager should realize that individuals look at situations in ways that are consistent with their past experience and their psychological expectations. As a result, defensive attitudes are formed not from logic, facts, or analysis but from defensive components that offer protection against real or imagined threats.

By recognizing the effect that experience and defensive attitudes have in conflict situations, the police manager is able to manage conflict effectively. He must realize that many defensive attitudes grow as a result of experience and can be changed through new experiences. Job rotation, allowing the subordinate to analyze situations, and personal counseling by the manager help the subordinate to discover new and better ways to deal with police problems. Statements such as "You have a negative attitude about dealing with the policies of this department and you must change" are rarely helpful.

*Group loyalty* is a major factor of human behavior. The police officer may feel a strong sense of belonging with her fellow officers and therefore has a strong sense of loyalty to them. The police manager should realize that even though the subordinate may understand a situation logically, she may be unable to accept it because of loyalty to peers. A subordinate may maintain a negative emotional attitude about a certain change or problem that exists within the department because a positive reaction would be considered disloyal to the group.

The police manager should realize that the key to resolving conflict between groups is to reach an understanding that encompasses groups, the management team, and the subordinates. He should avoid fixed positions and should attempt to maintain some experimental approach to conflict resolution so that alternative solutions can be examined logically whenever possible.

*Self-image* is another important factor. Each individual sees himself in a certain way and will usually attempt to maintain that image.

Consider the police manager who sees himself as being "tough-minded and practical." He may resist any solution that might be seen as "soft" or "theoretical," not because it is bad but because it would conflict with his own self-image. Some police managers argue that decisions must be made in only one way, and that changes can be brought about by using only one strategy. Upon careful examination, it becomes clear that the manager is primarily concerned with maintaining his self-image as a strong, direct, controlling leader.

*Saving face* is also important in conflict resolution. Police managers have to realize that, in a conflict situation, face saving may even become more important than problem solving. Face saving becomes an important issue when the police manager has assumed a fixed position, has argued strongly for that position, and then later realizes that the position was not the most desirable. The general philosophy of a bureaucracy is that managers are not supposed to make mistakes. If the manager admits that he was wrong, he places in jeopardy his position as an effective police manager. Therefore he may argue or attempt to avoid conflict in trying to find some way out of the dilemma he has created.

*Interpersonal relations* may have an important effect on the resolution of conflict situations. The police manager must be aware that if he enters into a conflict situation in an annoying or overbearing manner, he may force his subordinates into a fixed position. They will begin to argue on an emotional basis regardless of the content of the issue.

The police manager should always realize that individual differences and attitudes play an important part in determining the most effective strategy and approach to the resolution of conflict.

## The Psychology of Conflict Resolution

The police manager will find it desirable to establish basic criteria for effective problem solving before attempting to argue through minor points with subordinates. It becomes even more desirable to agree upon specific objectives before attempting to resolve conflict concerning details. The application of a systematic decision-making process is an appropriate starting point for conflict resolution.

In addition, the police manager must realize that the crucial factors in dealing with emotionally charged situations are the feelings, attitudes, and opinions of the people involved, not the approach the manager may take. One important ingredient that applies to both rational and emotional situations is the maintenance of an experimental attitude. The manager must be willing to try new ideas and approaches, even if they are inconsistent with his views. He must examine the situation to find the source of the conflict; he must approach it with understanding and interest rather than a win-or-lose attitude. In order to be more effective, the manager should attempt to explore and determine other people's points of view and ask them to discuss their experiences concerning the problem.

For example, two police captains may be meeting with the police manager to discuss the possibility of a new manpower allocation system. The police manager may list numerous reasons why the present scheduling system should be changed, yet both captains may strongly oppose this change solely because they would feel that they would be losing the respect of their subordinates if they were to accept the manager's position. The police manager, by not establishing a win-lose situation, would probably be able to resolve the conflict by bringing about some changes and at the same time guaranteeing that the captains did not lose the respect and trust of their subordinates.

The following steps can be of assistance to the police manager as he deals with rational differences in resolving conflict situations:

1. Deal with principles, not details.
2. Determine the criteria against which the judgment will be made.
3. Experiment with possible courses of action; do not just debate them.
4. Apply a rational decision-making process.

The police manager should always work with principles rather than details. It is important that the department have a set of policies, specific goals, and criteria from which to make decisions. By defining purposes, principles, and goals, the police manager can establish a foundation for agreement on specific issues.

The police manager should determine the criteria against which judgments will be made. He must answer the question: "What conditions will be present when we have adequately solved this problem?" Only through the establishment of criteria can the decisions be tested.

The police manager should have some logical way of experimenting or testing the possible solutions without arguing over them. With pretesting, the conflicting ideas can be compared; as a result, the final decision can often be made without a prolonged debate.

The police manager has to apply rational problem-solving processes. By the use of rational tools, conflict may in many instances be resolved.

## Dealing with Fixed Positions

The police manager should recognize that despite his best efforts, some conflict situations may never be resolved because of real differences in values, philosophies, expectations, goals, and needs of the persons involved. In other instances, the conflict may be caused by the differences in attitudes and opinions. In this situation, even effective strategies, cooperation, and experimental attitudes may prove to be ineffective in resolving the conflict.

Because such situations can and often do occur within a police department, the police manager should be aware of the techniques that can be used to deal with these conflicts. Some of the possibilities open to the police manager are:

1. Use of a third party
2. Use of power or authority
3. Compromise
4. Deferring action
5. Testing alternatives

*Use of a Third Party.*   When the police manager is unable to reach agreement in a conflict situation, it may be necessary for her to call in a third party. This third party may be a representative of higher-level management who has the authority to make decisions, can act as an arbitrator, and can decide which approach the department should take in resolving the conflict.

There are other third-party techniques. For example, it is possible to call in technical experts, consultants, or a completely objective third party. The key point in calling in a third party is to first agree upon the role he will play. The third party may have the power to make and enforce decisions, or he may be used only as a mediator to assist the police manager in exploring alternatives and reaching agreement.

*Use of Power or Authority.*   The police manager can also use his power and authority in dealing with subordinates. Here the police manager has to be careful that he does not alienate subordinates as a result of the conflict. The exercise of authority is exemplified in a statement such as the following: "I understand your position and I understand why we are not in agreement, but because of my responsibility, I have decided that we will follow the course of action outlined in Plan A."

When the police manager finds it necessary to exercise his authority in making a decision, he must be aware of the reactions of his subordinates. If an officer appears to be resisting the proposed changes, the manager must either replace him or see to it that he has nothing to do with the implementation process.

When the police manager and his subordinates have a history of working together in a cooperative manner, the occasional use of power and authority to resolve conflicts will usually elicit a positive response. If the police manager is able to implement some of the ideas of his subordinates, the use of power and authority becomes even more acceptable to them. The police manager should realize that even when he uses power and authority to resolve conflict and underlying disagreements still exist, there is still an excellent chance to develop mutually acceptable courses of action in implementing the decision.

*Compromise.*   When the police manager finds herself in conflict with someone of equal authority and power, one possible method of resolving it is for
each to find some middle-of-the-road position that is acceptable to both.
There are some dangers in this approach, however. The police manager
should be aware that the decision reached may be less effective than either
of the original alternatives. The value of compromise lies in the fact that it
allows the project to move ahead smoothly.

*Deferring Action.*   The police manager may find himself in the position of
strong disagreement with his subordinates or peers, and—because of the issues and their importance—he may find it necessary to defer action until
more experience can be obtained. With additional information, it may be
easier to reach an agreement. The police manager should be aware that to
"defer" action means that a decision *will* eventually be made. Many times
those involved will agree to defer a decision only to bury the issue forever.
The end result is that no decision is ever reached. It is important that even
though positions may be polarized, some technique be agreed upon to force
a final decision. Otherwise, the police department will eventually become
stagnant.

*Testing Alternatives.*   The last possibility available to the manager is to test
alternatives. This provides a factual base from which a decision can eventually
be made. Prior to these tests, it is important to establish criteria on the basis
of which the tests will be judged.

## Management Conflict Model[1]

The management conflict model examines two basic prerequisites to dealing
with conflict. The first is concern for relationship and the second is concern
for personal goals.

*Concern for Relationship.*   The police manager should be aware that his relationships with others play an important part in determining his behavior in
conflict situations. For example, if the police manager attaches importance to
continuing his relationship with those who oppose his view, he may react in
one way; if he does not consider the relationship to be particularly important,
then his actions and behavior may be completely opposite. The police manager should recognize that the way in which he deals with conflict reveals
how he feels about the others involved.

*Concern for Personal Goals.*   Conflict can also be interpreted as a clash of
personal goals. These collisions may occur in different ways and the goals may
be valued to different degrees.

   In some situations, the resolution of conflict may be mutually exclusive—
that is, it will cost one or the other person his or her personal goals. In
distributive collisions, on the other hand, the goals of each person in the

conflict may be similar but, because the "supply" is limited, it may not be possible to meet each person's demands. Conflict situations may also arise from the fact that the personal goals of two or more people are the same. For example, two managers may both have as their goal promotion to the position of captain.

Finally, there are value collisons—conflicts over what is right and what is wrong. Most police officers and managers agree that their conduct should be highly moral, but they may have conflicting ideas about the definition of moral behavior.

The police manager should recognize that there are numerous types of potential conflicts about goals and that the importance he gives to his personal goals will determine how he reacts to such conflicts. The manager's style in resolving conflict is also determined by how much he values his relationships with the others involved.

The conflict model also identifies five possible styles of management available to the police manager. Each style is dependent upon the value placed on the two concerns within the issue of conflict. The five styles are as follows:

1. Win–lose style
2. Yield–lose style
3. Lose–leave style
4. Compromise style
5. Synergistic style

Each style is shown graphically in Figure 16.1 and will be discussed in detail on the following pages.

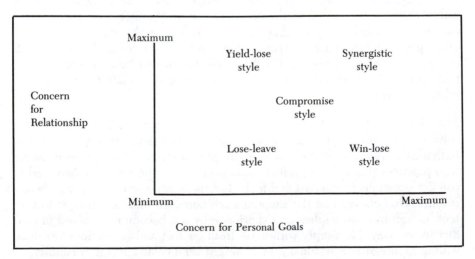

**Figure 16.1** Management Conflict Model
SOURCE: Adapted from Jay Hall and Martha Williams, *Styles of Management Inventory.* Teleometric Intl., Conroe, Texas.

*Win–Lose Style.* The police manager who believes in the win–lose style of management accepts the philosophy that differences between people are to be expected because some people have skills and abilities to do a job whereas others do not. Furthermore, the central issue in conflict is who is right and who is wrong. As a police manager, he believes that he owes it to himself and his subordinates to always be the winner in conflict situations, so that his opinions, philosophies, and goals, which are "right," will not be questioned. He believes that power, persuasion, and force are acceptable methods to be used to resolve conflicts. In fact, he believes that most people expect him, as a manager, to exercise such methods.

He believes that there are only two possible solutions to conflict: to win or to lose. He associates winning with his competence and his status. He therefore places prime importance upon personal goals to the exclusion of any serious concern for relationship. He believes that you must win at all costs because social survival within the police department is always at stake.

Usually his behavior patterns are aggressive, inflexible, and unreasonable in regard to the management of conflict. He emphasizes suppression and coercion and constantly protects his own personal goals. Furthermore, he does not consider the effect of any tactics he may use during conflicts until well after the conflict has been resolved.

*Yield–Lose Style.* The police manager who uses this style of management believes that conflict only drives people apart. As she enters into conflict, she feels that she must pay maximum attention to the relationship side of the conflict model and that it is her job to satisfy the needs and the desires of others in the conflict situation. She further believes that conflict means self-sacrifice, and she places the continuation of relationships above her own personal goals. This is the kind of police manager who tends to ignore conflict rather than bringing it out in the open. This type of police manager believes that her relationships with others are so fragile that she must appease the other people by ignoring, denying, or in some way avoiding the conflict. If, however, the conflict does persist, then she will submit because she believes that this is the most effective way of protecting her relationship with the others involved.

*Lose–Leave Style.* According to this type of manager, conflict is usually resolved as a result of past experiences, because of the personal power of the individuals involved, or because of their personal goals. The police manager who practices this style of conflict resolution is one who has been involved in conflict situations in the past and feels that there is no way he can win in any conflict. He believes that the situations are hopeless, and he attempts to protect himself from an unpleasant experience by not becoming involved in conflict in any way. He simply withdraws from conflict and is usually more than willing to forego any personal gain he might achieve as a result of conflict.

The manager who chooses this style feels that it is better to "roll with the punches and live to fight another day." The result is compliance without commitment.

*Compromise Style*. The police manager who accepts this philosophy believes that each member of the department must, at some point in time, disregard his or her personal goals for the advancement of the department and for the relationships that exist among members of the department. She encourages people to express their points of view, but she does not allow these views to block the progress of conflict resolution. This type of manager depends heavily upon her personality and her previous positive dealings with those involved.

The compromising police manager wants to win a little and lose a little. She accepts the fact that some loss must occur in any conflict, and the result is that she will attempt to reduce the loss by employing this philosophy. The police manager implies to all people involved that someday their turn will come to be the "winner." This police manager uses persuasion and manipulation in order to resolve conflict, and in many instances she will attempt to "play both ends against the middle." The result is confusion. Police managers using this style attempt to justify the ends (conflict resolution) by the means (compromise). The police manager who believes that she must always ask for more than she needs in her budget, in order to gain bargaining power for the future, is demonstrating the compromise style of conflict resolution. Unfortunately, many police managers are forced into this situation by the bureaucratic principles that are developed by tradition within many governmental agencies. Such compromise styles of conflict resolution bring about half-committed resolutions, and the game of conflict itself becomes more important than any gain that may be achieved for either the individual police manager or the department.

*Synergistic Style*. The police manager who uses the synergistic style believes that conflict is really a natural part of human behavior. The conflict itself is neither good nor bad, and it is usually nothing more than a symptom of some stronger issues that must be carefully analyzed and resolved. He also believes that conflict has a way of bringing people together, and that in many cases it produces creativity. The police manager who advocates this style of conflict management is one who attaches importance to the personal goals of those involved and maintains as well a concern for relationships. He does not view one as being exclusive of the other. In fact, he recognizes that a concern for both is most effective in resolving conflict.

Conflict is viewed as a lack of communication between the manager and other members of the department. This police manager believes that by working together to resolve differences, a creative solution can be developed. This manager has a tolerance for differences of opinions and believes that each individual has the right to differ with others, but he feels that if conflict does arise, there must be an agreement to resolve the conflict for the benefit of the department. The result is that others have a high degree of trust in him. This trust is the groundwork for the establishment of specific objectives and candid appraisals of the department's problem. There is a lot of encouragement to be open. The police manager who uses this style does not have a win-lose attitude but a win-win attitude. He realizes that the department as well as the individual will profit by resolving the conflict.

*Backup Systems.*   Although a police manager may believe in using one of the previously mentioned styles, in many instances he may find it necessary to use a secondary style of management for the resolution of conflict. The manager may prefer to depend primarily on a synergistic style, but if this fails, he will be forced to try an alternative or secondary approach.

Research seems to indicate that the styles of management should be applied in the following order: synergistic, compromise, yield–lose, win–lose, and lose-leave. The style that is ultimately chosen depends on the situation, the persons involved, the time available, and the police manager's philosophy.

---

## NOTE

1. Adapted from Jay Hall and Martha Williams, *Styles of Management Inventory.* Teleometrics, Intl., Conroe, Texas.

# CHAPTER 17

# *Organizational Development*

Organizational development is a planned change effort that involves the total operations of the police department. It requires an examination of its mission and its purpose as well as a commitment to a long-term effort for the growth and development of the department and its people. Organizational development focuses upon changing attitudes, behaviors, the structure of the department, the rules, and almost every facet of what is accomplished, how it is accomplished, and who is responsible for the accomplishments. The organizational development program can in some instances be viewed as a very threatening force within a department or as a positive method for growth.

All the management techniques discussed in the previous chapters of this text must be strongly considered prior to the decision to implement an organizational development program. The techniques mentioned—such as rational decision making, communications, and transactional analysis—must all be understood, and each must be reviewed in terms of whether it will play an important or a minor role in the organizational development program. Eventually, within the process, all of the issues covered in the text up to this point will be resolved one way or another.

An understanding of what must be accomplished, how to deal with conflict, and the theories behind the change process are all important in the management of change. Knowing what tools are available and how to use them to implement change may mean the difference between success and failure for the police manager. Some of these tools include the effective use of team decision making, the development of strategies for change, and the implementation of the change process.

Organizational development has been defined by many terms and clichés. One definition emphasizes that the goal of organizational development is to create an open, problem-solving climate throughout the police department. Another emphasizes the necessity for making decisions. Others emphasize the necessity for building trust among all levels of the department and the personnel involved.

In its simplest form, organizational development is a process whereby the police department decides specifically what objectives are to be reached in the upcoming few years, how these objects are to be reached, and how the resultant changes will be evaluated, in terms of overall departmental effectiveness. Organizational development emphasizes the improvement of the technical, rational, and human skills of all departmental employees. In many instances, it calls for the redesign of the department's formal structure.

## OVERVIEW

There are certain objectives that should be sought and achieved in any organizational development process. These include the following:

1. To create an open, problem-solving climate throughout the police department
2. To locate decision-making and problem-solving responsibilities as close as possible to the information sources
3. To build trust among police officers, supervisors, and commanders as well as among individual groups throughout the police department
4. To help the police managers to manage according to a planned future rather than according to past practices
5. To increase self-control and self-direction for all personnel within the police department, from the lowest rank up through police chief

Prior to entering into an organizational development process, the police manager must review certain factors. These include the ability of the police officers, supervisors, and managers within the department; the values of the community and the department itself; and any legal restrictions that might be placed upon the department regarding its development and growth.

The roles of other people must be carefully evaluated prior to a "yes" decision for organizational development. Key people, such as the city manager and the governing board, must be interviewed and their support gained. This includes civil service commissions, which also have some control as to how a police department must operate. In addition to the commitment of these key officials, the commitment of outside agencies, such as the personnel department and the finance department, is also required. It is possible that the skills necessary for a total organizational development program might not be contained either in the police department or in the city or county government. If this is true, there must be a commitment from some outside resource such as a college, a private consultant, or industry. Many cities and police departments throughout the United States have called upon industry for voluntary support in the implementation of their organizational development programs, and in most instances industry has responded in a very positive and helpful manner.

The organizational development program as it is implemented must affect numerous activities and people within the police department. The communication process must be carefully evaluated and the decision-making process must be reviewed to determine whether or not it is to continue in its present format. The attitudes of personnel within the agency toward the values of the community and the department—as well as their individual values—must be clarified. Productivity must be clearly defined for the individual police department, with goals and objectives established, present activities evaluated, more activities introduced if necessary, and new forms of management and leadership developed. The impact of an organizational development program is not slight, and it has lasting effects. The police manager must recognize, prior to entering into an organizational development program, that although there is much to be gained, the risks are extremely high. Once organizational development is entered into and people are involved in the day-to-day decision-making process, an attempt to revert back to an autocratic, central decision-making type of organization becomes extremely difficult.

## DEVELOPING LEADERS

If leadership is such an important function for the future, how can leaders in law enforcement be developed? Police departments can, through appropriate measures, develop effective leaders. They can take potential leaders and have them work closely with present leaders. Such one-to-one relationships help transmit the ideas of the present to the leaders of the future. If the police chief is willing to take the risks and devote the time needed to develop leaders—with the understanding that some may blossom while others fail—new leaders can certainly emerge.

The police department may view an organizational chart as something to be implemented in an upside-down fashion on a day-to-day basis. This process defines the leader as one who receives information and sees to it that the organization hews to its stated purposes and goals. Telling it "like it is"—or being truthful—is an important function of any police leader who wishes to develop leaders.

It is possible to take a talented individual (a lieutenant or captain) and assign him to work for six to nine months with a very responsible leader. In effect, the department would then have two leaders. If this process were repeated at least twice each year the number of leaders to be developed in a five-year period would grow, thereby providing sufficient leadership for many years to come.

## ORGANIZATIONAL CULTURE

Every police department has its own organizational culture, sometimes referred to as the "informal rules and regulations" or the policies that may not be outlined in black and white. A police chief must recognize that these guidelines, though unwritten, tend to help subordinates recognize the limitations of their positive and negative behavior. A police chief greatly assists the operation of his department by readily recognizing the organizational culture he intends to develop over the years. Any culture can be designed, but it is best if it evolves in harmony with the department's purpose, goals, and objectives.

A police chief, in recognizing or evaluating the organizational culture, has to be able to respond to certain issues. The first of these involves the reputation of the department—how it is viewed by the community, city council, and news media. Do they see it as an effective organization that operates to meet the needs of the community, or do they regard it negatively, possibly even as staffed by incompetent officers?

Another issue is that of status, which involves primarily the internal operations of the department. Are there special units that are regarded by others in the department as being more prestigious? For example, are those assigned to investigations considered to be "sharper" than those assigned to patrol? Is an assignment to a certain function such as jail operations or the front desk considered a punishment detail? Status also includes such issues as age. For example, are the younger officers considered immature while the older officers are regarded as the informal leaders—or is the opposite true? The future of the department may be dictated by the value structures of the younger officers, and the older officers may be viewed as obstacles in the way of progress. Educational levels are also to be considered. Is it more important, even though it is not mentioned in regulations, to be a college graduate, or are equal opportunities granted to noncollege people in assignment as well as promotion?

A third issue in organizational culture involves the style of management that is prevalent throughout the department. Is the police department predominantly viewed as an autocratic organization? Is it seen as being controlled from the top, or is the role of the police chief and commanders more in coordination? How are decisions reached within the department? Are they reached only at the top? Are they reached predominantly in the middle? Is the position of lieutenant or sergeant considered to be an important position, or is it one that is viewed as having little informal power? The fourth issue deals with the perception that police personnel have of the department's overall responsibilities to the community. In many smaller communities, law-enforcement agencies may view themselves as guardians of the peace, spending most of their time with citizens in the community. In larger areas, especially in high-crime districts, police officers may sometimes view themselves as strong crime fighters who do not have opportunities to become closely united with the community.

The police chief has to examine the unwritten policies of the department carefully. For example, how is honesty implemented? Is honesty more important than loyalty? Is it O.K. to be honest as one goes up the chain of command—for example, answering any question regarding opinions, facts, or feelings from a superior but avoiding the sharing of such information with subordinates? For example, a captain might be willing to share the opinion, during a staff meeting with his chief and other captains, that he believes a certain practice to be ineffective. However, is the chief decided to implement the practice anyway, the captain would then be obliged to withhold his true feelings from his subordinates.

In any issue of organizational culture, there are guidelines to define good and bad behavior, what is right and what is wrong. The police chief can become keenly attuned to this organizational culture by observing the manner in which people behave on a day-to-day basis. For example, when he enters a room such as the records center, do employees have a tendency to appear busy and to avoid talking to him? Does the chief normally receive an answer like "fine" when he asks how things are going within the department? The care of equipment is often a clue to the culture of the department. If a department is strongly committed to its purposes, equipment will generally be in good condition, reflecting the commitment of the personnel. But where people are dissatisfied, perhaps feeling that the commanders of the department are not supportive or that the community and the city administration do not understand their problems, they may become careless in the upkeep of equipment.

In conclusion, it is important for the police chief to understand the organizational culture and how it can serve as an asset. It is an area of police department operations that he may eventually be able to use to influence people, not only on a short-term basis but even after his tenure. It is an area where problems can easily be identified and solutions quickly implemented.

## FOUNDATIONS OF ORGANIZATIONAL DEVELOPMENT

As outlined by Wendell L. French and Cecil H. Bell, Jr.,[1] the organizational development program rests on eight major foundations.

First, organizational development is an ongoing, interactive process. By this is meant something that is dynamic, that is constantly changing, and that constantly requires people within the police department to learn new skills and, in many instances, to disregard old practices. Under this principle, organizational development is to be viewed by the police manager not as a one-time solution to all her problems but rather as something to be carried on continually, with a constant view to improving the effectiveness of the whole organization.

Second, organizational development is a form of applied behavioral science. The organizational development program utilizes principles from psychology, sociology, economics, political science, and business administration. This list is by no means exhaustive, and the amount of information obtained from each of these sciences is dependent upon the necessary information that will be required to make logical and effective decisions in the total change process.

Third, organizational development is a reeducative strategy of change. These changes are rational and will develop the reasoning skills of people within the agency, as well as their technical and psychological skills. The police manager must recognize that people within her department can, through a reeducation process, develop new principles, new standards, and a new set of norms.

Fourth, organizational development views the police department from the viewpoint of systems. Events in the everyday operations of the department are not viewed as isolated incidents but are recognized as occurring in relationship to other events or issues. For example, the fact that a police officer may be able to institute effective crime prevention programs relates directly to the selection process, basic training, in-service training, information that may be provided through technical crime prevention units within the agency, and the role that she—as opposed to the specialists, supervisors, and managers—is supposed to play in such a program. All these come together in order to properly implement a successful organizational development program. The police manager, by understanding the systems approach, recognizes that he cannot completely change one part of the police department without in some way strongly influencing other parts. He recognizes that if he wants to change the system under which the department presently operates, then he must change the entire system, not just individual parts or components within it.

Fifth, organizational development is day-to-day approach to planned change. By this is meant that the organizational development program is based upon data evaluated as it affects cooperation of the department. It emphasizes the data that must be evaluated and viewed through a rational process as opposed to mere guesswork. This data-based information is checked to show that it is not just feelings emanating from the parent or child ego states of managers or personnel of the agency but has been verified by the adult ego state and can be effectively used in the organizational developmental program.

Sixth, organizational development is experienced-based. The reason for this is that people learn how to implement changes by actually implementing them. They do not necessarily learn the changes merely by having them passed on through written memoranda or individual training programs, all of which, however, might be a part of the process. It is important to recognize that when the police officers, supervisors, and managers are involved in the real experiences of changing and developing the department, they then are completely caught up in the process, which involves their minds, actions, and desires. This experience-based learning requires an evaluation of the facts and the experiences as they are developed and reviewed.

Seventh, organizational development emphasizes goal setting and planning. It is important that both the police department and the people employed by the department understand the agency's goals and their own individual goals, so that the agency and the personnel can manage the affairs and activities of the department and compare them against these measurable and obtainable goals. This goal setting and planning must be begun at both the individual and departmental levels, thereby guaranteeing that the values of the department and the individual will coincide and that organizational development will be a success rather than a failure.

Eighth, organizational and development activities focus on work teams. These work teams, many times referred to as task forces, bring together beliefs and experiences from many levels and units of the police department. As a result of this new information and the development of decision-making teams, the effect of the organizational development program is both immediate and lasting. The effect strongly affects the individual behavior not only of those people on the task forces but also of other people who come in direct contact with these task forces through providing necessary information and through informal contacts on a day-to-day basis.


# STRATEGIES FOR ORGANIZATIONAL DEVELOPMENT

## Task Forces

In the implementation of an organizational development program, it is advisable to use *task forces*. Task forces are made up of six to ten people who are directly involved with the issue under study. For example, if the department wants to implement a new staff allocation system, personnel should be chosen from the command-level structure, from the operations-analysis or records function, from the investigative division, and from the uniform operations division. In this way, a cross section of the department is brought together to help develop a specific solution of a specific issue.

The use of task forces is a common management practice, and they are beginning to be used extensively by police departments throughout the country.

Task forces may be developed on specific issues and, when they have finished developing their recommendations, a task force to argue "why not" can also be created. In this way, both the positive and negative features of any new potential changes can be brought to light and discussed before action is taken.

## Management Workshops

Management development workshops are a common aspect of organizational development. Within these workshops, intragroup relations are stressed and goals are established so that team development processes, from the management team to the implementation team at the bottom of the organization, can be effectively introduced. This helps to upgrade the educational and skill levels of the people involved in the workshops.

The use of consultants as observers during these workshops can be useful. They may help participants bring forth issues without fear of reprisal from commanders in the department or from other persons involved in the workshop. To help analyze present practices, the use of special types of instruments developed for industry have proved helpful. The formal managerial grid instrument can be given to all managers within the department, scored, and the differences between the scoring at different levels of the department can be used as a starting point for management workshop discussions. Another example is questionnaires developed by police departments to analyze the present level of agency morale.

## Retreats

A common practice for organizational development is the use of retreats. Here commanders or other selected individuals leave the home environment of the department and go away to some setting where they will not be disturbed by everyday problems. They openly discuss where they feel the department is going and what changes they would like to see implemented. The retreat process has been used effectively by agencies in Charlotte, North Carolina; Los Angeles, California; New York City; and the Multnomah County Sheriff's Department in Oregon. Retreats are not formal in nature but usually have a specific purpose and a set time frame within which to achieve that purpose.

In some cities that have implemented team policing, the retreat process has been used to enable the individual team to plan their goals, objectives, and strategies for the upcoming year. In Charlotte, North Carolina, such retreats are held at the team level at least two or three times a year. They are held regularly at the command level and are planned as needed for major problems that might arise during the year.

Police departments sometimes use the retreat process for the preliminary planning of their budgets. In this way, the immediate future of the department is carefully planned prior to the actual budget request.

## UTILIZING TEAM DECISION MAKING

By and large, police managers are unaware of how they can effectively utilize team decision making. Because they are unaware of the group dynamics involved in joining a number of people in the decision-making process, they have uneasy feelings about the quality of such decisions and only pay lip service or make a moderate commitment to team decision making.

One of the more productive ways that the manager can help to bring about changes within her organization is through the effective use of decision-making teams at different levels within the agency. For example, chiefs who surround themselves with key personnel, assistant chiefs, or captains can delegate responsibility, bring about strong commitment, and develop alternative solutions through team decision making.

As top managers become effective in team decision making, they can develop individual decision making within their own units. The captains or assistant chiefs then become the link between top and middle management. As middle managers learn to use team decision making effectively, they become the final link in the chain between the top level and the bottom.

One way for the police manager to convince the members of his department that team decision making is beneficial is by showing them the results of studies that have been done. Research has produced enough information to demonstrate the important aspects and the high degree of effectiveness that can be gained through team decision making. Early research comparing individual to team decision-making performance indicated that the decisions made by a team effort had a higher degree of effectiveness than decisions made by an individual. The probability of reaching a good decision increases with the number of individuals who become involved. It was found that the individuals within the group help to cancel out the errors that each individual brings into the decision-making process. Extreme judgments are neutralized, so that extremely bad decisions and extremely good decisions are never reached. Instead, through team decision making, effective decisions are made consistently. The decision is more effective because each member of the team has a commitment to that decision.

It should be noted that there is no rule as to the number of persons who can effectively operate within a decision-making team. The numbers usually range from four to ten. More than ten usually tends to create serious inter-action problems, and time is wasted trying to make adjustments and compromises.

Team decision making becomes more effective depending upon the procedure that is chosen. Within the group process, there are five alternatives available to the police manager. First, she can receive input from each member of the group and then make the decision alone. This is an individual decision, and she has merely consulted with other members of the group to get their opinions, ideas, or feelings. Second, it is possible for the team to take an average of the figures suggested by individuals within the team and then to implement the decision reached on an average by all members. Third, the team can use minority control; that is, a few key members of the team serve as the controlling factor in making the decision. Fourth, the team can agree upon a majority rule for arriving at a decision. Fifth, the team can arrive at a decision by consensus.

As indicated in Figure 17.1, the effectiveness of the decision increases according to the method used. The individual decision is usually the least effective and the consensus is the most effective.

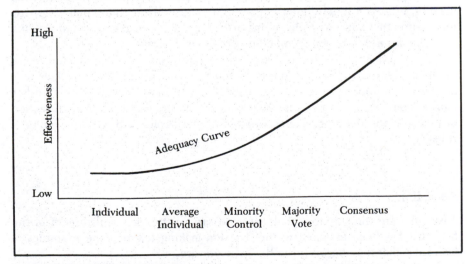

**Figure 17.1  Effective Decisions**

The police manager must realize that it is extremely difficult to have any of the last three techniques—minority control, majority vote, or consensus—in their pure form. In a department that relies on the minority-control technique, the decision-making team is usually ineffective because it becomes dependent on the abilities of the few key members of the team. For example, if the police manager listens to the opinions and ideas of one or two other team members only, the remaining members will lose interest in the whole process. Eventually, the "team" becomes those three people, and the others become rubber stamps.

The majority-vote technique relies more on the combined efforts and interaction of members of the decision-making team. Its decision is usually superior to that of the minority-control technique, since at least one more than half of the members must agree upon the decision. The interactions between members of the team are reflected in the final group decision. However, those members who have been outvoted are still unable to influence the final decision, and frustration still exists among members of the minority group. The police manager who uses the majority-vote technique must be careful not to cause or allow the members of his team to split into majority and minority groups. If this begins to occur, the police manager should take immediate steps to reevaluate the people on the decision-making team, the methods that are being used, and the criteria established by the team prior to entering into the decision-making process.

The consensus technique is a system in which all members of the decision-making team share equally in the final decision. Interaction among team members is encouraged, accepted, and utilized. No decision is accepted as final until each member of the team has given approval. As a result of these ground rules, the consensus technique produces decisions of superior quality to those achieved through minority rule or majority vote.

Because of the difficulty of implementing the consensus type of decision making, it is used less frequently than other procedures. Many police departments use the minority rule or majority vote in an effort to avoid conflict resulting from differences of opinion, values, or feelings.

In any effective decision-making team, there are needs which must be satisfied. Needs are directly related to the accomplishment of the task as well as to the development of strength within the decision-making team. In other words, there are two categories of activities that are related to the satisfaction of needs in the decision-making process: (1) task roles and (2) team-building roles.[2]

## Task Roles

Task roles are the activities that are necessary for the accomplishment of the task that has been assigned to the decision-making team. Some examples of task roles that may be taken by the manager are:

*Initiating activity*  In this role, the manager proposes solutions and suggests new ideas or gives new definitions of the problem so that all possible information relating to the issue can be brought out in the open.

*Seeking information*  In this role, the manager asks for clarification or suggestions, or he requests additional facts.

*Seeking opinions*  In this role, the manager looks for an expression of feeling from other members and seeks clarification of their values or ideas.

*Giving information*  The manager may offer facts or generalizations or give examples of his own experience so that other members of the team may have a clearer picture of the issues and the proposed solutions.

*Giving opinions*  The manager states an opinion or belief concerning a suggestion or the alternative solutions that have been recommended.

*Elaborating*  The manager clarifies the issues or alternative solutions, attempts to envision how the proposed solution may be implemented, and describes the effect it may have upon the police department as a whole.

*Coordinating*  The manager ties together the suggestions and activities of various members of the team.

*Summarizing*  The manager pulls together the related ideas or suggestions and formulates the overall plan on which the team must vote.

## Team-Building Roles

There are team-building and maintenance roles that must be performed by the manager in any team decision-making process. These are the functions that are required for strengthening and maintaining the team itself. These roles include:

*Giving encouragement*  The manager must be responsive to others, give praise for ideas that are worthy of praise and accept the contributions of other team members.

*Gatekeeper*  The manager should make it possible for all members to make a contribution to the team. She should also limit talking time so that each member of the team may have a chance to be heard.

*Setting standards*  The manager should express the standards that have been established for the team in order to avoid making decisions that will be in conflict with those standards.

*Following*  The manager must be prepared to go along with the decision of the team, to accept the ideas of other members, and to serve as a sounding board during team discussions.

*Summarizing*  The manager must be able to express group feelings and reactions to the team ideas or solutions.

There are also a series of behaviors that are really both task roles and team-building roles. These include:

*Evaluating*  The manager must compare the team decisions to the goals and objectives that were previously established by the team.

*Diagnosing*  The manager must be able to determine sources of difficulty, know what steps should be taken, and help the team analyze the main obstacles to progress.

*Consensus testing*  The manager must be able to determine by asking questions whether the team is nearing consensus on a decision or whether they are still extremely far away from agreement.

*Mediating*  The manager should be able to reconcile differences in points of view and be able to work out compromise solutions when necessary.

*Relieving tension*  The manager should have the ability to allay hostile and negative feelings that may exist within the team over a certain issue.

The police manager, in developing a decision-making team, should be aware of situations in which members of the team behave in a way that is not beneficial to the overall objectives and goals of the department. There may be occasions when the other members of the command-level staff or other decision-making teams may, by their comments or behavior, hinder the progress of the team.

Some members of the team may become aggressive and begin to work for status within the team by criticizing, blaming others, or showing hostility toward the team, the department, or an individual within the department. Another common form of negative behavior is that of seeking recognition as an individual. Some members may interfere with the progress of the team by going off on tangents or by citing personal experiences that are totally unrelated to the problem. Or they may argue and reject the ideas of others without considering the value of the ideas. Seeking sympathy is another type of negative behavior. The individual may try to induce another team member to be sympathetic to his problems or misfortunes when they have no bearing upon the progress of the team.

Competition, or overcompeting, is another type of behavior that the police manager should be aware of. One member may attempt to produce the "best ideas" all the time or to talk more than the others so that she will gain favor with the police manager who is leading the team discussion. At the other extreme is the member who seems indifferent or passive. In effect, this individual has withdrawn from the group.

The police manager must avoid placing blame on individuals who exhibit negative behavior patterns and are nonfunctional in regard to the purpose of the team. The manager must realize that such behavior is a symptom or a signal that the team itself is not being as effective as it could be.

One of the first tasks that a team should undertake is the establishment of criteria by which the team can measure its own effectiveness. Criteria should be graded on a scale of one to ten, ten being the highest. About once a month, the decision-making team should take the time to carefully evaluate where it is in relation to each of the criteria it has established. As each criterion or objective is achieved, new criteria can be added. Within a short time, the decision-making team should be functioning effectively, based upon the quality and ability of the people involved.

For a police manager to develop a decision-making team, he must have patience, understanding, and an ability to delegate responsibility to subordinates. The rewards from developing team decision making far outweigh the efforts necessary to implement the process.

Assuming that it becomes impossible for the decision-making team to arrive at a consensus decision, it is advisable for the chief of police and his key managers, working as a team, to arrive at a majority commitment to the decision and implementation. Usually a 75 percent majority is preferable to 50 percent plus one. This strengthens commitment.

## DEVELOPING ORGANIZATIONAL TEAMWORK

The police manager can bring about effective teamwork within his department by establishing systematic procedures. He must determine what is to be done, how it is to be done, who is to do it, and, eventually, how effectively it is being accomplished. This process of developing organizational teamwork can also provide a basis for reviewing the progress of change, for helping to identify problems, and for planning individual and group development.

The first step for the police manager is to clarify the work requirements. He must reach an agreement with subordinates as to the functions and responsibilities that are to be performed, the authority that will be given to the subordinates, and the expected results.

The development of the functions–authority–results (FARs) is the key to the careful development of organizational teamwork between the manager and his subordinates. A simple three-column table, as shown in Figure 17.2, can easily be established. In the first column, both the subordinate and the manager agree upon the tasks that the subordinate is responsible for performing. Next, the police manager must outline the authority he is willing to give to the subordinate. Authority may be broken down into levels: (1) the manager may require the subordinate to report before acting; (2) the subordinate may have the authority to act and then report to the manager; and (3) the subordinate may be given complete authority, meaning that he is responsible only for the overall results of his actions.

The police manager should recognize that the tasks may be quite similar for each of his subordinates but the levels of authority can be different. As the subordinate begins to exhibit an ability to accept responsibility, the level of authority can move from report–act to complete authority.

| Function | Authority | Result |
|---|---|---|
| Organizational structure | Act–report | Simplified structure |
| Budget preparation | Report–act | Prepare line-item budget |
| Assignment of personnel | Complete | Scheduled by incidents |
| Robbery prevention programs | Complete | 5% robbery reduction |

**Figure 17.2**   Function–Authority–Results (FARs)

Once this major step has been clarified and agreement has been reached on the FARs, then the manager can divide his attention between the management of tasks and the management of his subordinates. Under the broad category of management of personnel, he should evaluate and improve the performance of his subordinates. This comes under the third column.

It is also the manager's responsibility to assess the potential his subordinates have for future development. Working with his subordinate, the police manager should plan a career-development program for him. This program should indicate possible paths or promotions and the acceptance of added responsibilities within the framework of his present assignment. The purpose of this process is to guarantee the utilization of the abilities of the subordinate, ensuring growth for both the individual and the department.

In managing tasks, the second responsibility of the manager, he should review the work progress and the problems generated in attempting to carry out the FARs. Specific objectives must be set, and they must be carefully evaluated to determine whether or not they have been reached. It is important that problems be analyzed, that decisions be reached concerning the overcoming of obstacles, and that action be taken by both the manager and the subordinate to solve the problems in bringing about change.

Figure 17.3 indicates the process of organization for the manager. Through this process, the department is strengthened and the abilities of the individuals within the department are developed to their fullest.

## APPROACHES TO THE ORGANIZATIONAL DEVELOPMENT PROCESS

Approaches to change fall into two broad categories, those oriented toward changing people and those oriented to changing the structure or system.

People-oriented approaches include attempts to change the philosophies and attitudes of the individuals within the department. Many police agencies send key personnel to specialized schools with the hope that exposure to new information will enable them to perform assigned functions adequately. An agency may also provide consultants for the same purpose. But for the most part, this approach has not proved to be very successful for police departments.

In some instances it is necessary for the police manager to transfer individuals who hold key positions. By transferring personnel on a periodic basis, the manager can bring in "new blood" to initiate changes in the day-to-day operations. These periodic changes in position can be seen as a challenge and often produce a commitment to implementing new procedures. This approach seems to be more effective than attempting to change the individual who is presently holding the position.

Another people-oriented approach to change is team development. Starting with the managers at the top level, team training programs can be implemented. Each unit forms a cohesive team that forces evaluation of present practices and instills in the members a commitment to change and upgrade

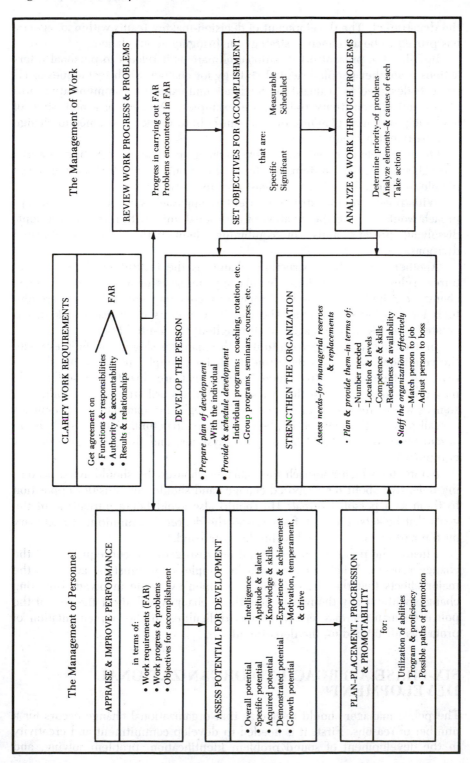

**Figure 17.3  The Foundations of Management**

the department. The development of decision-making teams within an agency has proved to be an effective strategy for bringing about change.

Revising the present organizational climate as it relates to personal interactions is another people-oriented strategy for change. Such techniques as (1) projects designed to evaluate the feedback and exposure communicative processes and (2) sensitivity training are examples. Developing a new style of leadership or a new planning process can help to reduce resistance to change in department personnel.

Other people-oriented strategies, such as pay raises, creating rewards through an evaluation system, or initiating a strong control system that forces people to change have been the least effective strategies.

With regard to the structure-oriented approaches for change, one approach would require the creation of additional units within the department, dissolving present units, or combining them with already established divisions.

Another approach for structural change is the institution of new procedures, rules, and regulations. By placing emphasis on enforcing the rules, changes can be implemented. Changes in technology and equipment are also tools for revising the system. The use of computers in decision making has created changes in police agencies throughout the United States.

In deciding which approach to use, the manager should carefully evaluate the conditions in his own department. If, for example, he feels that the climate for change is positive, then changes that are directed toward people may prove more effective than those directed toward structure. In other instances where resistance to change may be high, the manager may begin his overall process through the implementation of structural changes such as reorganization, development of computer systems, and the purchasing of new equipment.

No matter which approach the manager chooses, he should avoid becoming defensive about his proposed changes and should not consider opposition to them as a personal threat. He should also avoid being unrealistic in the goals that he sets, the time frames, and the degree of commitment necessary on the part of the personnel within his command.

Finally, the police manager should not disregard the consequences of the change process. Whatever approach he employs, he must be aware of the major effects that the strategy will have upon everyone involved. Initiating changes without any thought to how these changes will affect the rest of the police department may create serious difficulties in the implementation of programs for upgrading the department.

## SIX-PHASE APPROACH TO ORGANIZATIONAL DEVELOPMENT[3]

The police manager should recognize that organizational change occurs for a number of reasons. First, it is needed to develop commitment and creativity in the development of sound problem identification, problem solving, and decision making within the department. The organizational change should foster mental attitudes that will result in the achievement of goals and overall growth of the department.

Good interpersonal relations should be a strong part of any developmental process for change. The police manager should, through organizational development and change, establish standards and values that will continue to promote efforts of excellence and innovation within the agency.

The six-phase approach outlined here is a format for implementing organizational change.

## Phase One: Seminar and Workshop Training

Under this phase, all departmental personnel are introduced to the new concepts of management and to the rational tools they can use in implementing organizational change.

## Phase Two: Team Development

Under this phase, decision-making teams are established throughout the agency. It is mandatory that the team development begin at the top of the organization rather than in the middle or at the bottom. The personnel must learn how to work and cooperate as a team. They should develop the techniques and abilities necessary to arrive at consensus decisions and to begin to build confidence in their decision-making procedures.

## Phase Three: Horizontal and Vertical Linking of the Chain of Command

In this phase, the members of the numerous decision-making teams begin to regroup, forming new decision-making teams in order to bring the department together. Although each member has developed confidence in his initial team, the bringing together of new people at different levels will create new teams, each of which will have its own characteristics. It is in this process that the police captain, who had been involved with the uniform commander's decision-making team, now begins to play the role of team leader with his subordinates—lieutenants and sergeants—who have also established a decision-making team. This captain may also become involved as a member of other projects relating directly or indirectly to his assigned functions.

## Phase Four: Long-Range Organizational Blueprint

At this stage, the departmental concepts are tested for their validity and value. The management practices that are beneficial to the agency are developed, and a long-range plan for the future is produced. Goals and objectives are established and put into definite time frames.

The police manager must recognize that the implementation of phases one through four will take a minimum of one year, and—depending upon the size and condition of the agency—could take as long as three years.

## Phase Five: Implementation of Established Objectives

Under this phase, the numerous decision-making teams are totally integrated, the department is solidified, and the initial long-range goals are met. During this phase, the rational aspects of management by objectives, program budgeting, and the final major organizational structure are achieved.

## Phase Six: Stabilization

Under this phase, which usually comes approximately one year after phase five has been implemented, the agency moves into reevaluation. It is at this stage that the department is examined to see that there has been no reversion to the old ways.

This six-phase process should take from three to six years to implement.

These six steps describe a major organizational development process, and the police manager must be constantly aware of the need for minor changes within the department while it is going on.

# EXPECTATIONS OF ORGANIZATIONAL DEVELOPMENT

Once the organizational development program is implemented and begins to become effective, what can the police manager expect? First, he can expect improved job satisfaction for people within the department. This might not necessarily be true for 100 percent of the people, but it will certainly be true for a large majority of the personnel, including civilians, police officers, supervisors, and managers. Other major expectations could be increased productivity and the better use of the resources available to the police manager. He will now be able to address problems in a more logical and rational manner, and these problems can be carefully analyzed, identified, and possibly even prevented. At least partial solutions to the problems may be implemented as quickly as possible.

A major benefit of an effective organizational development program will be a clear understanding of the limits of the police service that can be provided by the police department based upon the resources it is given by the governing board. In this manner, the police chief and his managers will, on an annual basis, be able to show what types of calls for service they can answer, what the crime rate most probably will be within their community, and how much it will cost to bring about any major changes in the level of service or crime rate for the upcoming year. The organizational development program will not only increase the effectiveness of communications between the police department and outside agencies (including the governing board) but also force an open and effective communicative process within the police department itself.

If police departments are to meet the challenges of the future, they must accept the problems of the present and develop a method and system to bring about change, to deal with conflict, and to upgrade the quality of service they provide to the citizens of their community. The future of law enforcement depends on the police manager's ability to guide the department in meeting these challenges. He must be able to develop a department in which effectiveness is the key word, officers take pride in their work, and changes necessary for departmental improvement are implemented. Each member of the police profession must feel he or she is a worthwhile contributor to the overall growth of law enforcement.

In order for the criminal justice manager to become a successful person in his field, he must continue to mature. "Maturity" refers to many different aspects of growth. However, within the context of this discussion, it refers to the following elements:

Maturity is the ability to control anger and to settle differences without violence or destruction. Maturity is patience. It is the willingness to pass up immediate pleasure in favor of the long-term gain.

Maturity is perseverance, the ability to sweat out a project or a situation in spite of heavy opposition and discouraging setbacks. Maturity is the capacity to face unpleasantness and frustration, discomfort and defeat, without complaint or collapse.

Maturity is humility. It is being big enough to say "I was wrong." And, when right, the mature person need not experience the satisfaction of saying "I told you so." Maturity is the ability to make a decision and stand by it. The immature spend their lives exploring endless possibilities, then they do nothing.

Maturity means dependability, keeping one's word, and coming through in a crisis. The immature are masters of the alibi. They are confused and disorganized. Their lives are a maze of broken promises, former friends, unfinished business, and good intentions that somehow never materialize.

Maturity is the art of living in peace with that which we cannot change, the courage to change that which should be changed, and the wisdom to know the difference.

## NOTES

1. Wendell L. French and Cecil H. Bell, Jr., *Organization Development* (Englewood Cliffs, N.J.: Prentice-Hall, 1973)
2. D. Cartwright and A. Zander, *Group Dynamics, Research and Theory* (Evanston, Ill.: Row, Peterson & Company, 1960)
3. Robert R. Blake and Jane S. Mouton, *Grid Organization Development* (Houston, Texas: Gulf Publishing Company, 1968)

# CHAPTER 18

# *The Future*

The word "future" itself brings up ideas reminiscent of science fiction. It suggests a world of fantasy and evokes dreams that may eventually lead to action. The future cannot be predicted precisely, but without an anticipatory vision, it may seem frightening and unmanageable.

The future belongs to those who have the foresight to plan, the intelligence to implement their plans, and the courage to take personal risks in order to bring about improvements over the present or past.

The police leader of the future will deal with critical choices on a daily basis. His decisions will be basically positive but will also have a negative potential. In short, every leader must have the capacity to apply the lessons of the past to the problems that are yet to be faced.

A major issue for the police leader of the future will be the amount of control required to operate the individual agency. There are two areas in which, if a police leader loses control, he will no longer be able to direct departmental operations: finance and personnel. It is incumbent, therefore, upon the leader of the future to attempt in all ethical, legal, and moral ways to gain control over the financial resources of the department and over its personnel practices. In bureaucratic situations, tradeoffs may be required that call for compromise, as when the demands of law enforcement must bow to a level of equality with other agencies of city or county government. If law enforcement is really to reach its highest level of effectiveness, this must be done in other ways than by attempting to place law-enforcement agencies on a par with all others. The law itself has recognized that law-enforcement officers are required to operate at a higher legal standard than other members of government. This is because of the ultimate responsibility and trust placed in each officer at each moment of his or her life. If officers are to be accountable and if chiefs are to be accountable for the officers' behavior, then they must be able to implement the high standards required to bring about what we would consider to be truly professional law enforcement.

## SUCCESSFUL POLICE AGENCIES

In their book *In Search of Excellence*, Thomas J. Peters and Robert H. Waterman, Jr., studied a series of successful American companies and found that certain common factors tended to create an effective organizational culture and allowed the company to achieve its goals. In this author's experience over many years, these same criteria can generally be applied to a police department.

## Typical Factors

For years theorists have stated that the critical success factors included zero-base budgeting, management by objectives, matrix organization, the use of computers, strategic planning, and management science techniques. After looking at law-enforcement agencies throughout the country, the author has found that poor police departments use all of these strategies. So do good police departments. These strategies, however, are basically techniques that can be purchased or installed—much as a tire can be placed on a car or a stereo system in a home—without necessarily providing all the requisites for departmental effectiveness.

## Effective Factors

The following factors seem to be characteristic of police departments that are successful in reaching their stated goals and in developing a climate where people are committed to their work. The first and major factor is a bias on the part of the police chief toward some form of action. Words such as "we must delay" or "it may not be the right time" are not used in these departments. Instead, there is an emphasis upon performing now and the willingness to take some risks to achieve the department's important goals. Police leaders in the future, therefore, should have a bias toward such action.

The second factor is that effective police departments are usually simple in their organizational structure. They have a lean staff—that is, a small ratio of staff to line personnel—which requires line-assignment members such as patrol and investigations to make many decisions that affect the activities of the entire department. Personnel within the department are keenly aware of the leader's role, personality, and goals.

A third factor is that such departments are oriented toward productivity, and such productivity depends on the improvement of the people within the agency—not just on mechanical devices such as computers or fancy equipment. This is not to downgrade computers or fancy equipment but only to say that they do not determine the level of productivity. Only where each individual within the department develops the highest possible capability does productivity reach enormous heights. In such departments, people are treated as individuals regardless of whether they act in an individual or team capacity. In such departments, commanders of units are not told how to do their jobs but rather what they are expected to achieve. For example, a patrol shift may be told to reduce the number of armed robberies being committed in a certain area of the community during a certain time against a certain target, such as convenience stores. The manner in which this goal is reached is left up to the people who are responsible for the actual implementation.

Thus they become both autonomous and accountable. Individual officers know where they stand and also how well they are doing with the ideas that they have generated and put together as a group.

The author has also found that there is a fourth factor. The police leader emphasizes a few key goals and does not burden the department with so many rules and regulations that the big picture is lost. Instead, three to five goals are defined, such as reduction of the crime rate, quicker response time, and development of department personnel. The role of the leader is to see that these purposes are achieved. Almost every action that follows—whether initiated by police officers, supervisors, or mid-managers—is geared toward the achievement of the three major goals. An example is offered by the McDonald's food chain, which stresses that (1) its stores are to be kept clean, (2) people are to be kept moving in and out, and (3) each outlet is to sell its food at prices equal to or lower than those of other fast-food chains in the area. These three simple guidelines have helped to make an idea grow into a multibillion-dollar business.

In a similar way, a highly effective police department might stress the following goals: (1) that requests from the public are to receive the most immediate possible response, (2) that all police officers are to do their utmost always to be courteous, and (3) that the law is to be justly enforced.

Finally, while the police leader should have controls to see that work is completed, he should also be willing to loosen these controls when needed and to spend extra time in attempting to coordinate activities and communicate purposes. "Loose but tight" controls include the ability to allow personnel and the department to make judgments at any time to do whatever is best in a given situation. Rules are therefore viewed not as rigid controls but rather as guidelines. They may be observed most of the time, but people can still feel free to come up with new solutions to special problems so as to do whatever is best for the department and the community. This requires the police leader who can be both flexible and consistent—flexible in day-to-day operations but consistent in the overall direction of the department.

What, then, does all this suggest about the police leaders of the future? It would seem that police leaders will not be able to hide behind traditional practices. They will not be able to find easy acceptance by defining activities, such as the number of arrests or miles driven. These leaders may have to play a much stronger role, having to take and defend strong stands. They will have to build imaginative police departments that can continue to grow, develop, and help bring about a better life for all.

## LEADERSHIP VALUES

The police executives of the future will carefully examine their values and their relationships with other members of the law-enforcement profession, their individual agencies, and to the world at large. They will want to know exactly where they stand with regard to the following principles.

## Freedom

Our individual freedoms are guaranteed by the Constitution of the United States, and a major concern is their continued implementation. The role of the police executive will be to redefine continually the balance between individual freedoms and the rights of society as a whole. Police executives are responsible for seeing that their individual communities are safe and secure and that crime and its causes are kept at a minimum level. In the real world, however, the resources needed to eliminate crime and its causes will never be fully available. Moreover, the control of crime cannot be the sole responsibility of the police. Therefore it is up to the police executive to educate society about its responsibility and to determine what price that society is willing to pay, how much suffering society is willing to bear, and how much society is willing to sacrifice for the sake of crime prevention and control. Beyond feeling protected from the actual commission of crime, citizens are entitled to feel safe and secure within their communities. (It is also incumbent upon the police leader to create a work environment that allows police personnel to consider themselves worthwhile human beings who are continuing to develop their full career potential.)

## Dignity, Respect, and Trust

Police leaders must also believe that law-enforcement agencies can function with dignity, respect, and trust, inspiring respect from individual citizens and the community. In order to achieve this status, police agencies must strive for efficiency, effectiveness, and justice.

The police leader of the future must overcome the traditional idea that police officers are servants of the public. A more constructive view is that police officers are professional people in the same sense as other professionals who offer their communities special skills. This will increase the dignity of law-enforcement personnel and allow them to achieve a high level of effectiveness. This philosophy was successfully developed and implemented by Chief Ted Meyer of Pompano Beach, Florida. Within his first three years, dignity returned to officers as individuals and as a team. They became more effective and their productivity almost doubled.

## Accountability

Another value that will be strongly enforced in the future is that individuals are accountable for their actions.

Bureaucratic organizations tend to work toward three major goals: (1) to justify their existence, (2) to avoid conflict, and (3) to avoid making mistakes. Therefore the issue of individual accountability rarely arises; instead, the system is held to be accountable. The difficulty is that systems are run by people, and it is they who must change.

Bureaucracies are sometimes involved in so many peripheral activities that they never come to grips with their most important tasks and thus fail to fulfill their stated purposes.

A common example occurs at the level of first-line supervision in law-enforcement agencies. The leader of the future must be willing to hold supervisors and mid-managers accountable for their individual behavior and for the behavior of their subordinates, especially when they knew or should have known the actions of their subordinates. It is important that leaders of the future stress accountability and, with it, the necessary authority. That is, those who are held accountable must have the freedom to succeed and the freedom to fail. Accountability will probably be the most delicate but also one of the more important issues faced by the police leader of the future.

The future will demonstrate that police leaders who effectively strive to implement the major values and beliefs discussed above will achieve success in law enforcement and in our society. The individual department, the community, and the law-enforcement profession will be better off for their efforts.

## PERSONAL CHARACTERISTICS

Police leaders of the future must realize that they do not necessarily have any special insight—no special credentials that will guarantee their total success. Instead, they must possess certain characteristics.

In examining law-enforcement agencies for over twenty years, the author has come to the conclusion that effective leaders and those that will be effective in the future implement on a daily basis three major characteristics. These include (1) attitude, (2) courage, and (3) enthusiasm.

### Attitude

Attitude is defined as a position assumed for a specific purpose. The police leader of the future must assume the position of being a winner for the purpose of achieving. A winner is one who shapes the world; nonwinners are those who accept the world as it is; and losers are those who proceed to set impossible goals or no goals at all, thereby depriving themselves of success and guaranteeing failure. In order to develop this kind of attitude, police leaders must constantly seek the truth and must have the necessary skill to use this truth. Their attitude should include the strong commitment to implementing the truth, thereby guaranteeing the success they seek. Police leaders of the future need to recognize that they are whatever they think they are. If they firmly believe they can win, they will. If they believe that they are going to lose, they will lose.

Police leaders of the future can test their attitude, especially when they come face to face with an obstacle. If they stop behind the obstacle and stay there, committing their entire energies only to complaining about the presence of such an obstacle, they will probably lose. If, on the other hand, they have the winning attitude—the ability to go through the obstacle, around it, over it, and in some instances even under it—they will win. A winning attitude defines the purposes of the department as more important than its rules. If rules present an obstacle to the achievement of these purposes, rules can be changed.

Leaders with positive and winning attitudes do not say things like "They made me do it" or "We can't make it." They never use the words "I can't," since this can become a "cancer of the brain," bringing about failure in the present and in the long-term future. Police leaders recognize that a positive idea is unbeatable. Their attitude is one of accepting responsibility and being accountable for their individual behavior and the decisions necessary to run the agency.

## Courage

The second important characteristic is courage. Courage is defined as the inner strength to preserve one's legal, ethical, and moral values. These values must first be established; their priorities must be placed upon them. For example, will it be more important to be honest with people or to be tactful? Will it be more important to be honest and admit one's mistakes or to try to avoid criticism? The effective leader has the ability to be honest, to trust others and himself, to implement his attitudes with courage, and to practice self-discipline. Self-discipline is the ability to eliminate those parts of one's behavior that serve no useful purpose. The police leader who can speak to large groups and does so in an effective manner is not necessarily practicing self-discipline. However, such discipline is shown by the police leader who may feel uncomfortable in such situations but is still willing to take part in them, proceeds to practice, and does a good job.

When a police leader achieves courage, he has the ability to believe in the personnel of the department. The leader will have the courage to share ideas, set goals, and produce loose but necessary controls to see to it that ideas are effectively realized. He also has the ability to be open and honest with all. Courage is the ingredient that allows the leader and others to be accountable for their individual behavior.

A police leader recognizes that he or she has three separate aspects: goals, joys, and individual behavior patterns. There is what she wants to be, her potential for the future, and what others think she is. This latter part is nothing more than an approximation of the truth. Effective police leaders do not waste time and energy in trying to impress people but rather press forward to achieve their potential. They are willing to be what they really are.

It takes courage to deal with others in a police department. The police leader of the future must express such courage. She must attempt to praise people in the department and not spend time criticizing. A leader will walk the halls and speak both to people who report directly to her and to anyone else in the agency. The leader will take a few minutes each day to develop others' self-esteem. She must be willing to be honest, must recognize that personnel of the department hunger for the truth and for the opportunity to tell the truth. She will want to share their opinions, their judgment, their feelings, and the facts they know. Such steps demonstrate that she is satisfied with the present but looking forward to a more productive future.

It takes courage, but police leaders of the future will recognize that, in dealing with people, their true impressions must be reflected in their actual responses—otherwise they will come across as insincere.

### Enthusiasm

Enthusiasm is defined as a strong, positive sense of excitement and anticipation. It is the yeast that allows us to grow. It is the leadership quality upon which all others depend. With it, the police leader has everything; without it, he has very little. People with enthusiasm demonstrate it by the sparkle in their eyes, the swing in their walk, and the energy with which they implement their plans. Police leaders who develop alibis and excuses are usually dooming themselves to a life that lacks enthusiasm and to an eventual loss of respect and trust.

In order to possess and demonstrate such enthusiasm the leader must try to do things differently than we may have done them in the past. For example, when we feel down or depressed, we act in a depressive way that then makes us even more depressive. Instead, effective leaders begin to act enthusiastically about any project, about the work environment, about the people they work with and the opportunity to spread ideas and see people and projects grow. Once one begins to act in an enthusiastic manner and to feel enthusiastic, one continues to do so. The loser has a tendency to place his actions on top of his feelings, the winner has a tendency to place the feelings on top of the actions.

Effective police leaders are winners when they practice attitude, courage, and enthusiasm. It is rare to find an effective leader who was ever an enthusiastic loser. Instead enthusiasm makes one bubble over with the ability to win.

Enthusiasm is dangerous, but so is fire. Effective law enforcement did not really begin until people possessed the kind of enthusiasm that grew like a fire and made their departments the realities of their dreams. An enthusiastic police leader is possessed with a spirit that allows him to go further than others. He is a driving force that no power can overcome. It is the choice of the leader of the future to accept life enthusiastically, enjoy it, and to change it for the better or to accept the world and to follow the direction of others.

## POLICE CHIEF, CITY MANAGER, AND COUNCIL

### Police Chief to City Manager

Every police chief who reports to a city manager will eventually become aware of the role that he must play with the city manager. It is important, therefore, to understand the city manager's point of view—that is, what the city manager may expect from the police chief, what the city manager may expect from the council or commission, and, finally, what normally commissions or councils expect from their city manager.

In the first instance, the city manager has certain expectations from his chief of police. The chief must recognize that he is but one department head and in many instances can only spend a few hours on a weekly basis dealing with his city manager. In some instances, as in large communities, this contact may consist of only formal staff meetings and informal sessions over lunch. What, then, does the city manager really expect from his chief of police?

The average city manager expects the police chief to give professional advice. He expects the police chief to know law enforcement. Although he might not expect the chief individually to be able to answer all questions, he surely expects the police department to provide the office of the manager with a solution and other alternatives as well. The chief of police must therefore be able to effectively communicate to a nonpolice person, the city manager, in language that the city manager can understand.

A city manager expects the chief of police to present the police department's point of view. It is incumbent upon the police chief to know the department and the views of the police officers. The police chief is not expected to play games with his manager. He is not expected to use highly technical arguments when the real problem may be nothing more than a difference in points of view or an understanding of differences of opinion. Police chiefs should attempt to make themselves understood and, whenever possible, not become involved in highly emotional discussions, thereby creating feelings of anger on the part of one or the other.

The manager expects the police chief to understand the broader point of view. The manager will expect the police chief not only to recognize the need for budget restrictions within the police department but also to understand and analyze the budgetary problems that face the city as a whole. It is incumbent upon the police chief to learn something from other department heads concerning the priorities they may have and—just as important—what they consider to be necessary to serve the citizens of the community effectively.

The city manager expects the police chief to be a manager. He expects the police chief to assume necessary responsibility to take initiative and be accountable. Normally, a city manager would expect the police chief to make recommendations and not continually ask the city manager what he, the manager, wants done. The police chief should therefore have his information carefully analyzed before discussing any serious issue with the city manager. The police chief is expected to be candid with the city manager about what the manager needs to hear in order to pass information to other department heads, administrative personnel, and the council or commission. It is imperative that the police chief keep the city manager advised of serious issues such as high absenteeism or the effect of poor equipment before the city manager finds out about such issues by reading about them in the newspaper or listening to criticism from his council. It is usually better for a police chief to provide more information than less. When important facts are left out, these facts may come back to haunt both parties, not only in dealing with that issue but, more importantly, in dealing with the long-term issue of a relationship of trust.

It is incumbent upon the chief of police to attempt to be as understanding as possible about disagreements. It is advisable for a chief of police not to attempt to place a city manager in a corner so that he has but one alternative. Under all circumstances, share the information so that there are no big surprises for the city manager that could make him feel that he has been placed in such a corner.

In summary then, it is incumbent upon the city manager and chief of police, through day-to-day contacts, to develop a relationship of earned respect and trust in which honesty plays an important role.

## City Manager to Council

A city manager has expectations of his council or commission. He normally expects the council to advise him of what they expect the manager to accomplish. The manager would expect the council or commission to give the city manager instant feedback, especially when any problems exist. The city manager would expect his council to observe behaviors within city government, including those of police officers, and report back on those observations. The manager would further expect that when such issues do arise, they be brought to the city manager's attention rather than directly to department heads.

The city manager would expect the council to bring employee issues such as tardiness, sloppiness, or ineffective work habits to him for possible action. The city manager expects that the council will support the manager in increasing service levels, in reducing costs, and in improving the image of city government in general. Overall, the city manager expects his council to be supportive and positive not only in the program area but also in helping to develop new directions, so that the major purposes of city government can eventually be achieved.

## City Council to Manager

The police chief must also be aware that the typical city council or commission has certain expectations of the city manager. In many instances these expectations can only be fulfilled by a close working relationship between the city manager and the police chief.

Most councils expect their city managers to keep them as informed as possible as to what is going on. They would expect their manager to be abreast of problems, especially those that become public. For example, if there were a series of newspaper articles concerning the promotional process within the police department, they would expect the city manager to be aware of how the police department was dealing with these issues.

Councils expect the city manager to explain to them what the manager needs in order to perform his duties effectively. They expect the manager to make specific recommendations as to how an issue—such as the image of a department or the reduction of employee dissatisfaction—could be resolved.

City councils expect to evaluate the important key positions within city government. Normally this includes the position of chief of police. Therefore, the chief of police, in sharing as much as possible, is able to guarantee that the council itself will gain further knowledge of the performance of the police chief. A council expects the city manager to keep them abreast of any legal actions that may be brought against the city. For example, if a police union refuses to accept the promotional testing process and intends to file a lawsuit, it is incumbent upon the city manager to keep the council advised from the moment of possible rumors until the conclusion of any lawsuit.

In general, the city council expects the city manager to get everything done on time, at a low cost, and without disrupting service to the citizens. Obviously this is an impossible task. However, the police chief can help the city manager to try to achieve a high degree of success. Finally, the city council expects their manager to be in good health. Therefore it is incumbent upon the police chief to share the workload, not only running the police department but also in helping to run the entire city government. Otherwise, the city manager's job may become one in which people burn out and become ineffective after only two or three years, thereby adding to the problems of the chief of police.

## MODELS FOR THE FUTURE

If we are to look to the future, how can this be accomplished? The models that follow are but two ways of looking at the past and the present to help one predict the trends of the future.

### From Idea to Growth

The future of law enforcement may sometimes be characterized in the analogy of an individual who plants a garden. In the first step there is a vision. Then the ground is cleared and the garden is planned. The task of fostering growth in an organization is difficult and usually requires people who have courage and foresight. This kind of character was exhibited by the pioneers of our country.

Once the area has been plowed, seeds are planted. Without such seeds, flowers will never grow, and neither will law-enforcement agencies unless police leaders implement their ideas. The third step involves the actual growing and caring of the flowers. In law enforcement, this represents our daily activities. It represents our obligation to see to it that our plans and initial efforts are not allowed to wither and die.

It is incumbent upon the leader of the future to see to it that he or she spends time in plowing the field and generating new ideas, concepts, and goals. The leader trains the people and sees to it that necessary equipment is available and the agency works toward the overall goals and purposes of the police department. Finally, on a day-to-day basis, the leader of the future allows the flowers to grow—that is, personnel within the department are allowed to mature to reach their full potential and the department is allowed to reach its organizational potential.

## Factors–Areas–Trends

This model[1] addresses areas of the police leader's life that might be affected by the future and the factors that affect these areas.

These kinds of factors may, for example, include (1) inflation, (2) social trends, (3) technology, (4) crime, (5) civil litigation, and (6) the court system.

Broad areas that may be affected include (1) personal life, which includes police managers, their families, their careers, and their finances; (2) the community; (3) the government; (4) the economy; (5) society in general; and (6) law enforcement itself.

The police leader, by being able to compare each factor against the individual areas, will have some idea of what the next five to ten years may hold. An example of how this model may be applied is shown in Figure 18.1.

Once a series of factors are examined against areas, then trends can be developed. Trends can be in a straight line. For example, if the crime rate rises 2 percent each year for ten years, chances are pretty good that the trend will continue. Trends can also be cyclical in nature. Here they may go from boom to bust. An example would be the factor of inflation, when budgets at the police department will sometimes be high for two or three years. In harder economic times, budgets may be low, requiring the police leader to develop practices and procedures to balance resources with allocated funds.

Trends sometimes appear as an S curve. (See Figure 18.2.) That is, they start out slow, boom to a high degree, and then proceed to level off. An example might be the development of computers. They may have taken a few years to develop and implement, but then suddenly, as in home computers, they become an item that floods the market, thereby tending to create possible crime problems. Once the curve flattens out, however, the future will probably remain fairly stable. Finally, there is what is called the exponential curve. This trend starts out slowly but suddenly skyrockets and continues to grow. Such a curve might be what one would expect with an effective training program in some new technique or an organizational change. For example, going from a tall organizational structure to a flatter structure may, at first,

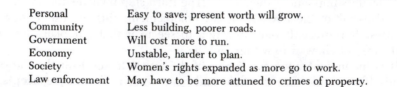

| Personal | Easy to save; present worth will grow. |
| Community | Less building, poorer roads. |
| Government | Will cost more to run. |
| Economy | Unstable, harder to plan. |
| Society | Women's rights expanded as more go to work. |
| Law enforcement | May have to be more attuned to crimes of property. |

**Figure 18.1**  Factors–Areas Affected by Inflation

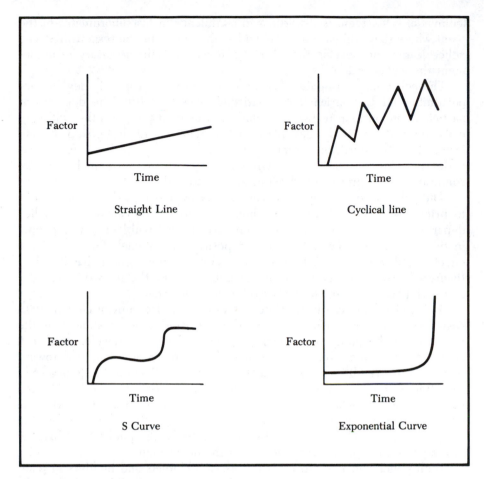

**Figure 18.2** Trend Lines

not produce any great degree of increased productivity. But once the change has been fully implemented, effectiveness suddenly begins to skyrocket.

By being able to apply factors to areas of his life, the police leader will be able to develop curves or trends upon which decisions for the future can be reached. The models by no means are a guarantee of exactness but can be used as devices from which discussions can be held, plans developed, and decisions reached.

## CONCLUSION

What, then, can the police chief of the future do first as a leader? As a department head, he can strive to develop individual responsibility and accountability in every member of the police department and as much as possible in every member of the community. He can see to it that the police department provides a positive role model for the entire community. This applies to the areas of honesty, service, and commitment. The police leader can develop feelings of self-esteem, self-worth, and confidence in his subordinates to the point where they will have freedom and at the same time be responsible. The police leader can develop the rational and human skills necessary to implement these standards.

The police leader can also lead the community. He can help develop opportunities for the enrichment of citizens' lives by letting the department participate in cultural, recreational, and development programs that will help make the community the best place to live. Through his leadership, he can foster strength, spirit, and community involvement in the law-enforcement endeavor. This can be done through openness with the news media, special community work projects, and public appreciation days.

The police leader can help the community by making a determined effort to bring together those who need help and those who can help. A police department can develop volunteers and services that will help young people in times of stress. One of the greatest positive role models for youth is an effective police officer. Walking the beat, although not popular, has its effectiveness because the individual officer gets to know the individual citizens and each plays a role of making the other feel important.

The police chief can further provide citizens and groups of citizens with easy access to information about how the department operates and how the resources at the police department can be utilized. The development of a simple hot line to answer questions and offer help can go a long way toward meeting this overall purpose. In the area of crime reduction, the police chief can attempt to make citizens aware of their roles in crime prevention through such programs as school participation and encouragement on the part of all citizens to report anything suspicious, especially any time they become the victims of crime. The leader can further encourage the public to utilize the crime-prevention programs generated by the department.

Both police and fire personnel can assist architects and builders in planning and designing structures so as to discourage crime and increase public safety. By making crime prevention a strong consideration in the designing of buildings, cars, and public areas such as airports the leader of the future can affect the entire community.

It may be incumbent in the future upon the police leader to involve the courts and correctional agencies in crime prevention. The police leader can take the attitude that everyone within the criminal justice system plays a role in the prevention and reduction of crime.

The role of the leader in the future may appear complicated, but it is challenging and rewarding.

The future belongs to those who are willing to accept its challenges.

---

## NOTE

1. Model developed at the Institute of Government, University of North Carolina, Chapel Hill, under the direction of C. Donald Liner.

# INDEX

# ABOUT THE AUTHOR

Ronald G. Lynch possesses Bachelor of Business Administration and Juris Doctor degrees from the University of Miami, Coral Gables, Florida. He has been a patrol officer, supervisor, and commander with the Metropolitan Dade County Police Department. He was a management consultant with the International Association of Chiefs of Police, and is presently assistant director of the Institute of Government, University of North Carolina, Chapel Hill. He assists police chiefs in bettering their agencies and consults with police departments across the country on general management issues.